THE CALIFORNIA
ELECTRICITY CRISIS

THE CALIFORNIA
ELECTRICITY CRISIS

James L. Sweeney

HOOVER INSTITUTION PRESS

STANFORD INSTITUTE FOR ECONOMIC POLICY RESEARCH

Stanford University
Stanford, California

Hoover Institution Press Publication No. 513

First printing 2002
07 06 05 04 03   9 8 7 6 5 4 3 2

Manufactured in the United States of America

The paper used in this publication meets the minimum requirements of
the American National Standard for Information Sciences—Permanence
of Paper for Printed Library Materials, ANSI Z39.48–1984.

Library of Congress Cataloging-in-Publication Data
Sweeney, James L.
The California electricity crisis / James L. Sweeney.
    p. cm.
Includes bibliographical references and index.
ISBN 0-8179-2911-8 (casebound : alk. paper)
ISBN 0-8179-2912-6 (pbk : alk. paper)
1. Electric utilities—Government policy—California. 2. Electric industries—
California. 3. Energy policy—California. I. Title.

HD9685.U63 C357 2002
333.793'2'09794—dc21
                                                2002006257

Contents

Figures and Tables

Acknowledgments

This book was made possible through the Hoover Institution on War, Revolution and Peace, the Stanford Institute for Economic Policy Research, and ExxonMobil Foundation. I would like to thank Ziad Alaywan, Severin Borenstein, Tom Casten, John Cogan, Linda Cohen, Robert Crow, Elizabeth Farrow, William Hogan, Hill Huntington, Jeffrey Jones, Paul Joskow, Lester Lave, Scott Lowe, Robert Naylor, Stephen Peck, Dmitri Perekhodstev, John Raisian, Gregory Rosston, John Shoven, George Shultz, and James Wilson. I particularly would like to thank Ralph Cavanagh, Jim Harding, and Robert Weisenmiller for extensive, deep, and detailed comments on earlier drafts. Most important, I would like to thank Aletha and Susan Sweeney for their encouragement. The invaluable ideas and assistance from these people have helped make this book possible. All errors, however, remain the responsibility of the author.

Foreword

The energy challenges facing the state of California dominated the news in the winter and spring of 2001. Brownouts, rolling black-outs, and uncertain supply leading to a virtual shutdown of the state's economy were on the horizon. The repercussions across the country were incalculable. Later in 2001, however, things changed dramatically. Moderate summer weather greatly reduced anticipated demand, conservation measures were initiated, and new power stations came on-line. Then, the events of September 11 changed our focus.

The underlying situation facing California remains problematic. Now, many citizens are alarmed by the long-term contracts the state established during the electricity crisis and assert that the state power brokers panicked and made bad deals that will have significant long-term consequences for the state's budget and economy.

The research program at the Hoover Institution incorporates nine Institutional Initiatives; one, Accountability of Government to Society, is based on the premise that government works for society, not the reverse. Researchers at Hoover study and monitor government's accountability to its citizens in terms of representation, limitations, and effectiveness; it is hard to think of a better area for study under this initiative than the California electricity crisis. Could this crisis have been avoided or, at least, anticipated? Did state and federal officials react quickly enough? Was their response appropriate? Were there market failures? These are the kinds of questions that Hoover fellows seek to answer.

The genesis of this project involved Hoover fellows John Cogan, John Shoven, and George P. Shultz and their discussions of an evolving crisis. John Shoven, who as well as being a Hoover fellow is the Wallace R. Hawley Director of the Stanford Institute for Economic Policy Research (SIEPR), suggested that this could be an area of research in which Hoover and SIEPR might combine their talents to address some important policy questions. James Sweeney, a fellow at Hoover and SIEPR and a Stanford professor, was drafted as the person to provide the main impetus for a study and dialogue, supplying the necessary historical perspective to address this issue. He does so graphically and clearly in this volume.

Hoover Institution overseer Thomas Stephenson, concerned about the evolving public policy implications of the energy crisis, encouraged us to pursue it. The financial support of Tom and Barbara Stephenson provided substantial wherewithal to address this issue comprehensively, leading to this book and the related Hoover/SIEPR conference addressing the California electricity questions.

Our partnership with SIEPR worked well; I want to thank John Shoven and Deputy Director Gregory Rosston for their teamwork. Finally, I acknowledge the assistance of my Hoover colleagues Patricia Baker, Marshall Blanchard, Jeffrey Jones, Richard Sousa, and Ann Wood; their contributions to the production of this eloquent volume were invaluable.

John Raisian
Director
Hoover Institution

1

INTRODUCTION
AND OVERVIEW

Since mid-year 2000, California's electricity problems have been a central concern in the state. Californians have faced blackouts, seen the state budgetary surplus decimated, watched as Northern California's largest natural gas and electric utility, Pacific Gas and Electric, filed for bankruptcy, wondered if and when Southern California Edison will follow the same route, listened to politicians debate how much to pay to purchase transmission lines from financially strapped utilities, and listened to state officials point fingers at myriad organizations and individuals for causing the crisis.

This book attempts to explain these events as an integrated saga that California has faced and is still facing. The saga began with an opportunity for California to restructure its electricity system to make it more flexible and responsive to changing economic conditions. Following the flawed implementation of this restructuring, California's political leadership failed in 2000 to respond effectively to the challenge of tight electricity markets, mismanaged the electricity crisis in 2001, and thereby saddled the state with heavy long-term, electricity-related financial obligations. As a result of the fundamental policy mistakes made by the state's governor and other political leaders, the saga continues, with California facing an electricity blight as it struggles to recover from its self-imposed wounds.

The electricity restructuring, often mischaracterized as "deregulation," included provisions that put the state and especially the investor-owned utilities in a risky economic situation. With delays in new generating-plant approvals, a failure throughout the western United States to match the growth in the consumption of electricity with new capacity, and problems with the newly created California wholesale markets, the downside risks became reality and California faced a difficult challenge.

Difficult challenges require wise political leadership. Such challenges require strong, courageous political leaders willing to make difficult and potentially politically unpopular choices. But that type of leadership never emerged in California. Rather than solving the challenge by taking appropriate steps, California's governor failed to act and then, once he started to act, overreacted. That failure of political leadership transformed the difficult challenge into California's energy crisis.

The "energy crisis" was a dual crisis: an electricity crisis associated with an insufficient supply to meet the demands of the California economy and the rest of the West, coupled with soaring wholesale prices, plus a financial crisis facing California's investor-owned electric utilities, the California state budget, and ultimately the taxpayers and electricity ratepayers of California.

During the height of the crisis and as the crisis subsided, the governor and the California legislature responded to the short-term crisis by enacting a group of long-term measures, which now threaten to create a continuing blight on the State of California. These measures collectively seem designed to turn California into a public power state rather than one characterized by a free market system for electricity.

The changes in California moved through four somewhat distinct, although overlapping, stages. The following four chapters of this book correspond to those four stages:

- California's Restructuring: Turning Opportunity into Risk
- The Challenge
- Through Crisis
- From Crisis to Blight

Each stage, and in fact the whole process, should be seen not as a random set of disconnected events but rather as a continuing sequence in which choices were made. At each juncture, there were problems to be solved, often because of earlier policy decisions. At each juncture, there were alternative actions that could have been taken. Given the political and economic forces at play at each juncture, logic underlay the decisions. The choices selected, however, often created new difficulties later. At each juncture, different choices could have led to very different outcomes, and perhaps different problems.

Although one group of events led to another in a causal chain, the results were far from preordained since very different choices were possible at almost all junctures. The totality of the system changes and the consequences for the State of California was the result of this sequence of public policy decisions. Unfortunately, the outcomes are now evolving in directions greatly different from the goals expressed by those instrumental in the initial restructuring.

The focus of this book is this series of policy decisions, the alternatives, and the consequences of the decisions, within the context of the process as a whole.

Figure 1.1 diagrams the chain of causation, linking one decision to the next. The various boxes represent issues, actions, or important system characteristics. The various colors of the boxes represent the four stages of development plus prior conditions. The arrows represent causal links, in the sense that the conditions associated with each action created forces or motivations that encouraged the next decision or constrained the next set of actions.

In green are issues underlying the restructuring decisions that culminated in Assembly Bill 1890 (AB 1890), passed by the legislature in August, signed by the governor in September 1996, and implemented in March 1998. In yellow are some of the important legal provisions of AB 1890 that created a high risk. In addition to these actions are factors or changes that created a challenge to the State of California; the most important ones are shown in orange boxes.

The red boxes represent the key factors or actions that represented the dual crisis: the electricity crisis and the financial crisis, including a group of these factors with a circular set of causation arrows. These factors mutually interacted, causing the system to spiral into a crisis. Indicated above the red boxes and shaping this whole process was the failure of political leadership.

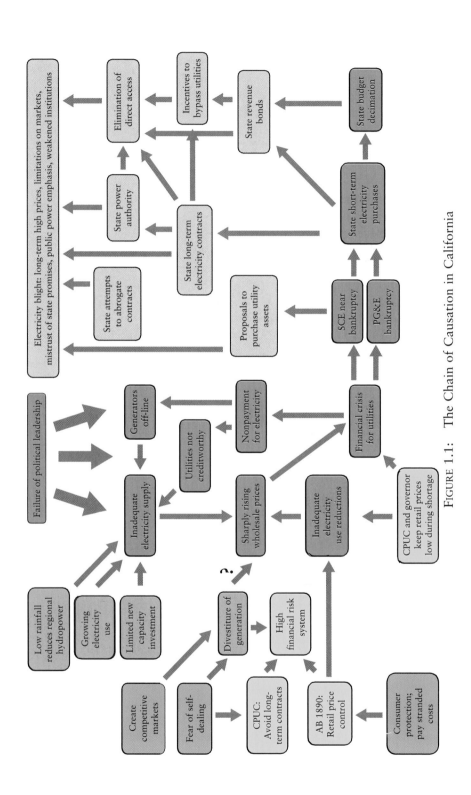

FIGURE 1.1:   The Chain of Causation in California

Finally, actions in gray boxes are described here as the growing long-term blight on the state. Taken together, these actions are changing California into a public power state, limiting market operation, and maintaining long-term high electricity prices. The process can be stopped. Future political leadership can determine how far down this road California will proceed.

The ultimate end state of California's energy system remains unknown. Will California continue down the path toward public power? Will it return to the market-oriented goals of the original restructuring? Or will California move to some fundamentally different electricity system? Any of these paths remain open to the state. Which path is chosen depends on a combination of private sector actions, California legislative and regulatory decisions, and federal governmental decisions. These then remain as collective choices for California.

What follows is an attempt to explain and make sense of the changes implemented at each stage of the process. This discussion will comprise Chapters 2 through 5. The final two chapters look to the future. Chapter 6 examines some of the policy issues that California should face that could help move it out of its present difficulty. Chapter 7 offers reflections based on this sequence of events. These reflections, it is hoped, will help other states contemplating restructuring their electricity systems. And perhaps some will be applicable to other major policy initiatives.

2

CALIFORNIA'S RESTRUCTURING

Turning Opportunity into Risk

At the beginning of the saga, California's electricity system operated in a manner similar to electricity systems throughout the United States. It included three large investor-owned utilities, collectively selling most of the electricity in California. Each investor-owned utility had a franchise in one of three separate parts of the state—Pacific Gas and Electric Company (PG&E) in Northern and central California, Southern California Edison (SCE) in coastal, central, and Southern California, and San Diego Gas and Electric (SDG&E) in San Diego. In addition, there were several much smaller investor-owned utilities, several electric co-ops, and numerous municipal utility systems, the largest of which were the Los Angeles Department of Water and Power (LADWP) and the Sacramento Municipal Utility District (SMUD) (see Table 2.1).

The investor-owned utilities serve 78 percent of the California customers and the municipal utilities serve 22 percent. The electric co-ops and the federal agencies collectively serve less than 0.1 percent of the customers. In terms of total megawatt-hours (MWh) of electricity, the investor-owned facilities sell 72 percent, the municipal utilities 24 percent, and the federal agencies 3 percent (see Table 2.1).

The average price of electricity was similar for investor-owned utilities and municipal utilities. As measured by the average revenue

7

TABLE 2.1
Retail Sellers of Electricity in California: 1999

Electric Utility	Number of Customers	Revenue ($ Thousands)	Sales (MWh)	Avg. Revenue ($/MWh)
Investor-owned Utilities				
Pacific Gas & Electric Co.	4,535,909	6,785,994	70,186,749	97
PacifiCorp	41,473	53,324	778,531	69
San Diego Gas & Electric Co.	1,184,844	1,415,141	14,718,306	96
Sierra Pacific Power Co.	43,877	38,826	506,280	77
Southern California Edison Co.	4,213,562	6,692,164	67,206,530	100
Southern California Water Co.	20,988	13,275	127,135	104
Total	10,040,653	14,998,724	153,523,531	98
Municipal Utilities				
Alameda, City of	32,569	38,979	371,326	105
Anaheim, City of	105,755	220,932	2,416,302	91
Azusa, City of	14,549	21,072	233,213	90
Banning, City of	9,523	13,501	118,821	114
Biggs, City of	656	787	7,340	107
Burbank, City of	51,488	106,360	1,029,003	103

Colton, City of	16,893	26,176	266,108	98
Glendale, City of	83,100	112,701	1,071,277	105
Gridley, City of	2,191	2,315	26,824	86
Healdsburg, City of	4,903	7,397	69,904	106
Imperial Irrigation District	93,486	193,531	2,384,949	81
Lassen Municipal Utility District	10,162	12,227	136,909	89
Lodi, City of	23,776	38,329	391,276	98
Lompoc, City of	14,455	12,336	125,717	98
Los Angeles, City of	1,385,396	2,080,736	20,056,691	104
Merced Irrigation District	148	5,362	113,305	47
Modesto Irrigation District	92,229	136,566	2,164,620	63
Needles, City of	2,907	4,907	60,967	81
Palo Alto, City of	27,723	66,503	1,124,025	59
Pasadena, City of	58,378	129,657	1,129,383	115
Redding, City of	38,295	68,937	683,493	101
Riverside, City of	92,644	160,773	1,647,509	98
Roseville, City of	36,243	60,003	819,570	73
Sacramento Municipal Utility District	503,615	722,046	9,284,751	78
San Francisco, City & County of	9	40,588	728,342	56
Santa Clara, City of	47,524	194,782	2,491,714	78
Shasta Lake, City of	3,916	5,004	65,305	77
Trinity Public Utilities District	6,464	5,606	77,498	72

TABLE 2.1 (continued)

Electric Utility	Number of Customers	Revenue ($ Thousands)	Sales (MWh)	Avg. Revenue ($/MWh)
Truckee Donner Public Utility District	10,324	8,615	122,029	71
Tuolumne County Public Power Agency	30	1,194	23,162	52
Turlock Irrigation District	66,456	105,366	1,415,162	75
Ukiah, City of	7,298	13,606	106,303	128
Vernon, City of	2,026	55,056	1,161,173	47
Total	2,845,131	4,671,950	51,923,971	90
Electric Co-ops				
Anza Electric Co-op, Inc.	3,468	5,138	34,693	148
Plumas-Sierra Rural Electric Co-op.	6,067	9,607	118,818	81
Surprise Valley Electric Corporation	3,923	4,594	88,802	52
Valley Electric Association, Inc.	29	337	7,081	48
Total	13,487	19,676	249,394	79
Federal Agencies				
Bonneville Power Administration	10	6,365	264,515	24
Western Area Power Administration	98	94,914	6,019,473	16
Total	108	101,279	6,283,988	16
State Total	12,899,380	19,791,632	211,981,140	93

SOURCE: Energy Information Administration

per MWh sold, the average retail price of electricity sold by the municipal utilities (including delivery services) was 8 percent less than it was for investor-owned utilities. Retail prices for municipal utilities varied over a wide range, from 30 percent above to 51 percent below the average investor-owned utility price. The largest municipal utility, LADWP, had an average price (more precisely, average revenue per MWh) 6 percent above the investor-owned utilities' average.

Each investor-owned or municipal utility operated as a local monopoly, selling electricity in its own exclusive franchise area, with no direct retail competition from other electricity sellers. The large investor-owned utilities, as well as some of the municipal utilities, were vertically integrated to include three separate functions: generation, transmission, and local distribution. A typical investor-owned utility generated most of its electricity (generation), moved that electricity on transmission lines to local areas where it was needed (transmission), and sold that electricity to industrial, commercial, and residential users (local distribution). Some municipal utilities operated as only local distribution companies; some participated in one or both of the other two functions—generation and transmission.

For investor-owned utilities, almost all significant financial decisions involving any of the three functions were subject to the jurisdiction and control of the statewide regulatory body, the California Public Utilities Commission (CPUC). Customers paid retail prices for electricity based on operating costs plus a regulated rate of return on the prudently incurred "used and useful" invested capital. The CPUC would review whether costs were prudent and determine the "fair" rate of return on invested capital that was meant to approximate a normal rate of return for companies facing equivalent risk. Thus pricing was based primarily on cost of service and only secondarily on market conditions.[1]

The significant decisions made by the publicly owned municipal utilities were subject to the jurisdiction and control of their

---

[1]Market conditions have a secondary role because of the dynamic nature of the rate-setting process. Each rate case sets retail prices based on conditions in some base year or years. These rates stay in place until the next rate case. Thus if sales increase in the future beyond expectations, profits for the utility will rise, and vice versa if sales decline. This provides an incentive to delay rate cases when sales and profits are higher than expected and to quickly initiate rate cases when sales and profits are low. In addition, the actual system creates incentives to block distributed generation investments that would reduce sales and to go slow on energy efficiency investments that would reduce sales of electricity.

appointed or elected governing bodies. Thus, their strategies could be based on local decision making, rather than on statewide regulations. They typically were operated, however, so that over a span of several years their revenues roughly equaled their total costs of operation. Thus, for municipal utilities as well as for investor-owned utilities, pricing was based primarily on cost of service and only secondarily on market conditions.

This particular type of industrial organization—utilities operating as regulated monopolies—had been justified for many decades by the increasing-returns-to-scale[2] nature of electricity generation, transmission, and distribution.

Retail distribution (the provision of delivery services: wires, transformers, and other physical equipment) provides the most obvious example of increasing returns to scale in the electric industry. A customer could double the amount of electricity used with no increase in the cost of providing wires to a home. Equivalently, if two competing companies were each to run electric wires down the same streets to compete for customers, total cost and cost per customer would increase even with no change in the quantity of electricity delivered. Cost would be lowest if only one company were providing the wires, transformers, and other physical equipment for local distribution of centrally generated electricity. Thus local distribution of centrally generated electricity is generally considered to be a natural monopoly and, as such, is typically allowed to operate as a monopoly franchise, subject to regulatory oversight, in California, as in other states.[3]

As distinct from electricity distribution services, retail electricity is not characterized by increasing returns to scale. To double the amount of electricity sold, a retailer would need to double the amount of electricity acquired at wholesale. For wholesale electricity prices held fixed, doubling the acquisition of electricity would double the total cost of acquiring the electricity. Thus the cost per MWh sold at retail neither increases nor decreases (at

---

[2]Increasing returns to scale characterizes an industry if increasing the size of individual firms reduces the average cost of the product.

[3]This argument cannot legitimately be generalized to include distributed generation of electricity at the point of end use. Distributed generation includes both the generation and distribution function. In some cases, the addition of distributed generation to systems with existing distribution networks may reduce total system costs. Nevertheless, natural monopoly arguments have been used by some utilities to limit competition from distributed generation.

least not significantly) as the scale of retail operations changes. Retail sale of the commodity (electricity itself) is not characterized by increasing returns to scale, and thus the retail electricity sales function cannot be viewed as a natural monopoly.

In principle, the regulatory system could logically separate delivery services from the retail sales of electricity itself. The retail sales function would be amenable to organization as a competitive industry even though the delivery function was not organized in a competitive market structure.

Typically, however, delivery services and the electricity were bundled: customers were charged a price for the combination of electricity and delivery services. In this way, the natural monopoly franchise for delivery services was extended into monopoly franchises for delivery services and for electricity. California operated this way, as did most states.

Increasing returns to scale also characterizes the transmission of electricity, up to a point. Electricity moves on high-voltage transmission lines integrated into an electricity grid. A significant cost of this transmission system is paying for the right-of-way on which to build transmission lines. When the transmission lines are operating well below capacity, it would cost little to move additional electricity through these lines. Even at capacity, installing additional high-voltage wires on an existing transmission link costs substantially less than required to establish the link in the first place. Thus transmission also seems to be appropriately organized as a monopoly along a given transmission path, as it is in California.

Finally, electricity generation also seemed to have the increasing returns to scale characteristic of a natural monopoly. For many years the conventional wisdom was that the larger the electric generating plant, the lower the overall cost of electricity generation. Bigger was cheaper. This increasing returns to scale characteristic of electricity generation led to the common belief that electricity generation should be organized as a monopoly.

Given that all three components of the electricity supply system were operated as monopolies, there was a tendency, although not a necessity, for these three elements to be vertically integrated into a single company.[4] The first reason for this was the need for coordination in planning for capital investments and

---

[4]Many municipal utilities were not vertically integrated even though all three large investor-owned utilities were.

operations. The amount of electricity sold by the distribution firm determined the amount of generation and transmission capacity needed. The location of transmission facilities and generation facilities required coordination to minimize overall cost. This need for coordination and for appropriate information flows helped justify combining these three entities into one vertically integrated company.

A second, and related, reason for vertical integration was based on reducing transactions costs. Three separate monopolies, all integrated into one supply chain, might choose to operate so as to gain financial advantages over one another. Although this strategic problem could be controlled through the regulatory process, integrating the three entities into one company would reduce or eliminate those incentives and the resulting need for regulatory oversight.

Although the investor-owned utilities in California, and in the rest of the nation, operated as vertically integrated monopolies, they did purchase some electricity from external sources. These purchases involved a mix of long- and medium-term contracts, plus spot market purchases or sales, to match unexpected variations in their sales of electricity. In particular, California utilities had long-term contracts to purchase hydroelectric power from the Bonneville Power Administration (BPA), a federal power-marketing agency. BPA sells power generated primarily from federal hydroelectric projects in the federal Columbia River Power System.[5] Both municipal utilities and investor-owned utilities also had other contracts to purchase electricity from federal projects. California traditionally sold electricity to entities in the Pacific Northwest in the winter, when demand there peaked, and purchased electricity from the Pacific Northwest during the summer, when California demand peaked. Other than these low-priced sources of electricity, however, California's investor-owned electric utilities historically tended to acquire electricity from their own generating units.

THE CHANGING FEDERAL REGULATORY STRUCTURE

PURPA

In 1973, energy markets, particularly oil markets, were severely shaken by the sudden jump in oil prices resulting from the Organization of Petroleum Exporting Countries (OPEC)–organized

---

[5]The largest of these federal dams is the Grand Coulee Dam.

reduction in world oil production. President Richard Nixon declared "Project Independence," and the United States began searching for means of reducing its dependence on oil and natural gas. In 1973, oil accounted for about 20 percent of the fossil fuels used for electricity generation; natural gas accounted for another 20 percent. Although natural gas was not imported in large quantities, U.S. policies were shaped by a general belief that natural gas would be in short supply and that, as a "premium fuel," natural gas should not be used for electricity generation. The efforts to reduce the use of oil and natural gas left nuclear power, coal, and various renewable sources of energy as alternative primary sources, plus energy-efficiency investments that provided energy services using smaller amounts of electricity.

In response to these public policy goals, Congress passed several laws designed to promote nuclear power, coal, energy efficiency, and small-scale renewable energy sources (wood waste, solar, wind) and to discourage the use of oil and gas.[6] Many people, however, feared that utilities would favor their own generation and avoid adopting the generation technologies Congress wished to promote. The Public Utility Regulatory Policies Act (PURPA) of 1978 was enacted primarily to promote development of small-scale renewable sources of energy for electricity generation. Cogeneration[7] was included as a means of more efficiently converting primary energy into electricity and usable heat. PURPA mandated state regulatory commissions to establish procedures requiring electric utilities to interconnect with and buy capacity and energy offered by any nonutility facility that qualified under PURPA. These so-called qualifying facilities, or QFs, were typically

---

[6]The Powerplant and Industrial Fuel Use Act of 1978 includes a provision: "Except to such extent as may be authorized under part B, no new electric powerplant may be constructed or operated as a base load powerplant without the capability to use coal or another alternate fuel as a primary energy source." "Alternative fuel" within the definition of that act excludes oil and natural gas. The act explicitly did not apply to nuclear-powered plants. And it provided a permanent exemption for cogeneration plants. (U.S. Code Title 42, Chapter 92, Section 8301–8354.)

[7]Cogeneration units are those that both generate electricity and use the energy not converted to electricity for purposes such as space or water heating or industrial process heating. In so doing, a large fraction of the input energy is harnessed for desirable functions. Many cogeneration plants are based on natural gas, but PURPA promoted cogeneration based on any primary fuel.

small generating facilities based on renewable energy, waste products, or natural-gas-fired cogeneration units.

Utilities were required by PURPA to pay a price for electricity from QFs equal to the "avoided cost" of electricity generation, which was meant to be the total costs that a utility would avoid by purchasing electricity from these small alternative sources. The state regulatory commissions were allowed by PURPA to interpret the dollar price that corresponded to avoided cost and the precise conditions under which the electricity and capacity must be purchased.

Impacts well beyond the limited public policy goal that motivated its passage were achieved by PURPA. PURPA started to change the structure of the electric industry, providing the first challenge to the tightly integrated vertical monopoly structure.

OPENING TRANSMISSION NETWORKS

With the success of PURPA, by the mid-1980s analysts realized that it was not necessary to operate electricity generation as a regulated monopoly and that there was an opportunity to create a competitive electric generation industry. By then, utility executives understood the high capital costs of nuclear power; no utilities were proposing new nuclear power plant construction. Natural gas had become broadly available throughout the United States and was no longer seen as a premium fuel; its use in new electricity-generating plants was no longer prohibited under federal law.[8] Thus it became possible to construct gas-fired power plants. Combustion turbines had become more efficient, particularly in a combined-cycle mode. These turbines could be built in modules—one turbine, then another, then a steam cycle. This modular construction allowed for more flexibility and the construction of smaller, very efficient plants. However, although utilities typically had not been taking advantage of that opportunity, once PURPA opened the way for independent power producers, these firms began exploiting the profit opportunities of using the waste heat from turbines in combined-cycle plants. Thus the assumption that electricity generation exhibited increasing returns to scale was no longer seen as valid. Consequently, the idea

---

[8]In 1987, the Powerplant and Industrial Fuel Use Act was amended to permit electric utilities to burn oil or natural gas in new baseload generating facilities, if the plants could permit future voluntary conversion to coal. Even before that time, however, exemptions to the restriction had been routinely granted.

of electricity generation as a natural monopoly was no longer consistent with technical reality.

However, utilities still controlled all electricity transmission lines, which were still seen as natural monopolies. A utility that wished to stifle competition in electricity generation could do so by refusing to allow its competitors to transmit electricity along its transmission lines. Thus creating a truly competitive market for electricity generation required federal officials to deal with issues of utility control of transmission lines.

The first step was the Energy Policy Act (EPACT) of 1992. Among its many provisions, EPACT opened access by nonutilities to the transmission networks. And in 1996, the Federal Energy Regulatory Commission (FERC) issued Order 888, which much more generally opened transmission access to nonutilities. These regulatory changes together started to transform the electricity transmission system into a common carrier system. With EPACT and Order 888, it became much more difficult to control electricity generation markets by controlling electricity transmission. Utilities still made the investment decisions for transmission facilities and thus could still exercise some control over generation markets, but this form of control was less effective than direct control over access to transmission lines. These two changes were fundamental for establishing the opportunity for wholesale competition in electricity.

IMPACTS ON CALIFORNIA ELECTRICITY BEFORE RESTRUCTURING

In California, the CPUC aggressively implemented PURPA, setting high prices for electricity purchased by the investor-owned utilities[9] and requiring the investor-owned utilities to sign contracts based on standard offers with guaranteed prices that rose sharply over time.[10]

---

[9]Since the CPUC did not regulate the municipal utilities, these high prices were not relevant to these entities.

[10]Under Interim Standard Offer No. 4 (ISO4), a QF based on renewable energy could sign a contract based on a fixed forecast of future electricity price. Such a QF entering a contract would be guaranteed $57/MWh in 1985, $81/MWh in 1990, and $109/MWh in 1994. After ten years the contract price reverted to the short-run avoided cost, which typically would be far lower than the fixed-price guarantee. Gas-fired cogeneration units were not treated nearly as generously but were generally paid an annual average of about $25/MWh for capacity and about $25–$30/MWh for energy.

The financial incentives and guaranteed market for QF electricity, coupled with tax incentives established by the federal government, created a significant industry of renewable electricity generation in California, including wind farms and wood waste–fueled generators. These policy changes also led to large increases in cogeneration capacity,[11] which was largely natural gas–fired. By the end of 1994, 20 percent of the electricity generation capacity in California was from QFs, 11.5 percent of which was cogeneration; 8.3 percent was renewable generation capacity, the largest inventory of renewable generation capacity in the nation.

However, with long-term contractual obligations to purchase electricity from QFs at a high cost, by the early 1990s the utilities were facing a high average cost of electricity generation. In addition, California utilities had invested in nuclear power plants, whose construction costs turned out to be far greater than initially predicted, further increasing the average cost of electricity generation.

These factors together helped make California's retail prices among the highest in the nation. For retail prices,[12] or, more precisely, a state-by-state comparison of the 1998 average revenue per kilowatt-hour (KWh, measured in cents per KWh) sold to residential customers, see Figure 2.1. Only in California, Alaska, Hawaii, and the northeastern states did average retail prices exceed 8 cents/KWh ($80/MWh). California's average revenue was 9 cents/KWh ($90/MWh).

MOTIVATIONS FOR CALIFORNIA ELECTRICITY DEREGULATION

GENERATION/WHOLESALE MARKETS

The high retail price of electricity in California, relative to that of the rest of the nation, was one argument for California's electric system being deregulated to create a more competitive, and

---

[11]Cogeneration now is the single biggest source of PURPA electricity-generation capacity in California. Of the roughly 10,200 megawatts (MW) of total QF nameplate capacity in California in 2001, about 5,700 MW came from cogeneration and 4,500 MW from renewables such as wind or organic wastes. (Data from California Energy Commission database of electricity-generating plants on-line in California.)

[12]Source: U.S. Department of Energy, Energy Information Administration, *Electric Power Annual* 1 (1998).

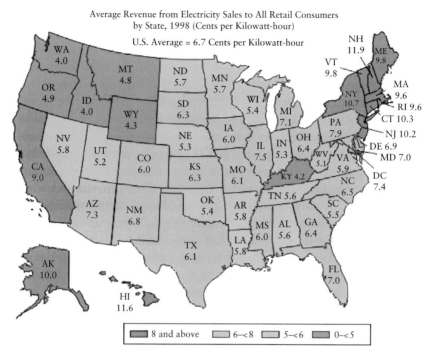

Average Revenue from Electricity Sales to All Retail Consumers
by State, 1998 (Cents per Kilowatt-hour)

FIGURE 2.1:   Average Revenue from Electricity Sales to
All Retail Consumers

SOURCE: Energy Information Administration, U.S. Department of Energy

presumably lower-cost, electricity system. The concern about high retail costs became an argument about electricity generation because major contributors to the high retail price in California were the high average cost of generating electricity and the high prices embedded in contracts for purchasing electricity under PURPA contracts. Many advocates of electricity-generation deregulation expected deregulation to reduce retail prices of electricity quickly.

But this expectation was based on a fundamental fallacy, implicitly assuming that deregulation in the present could somehow correct the historical problems that had led to the high generation costs and the high costs of purchasing bulk power under contracts. The costly investments in nuclear power plants and the long-term contracts for QFs, however, could not be reversed. At the time of the restructuring debate, the state was no longer investing in new nuclear power plants. New cogeneration plants and renewable energy investments were being made when such investments were expected by their developers to be economically attractive. The high-price standard offers under PURPA were no longer required for new contracts. If the problem was higher prices caused by the historical nuclear power plant investments and QFs contracts, restructuring was not the answer.

Moreover, if California could have gone back in time to restructure the wholesale electricity markets before it invested in the nuclear power plants and the QF contracts, it could probably not have avoided those high electricity costs. After oil prices jumped in the mid-1970s and early 1980s, oil was no longer an economically attractive source of energy for electricity generation. Initially, natural gas was not available in large quantities, and beginning in 1978, federal law precluded its use in new baseload electricity-generating units. The sites for developing high-head hydroelectric power plants in California had already been well developed. Coal was not a good option: California had no indigenous coal; cooling water needed for coal-fired units was limited, except on California's coasts; building new railroad lines to haul coal to California's coasts would have been very costly; the environmental impacts of coal-fired facilities on California's coastline would have been unacceptable; and the problems of transporting vast quantities of coal to those plants by railroad would have been overwhelming. The United States had been investing in nuclear power plants believing that nuclear power would be the least costly method of generating electricity, which turned out to be false. Moreover, the geologically active faults near the California coastline made designing and constructing nuclear power plants difficult. Thus, the most attractive options for new generation capacity were renewables and cogeneration. Those supply sources, combined with energy efficiency programs— programs that reduced the need for new generation—were probably the best choices.

The cost of contracts to purchase electricity from QFs could have been significantly lower if the CPUC had chosen a more realistic calculation of the avoided cost of electricity. And even restructuring electricity markets was unlikely to have forced CPUC away from its politically inspired high calculations of avoided cost.

In short, even if California could have gone back in time and restructured electricity markets in the mid-1970s, whether the particular factors that led to high electricity prices in California would have been significantly different as of the 1990s is dubious.

The more subtle argument, however, was that deregulation would reduce costs, although the cost reductions would be gradual, not the instant cost decreases some expected. The regulatory system probably did not provide strong enough incentives for utility-owned electricity generators to minimize costs and thus probably did not lead to the lowest-cost mix of energy generation technologies. Some utilities were probably favoring their own generation over generation by independent power producers and thus not minimizing cost. There remained incentives and opportunities for utilities to block distributed generation and to rely instead on central-station power, even if distributed generation had lower overall costs. Whether the regulated system was leading to too much investment in capital-intensive generation, and too much investment in generation relative to expenditures on demand management, was a more subtle debate. However, economists and other industry analysts argued that creating competition could change economic incentives facing the utilities and thus gradually reduce costs of electricity generation, which in turn would gradually reduce retail prices. This argument, although not proven, was probably valid, even though the hope of fast cost savings was probably never realistic.

In addition, many asserted that the expansion of wholesale markets would encourage investment by independent power producers in new generating capacity. In the early 1990s there was a surplus of California electricity-generating capacity (including expected electricity imports), albeit a small one. However, most analysts anticipated that the healthy California economy would continue to need more electricity over the years and doubted whether the old regulated system would be responsive enough to those needs. Many also argued that the old regulated system would lead to utilities discouraging new investment by independent power producers.[13] The

---

[13]Traditionally rate-of-return–regulated utilities invest in more generation than might be expected under a purely competitive regime. However, their incentive to reduce purchases from independent power producers could reduce total investment in new generation. For example, in 1993, the CPUC directed the utilities to issue a solicitation for a little over 1,000 MW of electricity. Bids by QFs undercut the costs of the utility projects with a price of about $44/MWh. But SCE (and to a lesser extent, SDG&E) successfully resisted entering the new contracts, asserting that no new capacity was needed, since conservation could meet any new needs.

expansion of a competitive wholesale market was intended as a long-term solution to a long-term problem.

The nationwide trends toward smaller, modular electric generation units were evident in California. During the 1980s the combination of broadly available natural gas and technological change had led independent power producers in California to invest in smaller gas-fired plants that could be distributed throughout the state. Electricity thus could be generated close to where it was needed, saving costs of expanding electricity transmission lines.[14] It had become clear in California that bigger was no longer cheaper and thus that electricity generation was not a natural monopoly. Since most new investment in electricity generation was by independent power producers, not utilities, the deregulation of electricity generation and the expansion of wholesale markets supported this pronounced trend.

Thus, there was the opportunity in California to deregulate electricity generation and to expand the scope of the existing competitive portion of the industry. Expanding competition in electricity generation was expected to create incentives for cost cutting, to encourage investments in new generating capacity by independent power producers, and to provide a flexible system for a dynamic California economy.

STRANDED COSTS

The prospect of low wholesale electricity prices, coupled with high costs for some past investments, created challenges for deregulation. If future costs would be low for new generation, then future wholesale prices could be expected to be low as well. However, with low wholesale costs, the existing high-cost generating units might no longer be economically viable in a competitive environment. The investment costs incurred by the utilities in constructing these plants would be "stranded." Utilities would incur losses because of these stranded costs, absent policy intervention.

The issue of stranded costs was not fundamentally a problem of "going forward" costs—future total costs of electricity generation ignoring sunk costs—even if those costs might be very high for

---

[14]Such localized, small-scale generation could also reduce the need for new transmission lines with their very large costs and their possible environmental impacts.

some of the units. If wholesale electricity prices turned out to be lower than the per MWh going forward costs of these plants, in a competitive environment the plants would shut down and their entire remaining book value would be a loss to their owners. However, such plants *should* be shut down for economic efficiency reasons: the value of electricity they produced would be less than the additional cost to produce that electricity. By contrast, if the wholesale electricity prices turned out to be higher than the going forward costs of these plants, they could sell electricity at the wholesale price and generation would thus be more profitable than shutting down. These plants could compete in a market environment, as would be desirable for economic efficiency. However, there would still be a fixed loss: the owner would not be able to recover all of the remaining book value. Although the loss would be strictly less than the book value, it might still be large.

These fixed losses were sunk costs and therefore not expected to influence the market-clearing price. But someone would have to bear the losses. Who should bear these losses—the utilities or their customers—was a politically important issue. Thus, the issue of stranded costs was simply who should bear the burden of those fixed costs.

Given the issue of stranded costs, several possible alternatives were consistent with the deregulation of generation. One would be to allow the utility to include those costs in retail prices, keeping the retail prices high, just as they would be absent restructuring. That solution would motivate customers to bypass those utilities with large stranded costs and purchase directly from generators or generate electricity themselves, say, by investing in cogeneration units. The customers most able to do so would be the large industrial users of electricity that could go directly to new electricity generators and could enter contracts based on the lower costs of new generation or could invest in cogeneration units near the point of use. If enough large customers bypassed the utilities, these utilities would sell electricity primarily to residential and small commercial consumers; small users would thus pay most of the stranded costs. Many consumer groups, not surprisingly, opposed this option.

Another option would be to require the utility to write off the assets as losses, requiring stockholders to face the consequences of stranded costs. The utilities argued persuasively that it would be fundamentally inequitable for their investors to bear all the stranded costs of long-term contracts and generating investments that, in many instances, were forced on them under the old "regulatory compact." They argued that they should be able to recover all of these "prudently incurred" investments because there had been an implicit contract between the regulators and the utilities under which utilities would make investments to serve the needs of ratepayers and ratepayers would pay back the costs of those investments, plus a fair rate of return on the investments, over the life of the equipment. By contrast, those who advocated requiring the utilities to bear those losses argued that the utilities were not blameless in the past investments, that they had proposed most of the investments themselves, that they had mismanaged the long-term contracting for QFs, and that many of the investments were simply mistakes by the utilities. Their recommendation was that the investors in those utilities, not the ratepayers, should be required to bear the stranded costs.

This debate—who should pay the burden of historical investments, now uneconomical—became central to the subsequent regulatory hearings and legislation. In addition, calculations of the magnitude of stranded costs, by necessity, include many subjective elements. No one could predict with any confidence future sales prices over time of wholesale electricity or future natural gas prices. Thus issues of how to calculate stranded costs and how to reduce the need to calculate stranded costs also remained important. Once the crisis occurred, the theme returned. Looking to the future, this class of issues remains central to the policy options, because the State of California incurred large financial obligations during the crisis, obligations that are likely to be losses for someone. We return to these questions in subsequent sections and chapters.

RETAIL SALES

In addition to expanding competition in electricity generation, there was the possibility of creating competitive markets for retail electricity. During the 1980s, there was a growing recognition that electricity as a commodity could be unbundled from electricity distribution services. One could envision a local distribution company that provided electricity distribution services as a monopoly, with those services being subject to regulatory oversight, and simultaneously a market in which many firms competed with one another to sell electricity, with that electricity delivered by the monopoly distribution company. In fact, Chile had put such a system in place in the early 1980s, followed by the United Kingdom and Argentina in the late 1980s. Australia and New Zealand had also unbundled electricity in this fashion,[15] making it clear that there was an opportunity for retail competition.

Such competition offered the possibility that competing retailers would provide differentiated energy services that would be attractive to consumers. Some retailers could provide "green power" to environmentally conscious consumers. Others could bundle energy efficiency measures with electricity to help consumers reduce the overall cost of obtaining energy services (for example, warmth, lighting, cooking, clothes drying, refrigeration). Some retailers could provide highly reliable electricity to the industrial or commercial customers for whom reliability was essential or interruptible service to those customers willing to accept service interruptions in exchange for a lower overall bill. Some could sell electricity at real-time prices for those customers that wished lowest average cost but did not mind price variability, and others could sell electricity at guaranteed prices, essentially selling risk management services bundled with electricity. A competitive retail market could enhance consumer options and create a more flexible system.

Thus, in the 1990s, the opportunity and the motivation arose to restructure both the generation function and the local distribution function of the California electricity industry. These factors set the stage for the debate on how to deregulate or restructure the California electricity system.

CALIFORNIA PUBLIC UTILITIES
COMMISSION LEADERSHIP

It was California's regulatory agency, the CPUC, that spearheaded the move toward electricity deregulation in California. Contrary to the common view of regulatory agencies as bodies working to preserve their own power, the CPUC, or at least CPUC commissioners and staff in the early and mid-1990s, took aggressive leadership on a course of action that promised to reduce their authority over

---

[15]For a discussion of restructuring efforts in other countries, see Robert Thomas Crow, "Not Invented Here: What California Can Learn from Elsewhere about Restructuring Electricity Supply," (Working paper at Stanford Institute for Economic Policy Research, December 2001); available at http://siepr.stanford.edu/papers/pdf/01-10.html.

electricity markets. The deregulation that they envisioned (and at that time it was still deregulation, not simply restructuring) would rely more on competitive market forces in both wholesale and retail electricity markets and less on governmental control over electricity production and use.

YELLOW BOOK AND BLUE BOOK

In April 1992, the CPUC initiated a review of trends in the electric industry, which initially resulted in a staff report[16] published in February 1993. This report, commonly referred to as the "Yellow Book," outlined a set of broad strategies for restructuring the electricity industry to rely more fully on market forces.

Following the Yellow Book was a CPUC Order proposing a process of restructuring California's electricity industry. This Order,[17] often referred to as the "Blue Book," issued in April 1994, envisioned competitive retail markets, in which "customers would have choice among competing generation providers,"[18] with electricity generated through a competitive wholesale market. However, the Yellow Book and subsequent restructuring Orders all maintained the utilities as monopoly providers of delivery services.

The Blue Book laid the foundation for California's subsequent electricity restructuring, proposing several fundamental changes, including replacing cost-of-service regulation with performance-based regulation, wherever regulation was needed, thereby strengthening regulated utility incentives for cost reduction. At the retail level, the Blue Book proposed to grant all purchasers of electricity voluntary and direct access to electricity suppliers in a time-phased manner. In addition, retail customers would be able to purchase electricity from the local utility. The Blue Book envisioned that both the regulated utility (operating wherever possible under performance-based regula-

---

[16]California Public Utilities Commission. "California's Electric Services Industry: Perspectives on the Past, Strategies for the Future" (February 3, 1993).

[17]California Public Utilities Commission. "Order Instituting Rulemaking on the Commission's Proposed Policies Governing Restructuring California's Electric Services Industry and Reforming Regulation" and "Order Instituting Investigation on the Commission's Proposed Policies Governing Restructuring California's Electric Services Industry and Reforming Regulation," R.94-04-031/I.04-04-032.

[18]Quotation from Decision 95-12-063 (December 20, 1995). A more complete discussion of this procedural history appears in that document.

tion) and unregulated retail purchases would coexist. Electricity generation would be fundamentally deregulated. Wholesale prices would be kept "just and reasonable" by the discipline of competitive wholesale markets.

The Blue Book addressed the issue of stranded costs by proposing a financial transfer from the utility customers to the generation side of the utilities, a solution that essentially remained through the subsequent legislation. The financial transfer would be in the form of a limited-time "competition transition charge." Each retail customer in the utility's service area would be required to pay the competition transition cost for all electricity purchased. That charge could not be bypassed: even if a customer were no longer served by the utility, whatever entity sold that customer electricity would be required to collect the competition transition charge. Thus, although the total amount of money collected by the competition transition charge would depend on the total amount of electricity sold at retail, it would not depend on whether the incumbent utility or some other firm sold the electricity.

The utility would receive all money collected through the competition transition charge, allowing it to recover stranded costs. The competition charge would pay for the entire stranded costs for the given utility over a target number of years. Thus, under the Blue Book proposal, the CPUC would estimate the total of stranded costs for a given utility and the total amount of electricity that would be purchased by customers in the utility's service area over the target number of years. The estimate of total stranded costs would be divided by the estimate of future electricity sales to determine a competition transition charge (CTC) assessed in proportion to the amount of electricity sold.[19]

The total stranded costs depended on the market-determined wholesale price of electricity. If the wholesale price were very low, then the total stranded costs could be as large as the total of book values of the old plants owned by the utilities plus costs associated with the QF contracts. Conversely, if the wholesale price were very high, then the total stranded costs might be negligible. Thus, the size of the CTC would depend on the expected

---

[19]The calculation would account for financial discounting of future cash flows by allowing the stranded costs to earn a financial return that would itself be included as part of the calculation of the CTC.

wholesale price and thus would need to be periodically adjusted to changing wholesale prices.

In many ways, the CTC looked like a temporary tax on electricity use that was different in each investor-owned utility's service area, depending on the magnitude of the stranded costs of that utility, and differed with the prevailing wholesale price. Unlike most taxes, the revenues would go directly to those utilities with stranded costs, not to a government entity.

If all a utility's customers remained with the utility and none switched to other suppliers, then the CTC would simply take money from the retail side of that utility and pass exactly the same amount of money to the generation side. The CTC would have no financial consequences for the utility as a whole unless it caused the retail price to change (which it would not under most regulatory regimes).

The CTC would be financially beneficial to the utility, however, if some retail customers switched electricity retailers, no longer purchasing from the incumbent utility. These customers would continue to pay the CTC, and the money so collected would be paid to the generation side of the utility. The payments to the generation side of the utility for stranded costs would be invariant to the fraction of customers who remained with the utility and the fraction that purchased from other retailers or entered direct contracts with generators.

DECISION 95-05-045

Although the Blue Book laid the foundation for the restructuring, many steps were required to complete the process, each of which seemed to add more complexity to the restructured system. In May 1995, the CPUC issued a Decision that laid out two broad policy alternatives for organizing restructured wholesale markets and transmission management: a preferred (majority) policy and an alternative proposed policy.[20]

The preferred structure was a wholesale power pool, managed by an independent system operator (ISO) that would dispatch generation based on a day-ahead bidding mechanism and would arrange transmission access for generators that bid to sell electricity at prices no greater than the market-clearing price. Under this proposal, management of the grid, dispatch of generators, and wholesale trading would be integrated functions.

---

[20]CPUC Decision D.95-05-045.

Wholesale prices for electricity could vary sharply with supply and demand conditions, with risk for both generators and consumers. Risk management would be available through financial instruments to hedge prices. These instruments, in principle, would be immediately available to any parties that mutually agreed on them, but the CPUC was to take no responsibility for establishing markets for such hedge instruments. Energy traders and marketers, such as Enron Corporation, seemed prepared to organize such markets. The new system would allow physical, bilateral contracts that, after two years, could be used for risk management.

The alternative policy recommended consumer choice through direct access contracts. This plan would allow physical, bilateral contracts, separate from any pool bidding, to be available immediately. This alternative would allow the opportunity for competing operators of the transmission grid, with a role for the ISO only when there were transmission constraints. Under this alternative, financial instruments to hedge prices could still be available and risk management through long-term bilateral contracts would have been available to those customers who were able to negotiate such contracts.

Memo of Understanding

In September 1995, four major participants—a utility, a group of generators, and two electricity user groups[21]—presented a Memorandum of Understanding (MOU) with their joint recommendations. Although it addressed virtually all elements of the proposed restructuring, the MOU focused on market structure and stranded cost issues.[22] The proposed market structure combined features of the preferred and of the alternative proposals from May 1995. The new proposed system would be more complex and less coordinated than would either the preferred or the alternative proposals.

---

[21]The MOU was submitted by Southern California Edison (SCE), the California Manufacturers Association (CMA), the California Large Energy Consumers Association (CLECA), and the Independent Energy Producers (IEP).

[22]For more discussion of these changes, see William W. Hogan, "Electricity Market Restructuring: Reforms of Reforms," Harvard University, May 25, 2001.

The MOU proposed creation of a power exchange (PX), creation of an ISO, and early phase-in of direct bilateral contracts between generators and individual customers or distribution companies. Importantly, under this proposal, the ISO and the PX would be separate entities, operating independently of each other. The PX would develop a visible electricity spot market with transparent electricity prices. It would be open to all suppliers, both within and outside of California. The ISO would manage the grid.

This organization structure—with management of the grid, dispatch of generators, and wholesale trading functions kept separate—was very different from the systems that had been adopted in other countries that had restructured their markets. Normally, these functions, which are integral parts of a smoothly functioning system, would be tightly integrated into one organization. This structure created the great risk that the functions would not be well coordinated with one another.

The resulting inefficiencies in these markets would provide opportunities for energy traders, such as Enron, to operate profitably; market inefficiencies could create profit opportunities through arbitrage and through selling financial instruments for managing the increased risks. Such profit opportunities to traders would stem directly from the costs the inefficiencies would otherwise impose on generators or consumers. It was a most remarkable public policy concept: California was creating market inefficiencies to make the system profitable for arbitrageurs (more-benign explanations for this separation are difficult to conceive).

CPUC Restructuring Order of 1995: The Preferred Policy Decision

A continued set of hearings and public submissions led to a final CPUC restructuring Order,[23] issued in December 1995, often referred to as "the preferred policy decision." The Order followed the MOU recommendation to separate the ISO (to manage the grid) and the PX (to create wholesale markets). The organizational separation of the two closely connected functions, unique to California, promised to create an extremely complex and

---

[23]*Order Instituting Rulemaking on the Commission's Proposed Policies Governing Restructuring California's Electric Services Industry and Reforming Regulation.* Decision 95-12-063 (December 20, 1995) as modified by D.96-01-009 (January 10, 1996).

untested system. Like the Blue Book, the restructuring Order proposed to deal with stranded costs through a CTC designed to allow utilities to recoup all stranded costs[24] by the year 2005, a long transition period.

At the retail level, like the Blue Book, the CPUC envisioned a system in which consumers would face many options for electricity purchases. Consumers could continue to rely completely on a local distribution company to purchase and deliver electricity or could opt for direct access through bilateral contracts. Those relying on a local distribution company could agree to either pay the average cost of electricity throughout the year or pay a real-time price, a price that varied on an hour-by-hour basis with changing wholesale market conditions. Those paying a real-time price could choose hedging contracts with third parties to reduce the risk.

The CPUC restructuring Order included one provision that some have interpreted as imposing a price cap on retail electricity prices. The language of the Order is as follows:

> *One of the goals of this proceeding is to lower the price consumers pay for electricity. Recovery of transition costs frustrates this goal because it is possible that the surcharge will exceed price decreases in a given year, resulting in higher electricity-related costs for consumers. To avoid this result, we will cap transition cost recovery so that the price for electricity does not rise, on a kWh basis, above current rate levels in effect as of January 1, 1996 without adjustment for inflation.*[25]

This provision would have limited the size of the CTC, assuring that if the CTC otherwise would have increased electricity prices above the January 1966 levels, then the magnitude of the CTC would be reduced. The precise language suggests that this provision was not intended to prevent increasing wholesale costs from being passed through to retail prices but only to limit the size of the CTC. Thus, it was not strictly a cap on retail prices but a cap on the CTC.

---

[24]In addition, long-term contractual obligations entered into before January 1, 1996, would be recovered over a longer time period.

[25]Decision 95-12-063 (December 20, 1995) as modified by CPUC Decision D.96-01-009, p. 139.

Electricity distribution functions would remain with the utilities and would be regulated by the CPUC. The regulated distribution costs would include a separate unavoidable component of retail rates that would have provided funds for other social goals: a Public Interest Energy Research Program (PIER) and demand-side management programs to promote energy efficiency.

This restructuring Order had set the framework in place but not the implementation details. That phase was left to a sequence of other CPUC decisions, including the 1996 Decision, commonly referred to as the "Roadmap Decision,"[26] which set in place a process for forming working groups of interested stakeholders to identify and discuss options for addressing many of the implementation issues. Thus, even after the restructuring Order and the passage of Assembly Bill 1890 (discussed in the next section), the CPUC continued to take the lead in translating the framework of the restructuring Decision and of the legislation into operational rules. Later sections of this book discuss impacts of the CPUC implementation.

ASSEMBLY BILL 1890

Although the CPUC had issued the restructuring Order, such a fundamental reform would be politically more viable if it were the product of legislation, not simply regulatory rulemaking. Soon after the CPUC restructuring Order, the state legislature embraced this role. State senator Steve Peace (D-El Cajon), a highly respected legislator, deeply knowledgeable about energy issues, provided the leadership throughout the process.

The legislative process culminated in Assembly Bill 1890 (AB 1890), formally authored by state assembly member James Brulte (R-Rancho Cucamonga). This measure was passed by the California legislature and signed into law in September 1996 by then-Governor Pete Wilson. It became effective in March 1998.

The bipartisan nature of the restructuring legislation was striking. Primary leadership for the entire legislative package came from a Democratic member of the state senate, Steve Peace; in the state assembly, a Republican, Jim Brulte (now a state senator), authored the bill. The bill passed with no dissenting votes from legislators of either party. A Republican governor, Pete Wilson,

---

[26]CPUC Decision D.96-03-022.

signed the bill. Moreover, the bipartisan legislation built on a very open, very public process led by the CPUC. Although, in retrospect, many commentators critical of California's restructuring have blamed Governor Wilson or Senator Peace, in reality the strengths and weaknesses of the restructuring were the result of a remarkably open and bipartisan process involving hundreds of participants from both political parties and many with no particular party affiliation.

The legislative process started from the CPUC restructuring Order of 1995 but modified several central provisions and added its own features. Most electricity, AB 1890 recognized, was generated, transmitted, and distributed by private corporations. Given this recognition, like the various CPUC Orders leading up to AB 1890, this legislation was designed not to change the dominantly private ownership of the electricity system; rather it was designed to allow competition in places where it seemed appropriate.

Like the CPUC restructuring Order, AB 1890 promised to reduce sharply the degree of vertical integration in the industry. Under AB 1890, a utility could still include the three separate functions: generation, transmission, and local distribution. Ownership of the three functions, however, would not translate to decision making coordinated among these functions. Decision making and control of its transmission function would be in the hands of the ISO, not the utility owning the transmission lines. The market structure provided incentives for local distribution decisions to be made separately from fossil fuel–fired electricity generation decisions,[27] so that a utility that both generated electricity from fossil fuel–fired plants and sold electricity at retail would operate as if two separate companies owned these two functions.

This separation of generation and local distribution was accomplished by requiring the utility to sell through the PX or the ISO all electricity it generated using fossil fuel–fired plants. The following language was included in AB 1890:

All "going forward costs" of fossil plant operation, including operation and maintenance, administrative and general, fuel and fuel transportation costs, shall be recovered solely

---

[27]Hydroelectric generation could still be coordinated with retail sales and would thus provide the utility some opportunity of changing production with changes in load.

from independent Power Exchange Revenues or from contracts with the Independent System Operator.[28]

If the investor-owned utility needed all the electricity it generated for sales to its retail customers, it was still forced to sell that electricity through the PX or ISO and purchase that same amount of electricity back. The market-clearing conditions operated independently of the identity of buyers or sellers. Thus, in selling electricity, the utility would be unable to show itself any preference as a buyer; in buying the electricity, the utility would be unable to show itself any preference as a seller.

As proposed by the CPUC restructuring Order, AB 1890 separated distribution services from retail sales of electricity. The act confirmed that distribution services would continue to be subject to CPUC regulatory authority. Distribution service would include a charge proportional to electricity use to pay for public benefit programs. These included (1) $228 million a year to pay for energy efficiency and conservation activities that had been supported by utilities, financed through their retail rates; (2) $62 million a year to create the Public Interest Energy Research program, to be managed by the California Energy Commission; and (3) $109 million a year to support emerging renewable electricity generation technologies. The total charge would be somewhat less than 3 percent of the total revenues of the investor-owned utilities and the majority had already been included in retail electricity prices prior to restructuring.

The act promised to create competition for retail electricity sales by authorizing direct transactions between electricity suppliers and end-use customers and by allowing electricity aggregators. The investor-owned utility would be the default seller of electricity. Direct access was to start simultaneously with the initiation of the PX and the ISO and was to be phased in for all customer classes by January 2002. The CPUC was directed to authorize aggregation of customer electrical load for all customer classes. Aggregation would be allowed by private-sector marketers or by cities or other public agencies, as long as individual customers could freely choose to remain with the local utility or to purchase electricity from the

---

[28]Although this language does not strictly require that all electricity the utility generates be sold through the PX or the CAISO, it ensures that the utility can recover none of its costs if it fails to do so. That economic incentive is as strong as a strict requirement.

aggregator. The transition period, during which the stranded costs would be recovered, was made much shorter than that proposed under the CPUC restructuring Order. This period would end no later than March 31, 2002, or whenever the stranded costs had been fully recovered,[29] whichever came first.

The cap on the CTC was transformed by AB 1890 into a retail price cap for electricity, a subtle but important change. It was required by AB 1890 that the investor-owned utilities' electricity prices for residential and small commercial customers would be reduced immediately by at least 10 percent below their June 10, 1996, levels. Since the retail electricity price and the price for distribution services were about the same, this requirement that the bundled rates be reduced by 10 percent translated to a requirement that the retail electricity price be reduced by about 20 percent. For other customers the retail prices could not increase above their June 10, 1996, levels.

In order to recover its stranded costs, each utility would propose to the CPUC a cost recovery plan that included the capped retail prices described above. Significantly, in order for the cost recovery plan to be approved, it had to meet the following criterion:

These rate levels for each customer class, rate schedule, contract, or tariff option shall remain in effect until the earlier of March 31, 2002, or the date on which the commission-authorized costs for utility generation-related assets and obligations have been fully recovered.[30]

Thus, under AB 1890, recovery of stranded costs required utilities to formulate and the CPUC to approve a plan in which retail rates would remain constant until the stranded costs were fully recovered.

The system was designed with the anticipation that the CTC would lead to financial accumulations each year and that the stranded costs would be paid over a limited transition period. However, wholesale prices could not be predicted. In the legislation, there was no provision for what might happen if the wholesale price exceeded the capped retail price, perhaps by a large amount, so that a utility could not pay for the authorized stranded costs or even preserve any financial assets, as happened during the electricity crisis.

---

[29]The utility would be at risk for costs not recovered by March 31, 2002.
[30]Section 10 of AB 1890.

However, AB 1890 imposed no restrictions to stop the CPUC from modifying or abandoning the stranded cost recovery plan once it had been approved, if so requested by the utility. In particular, since the CPUC could agree to reduce the amount of stranded costs to be recovered, it had the ability, if requested by a utility, to reduce authorized stranded costs to just the amount that had already been recovered. This reduction would terminate the requirement that retail rates for that utility remain at their price-capped level and would allow the CPUC to raise retail prices if needed.

High wholesale prices turned out to be a very large risk. But the risk may have been severely underestimated or completely unrecognized by many participants in the process. The utilities (or their parent corporations) could have protected themselves against high wholesale prices by entering contracts for financial hedges, designed to cover the risks of buying power from a volatile spot market while selling it at a frozen retail rate. However, although such hedge contracts were offered to utilities, they rejected these offers, apparently believing that the hedges included overestimates of the risks and thus that the prices of the hedges were too high.

In addition, an important safeguard could avoid the anomalous situation of skyrocketing wholesale prices—draining utilities of all financial assets and bringing them to the verge of bankruptcy, while retail price caps were enforced on grounds that the utility was still entitled to recover additional stranded costs. The CPUC could simply reduce allowable stranded cost recovery, terminate the transition period, and raise retail rates. However, the participants in the process probably did not recognize the risk that the CPUC would fail to act in such a way when necessary.

Like the CPUC restructuring Order, AB 1890 kept organizationally separate the management of the grid, dispatch of generators, and wholesale trading. It directed the CPUC to work with the utilities to develop a PX that was to be governed by a board that included representatives of the various stakeholder organizations in California that might be affected by operation of the PX. Otherwise, AB 1890 gave very little guidance about its functions. The only explicit language in AB 1890 was the following:

> *The Power Exchange shall provide an efficient competitive auction, open on a nondiscriminatory basis to all suppliers, that meets the loads of all exchange customers at efficient prices.*[31]

---

[31]This and the following quotation are from Section 10 of AB 1890.

In particular, there was no further guidance about the competitive auction, the bidding structure, or the length of the advance period during which electricity could be purchased. Such implementation issues were left to the CPUC, the PX board, and the FERC, the federal organization that ultimately had the authority to approve or reject any plans developed in California.

Under AB 1890, the transmission system would continue to be owned by investor-owned utilities but would be subject to FERC review. The CPUC was directed by AB 1890 to work with the utilities to develop an independent not-for-profit ISO to control the use of the transmission system. That ISO would also be governed by a stakeholder board including representatives of the affected various parties. This organization ultimately became the California Independent System Operator (CAISO).

The technical functions of CAISO were described in some detail by AB 1890, but it gave no guidance as to its market functions. The only language in AB 1890 hinting at the need for market functions was the following:

> *The Independent System Operator shall ensure that additional filings at the Federal Energy Regulatory Commission request confirmation of the relevant provisions of this chapter and seek the authority needed to give the Independent System Operator the ability to secure generating and transmission resources necessary to guarantee achievement of planning and operating reserve criteria no less stringent than those established by the Western Systems Coordinating Council and the North American Electric Reliability Council.*

As with the PX, AB 1890 left implementation issues to the CPUC, the CAISO board, and the FERC.

The restructuring plan implied that the ultimate control over the design and operation of both the PX and CAISO would be with the FERC, the federal agency with regulatory power for wholesale markets for electricity,[32] rather than with the State of California. Nevertheless, the design and operating principles would be crafted in California.

---

[32]The FERC has jurisdiction over sales of electricity for resale—wholesale electricity—and the state retains jurisdiction over retail sales of electricity and strictly intrastate electricity transmission.

The CPUC was directed by AB 1890 to work with the utilities to obtain authorization from the FERC for creating the CAISO and the PX. In April 1996, the three investor-owned utilities—PG&E, SCE, and SDG&E—submitted requests to the FERC[33] requesting approval of those restructuring elements subject to FERC jurisdiction. These included creation of the PX, authority to sell electricity through the PX at market rates, the creation of the CAISO, the vesting of operational control of transmission with the CAISO, approval of PX and CAISO tariffs, and the jurisdictional split, with the FERC regulating the wholesale markets and CPUC regulating the retail markets. The FERC largely approved these proposals, and in 1997 it authorized the first limited operation of the CAISO and the PX.

The set of regulatory changes, culminating in AB 1890, promised to fundamentally change the electricity system from one strictly regulated from "cradle to grave" into one in which market forces would play the primary role once each utility passed its transition period. Wholesale markets were intended to allow competition to determine supply, demand, and prices of electricity in wholesale transactions. Although analysts envisioned that most retail customers would continue obtaining their electricity bundled with distribution services sold by regulated utilities, the seeds for a competitive retail market were planted.

The set of changes thus was designed to transform the system while grappling with transition problems of moving from a system of vertically integrated regulated monopolies to a competitive one. This was to be a fundamental and radical transformation of the system that required leaders to face a series of challenges. In facing these challenges, new problems were created, as discussed in subsequent sections.

The framework for the fundamental transformation was thus set by AB 1890. However, it was simply a framework, not a set of detailed designs for system implementation. The structure of the PX and CAISO, as well as the markets they were to operate, was left to stakeholder committees and the CUPC, with the FERC to approve or disapprove the designs. Careful delineation of the

---

[33]FERC Docket Nos. ER96-1663-000 and EC96-19-000. The applications were filed after the CPUC restructuring Order but before passage of AB 1890. These applications were approved only after AB 1890 was signed into law. FERC took due note of the passage of AB 1890 during its proceedings.

jurisdictional split between federal and state regulators was left to the various parties to work out.

The parties were left by AB 1890 with many complex and potentially divisive issues to work out and very little time to accomplish that end. It came into effect only eighteen months after it was signed. With such a tight implementation schedule, the original applications to the FERC were filed while the California legislature was still considering AB 1890. Once the FERC approved the applications, the large size and diversity of the part-time stakeholder boards made it difficult, if not impossible, to seriously rethink or revise the original structure. Working out jurisdictional conflicts within the short time frame was close to hopeless.

The following examines these various system components in depth.

WHOLESALE MARKETS UNDER THE RESTRUCTURED SYSTEM

The restructured system required several markets and market institutions for buying and selling electricity at the wholesale level. Much work was needed to implement this complex system. Because the system had been newly designed, it was reasonable to expect that some elements would be flawed and thus require modification. In addition, because the particular market institutions and the relationship between these institutions could not initially be completely understood, significant risks were associated with these wholesale markets.

THE CALIFORNIA POWER EXCHANGE (PX)

The investor-owned utilities and the CPUC developed, and the FERC approved, plans for the PX and for the wholesale markets that the PX would manage. The PX organized a set of competitive auctions, open on a nondiscriminatory basis to all suppliers.[34] The PX initially established one-day-ahead and day-of wholesale markets for electricity. Only much later did it establish markets that allowed contractual agreements extending longer than one day in advance.

---

[34]The three large investor-owned utilities were required to sell through the PX. For all entities other than the three large investor-owned utilities, use of the PX was optional.

For both the one-day-ahead and day-of wholesale markets, the PX accepted bids to sell electricity hour by hour and bids to purchase electricity hour by hour. Prices for each hour were determined on a market-clearing basis, with all buyers for a given hour paying the same market-clearing price and all sellers receiving the same market-clearing price.

In this market, each generator would bid to sell its available supplies at some offer price,[35] and each utility (or other load-serving entity) would bid to purchase electricity at some offer price.[36] Once the market-clearing price was determined, all bids to sell with offer prices lower than or equal to the market-clearing price and all bids to purchase with offer prices greater than or equal to the market-clearing price would be accepted; all sales bids with higher offer prices or purchase bids with lower offer prices would be rejected. The market-clearing price was the lowest price that would provide enough electricity from accepted sales bids to satisfy all the accepted purchase bids.

This market-clearing price setting can also be envisioned in an equivalent way. The sales bids would be ranked from lowest offer price to highest offer price—that is, in their merit order. The purchase bids would be ranked from their highest offer price to the lowest offer price, in their merit order. Equivalently, for purchasers that simply offered to buy a fixed quantity, the quantities would just be added up. At some price, the total of sales bids up to that point in their merit order would be equal to the total of purchase bids down to that point in their merit order. That price would be the market-clearing price.

All sellers would receive the market-clearing price for their electricity, even if they bid less than that price; all buyers would pay the market-clearing price, even if they bid more than that price. This one-price market system was fashioned after typical commodity markets, in the recognition that bulk power was a nondifferentiated commodity.

---

[35]Most of these offer prices would be determined by the owner of the generator itself, although some generators, designated as "must run," would be required to set offer prices equal to zero.

[36]In practice, utilities could simply state a quantity of electricity they wished to purchase. That would be equivalent to a purchase bid at some very high price, a price ensured to be higher than the market-clearing price.

The theory behind such a bidding system is that all bids to sell electricity would be priced at the marginal cost of that electricity.[37] This theory was based on the observation that a supplier, bidding its total quantity at a single price in a competitive market, could make the most profit by bidding at a price equal to its marginal cost for producing that electricity. Increasing the sales bid above marginal cost would not increase the payment the supplier would receive from that sale—since all payments would be equal to the market-clearing price—but could cause the firm to lose a profitable sale. Bidding at a lower price than marginal cost would also not change the revenues if the bid were lower than the market-clearing price. However, such a bid could result in the firm selling electricity at a price lower than its marginal cost and thus losing money. Therefore, for a firm operating competitively, bidding a price equal to its marginal cost would lead to the greatest profit. For such firms bidding in a competitive market to sell electricity, there was a strong incentive to offer to sell at the marginal generation cost.[38]

This system was designed to simulate a perfectly competitive commodity market in which a price would be known and each firm would be able to sell its commodity at that price. It would choose to do so if its marginal cost (including any opportunity cost) were lower than its price. In theory, such a competitive market would be desirable for the wholesale electricity markets and would result in the lowest total cost to generate a given amount of electricity.

There were several alternatives to such an auction system. One alternative, in principle, would have been to set up a normal commodities futures market. People would enter bids to

---

[37]The theory was also based on the symmetric assumption that all bids to purchase electricity would be priced at just the marginal value to the user. However, the regulatory system for retail sales of electricity ensured that assumption was never valid.

[38]The theory would be precisely correct only if there were a continuum of bid prices so that if the highest successful bidder were to increase its bid price at all, it would then become higher than the next more expensive bid. If, however, there was any gap between the highest successful bid and the next more expensive bid, the firm could make more profit by bidding a tiny amount below the next bidder, not by bidding at marginal cost. But if a firm did not know exactly the prices others were planning on bidding, such a strategy would not be possible. In that case there would still be an incentive to bid just a bit more than the marginal cost.

buy and sell, prices would adjust, and ultimately equilibrium would be reached. However, such an adjustment process would take time, and electricity markets had to adjust on a much faster time scale than would normal commodity markets. Markets would need to clear on an hourly basis; there were twenty-four separate markets to clear for each day. Moreover, all adjustments would have to be completed, starting at most one day before the day of electricity delivery. Thus, prices would need to adjust very quickly. The only viable method was a computer-based system that calculated market-clearing prices and matched buyers and sellers of electricity for each hour, which would simulate the workings of a competitive commodities market without actually being one. The single price auction was designed to serve that function.

A second alternative would be to design the system to pay bidders just what they bid, rather than to pay them the market-clearing price. Under such an alternative, just as under the market-clearing system, bids would be arrayed in merit order until sufficient quantities were available to satisfy the bids to purchase electricity. This point in the merit order would determine a cut-off price. Any bids higher than the cut-off price would be disregarded, just as under the market-clearing system, whereas any bids lower would be accepted. Bidders would be paid the price they bid rather than the market-clearing price. The total cost of all purchases would be averaged, and the buyers would each pay the average bid price.

Many have argued that a system of paying on an as-bid basis, rather than on a market-clearing basis, would result in smaller total payments by the buyers of electricity. After all, those bidding to sell at prices below the cut-off price would not receive the cut-off price but would receive only their bid prices. The fallacy of that reasoning is that it implicitly assumes that the sellers of electricity would offer the same bids under an as-bid system as they would under a market-clearing system. In fact, the bidding strategies would be very different under the two systems.

Under an as-bid system, each firm makes the most profit by guessing the cut-off price and bidding at or just below that price, as long as the cut-off price is at least as high as its marginal cost. Thus, even in a competitive market, suppliers would *not* bid at their marginal costs.

If all firms could guess the cut-off price perfectly, each firm whose marginal cost was no larger than the cut-off would bid the cut-off price and each would be paid the cut-off price.[39] The cut-off price would be the same as the market-clearing price. Thus if each firm could guess the cut-off price perfectly, an as-bid system would result in the same payments as would a market-clearing system. The advantage often postulated for such a system would disappear under the best circumstance: perfect guessing.

Although each firm would learn much from observing the results of the hourly bids, twenty-four a day, there would undoubtedly be mistakes, and to compensate, firms would bid somewhat below their estimate of the cut-off price. Some lower-cost firms would guess incorrectly and bid above the cut-off price, thereby leading to increases in the cut-off price. Thus, some higher-cost firms would generate electricity and some lower-cost firms would remain idle. The total cost of generating the given quantity of electricity would therefore be increased above the cost in a market-clearing system.

The net result would be some variability in the prices paid for electricity at any hour, with some prices higher than what would have been the market-clearing price and some possibly lower. Whether such a system would increase or decrease the total payments for obtaining a given quantity of electricity would depend on the precise bidding strategies of the various market participants. However, an as-bid system could be expected to increase the total cost of generating electricity and would therefore be less efficient than a one-price market-clearing system.[40]

There was another difficulty with the auction system, arising because the system was based on hour-by-hour bidding and hour-by-hour market clearing. Some generating plants, typically operating as base-load plants, have very long and very costly periods for ramping up from no production to full capacity. These plants might be profitable to operate if they received at least a particular price, say, $30/MWh, for a large fraction of the day or for all of the peak period of a day. However, if they were operating only a few hours, even at a higher price, say, $40/MWh, they might not be profitable to operate, since the fixed costs of ramping up could be greater than the profit earned during those more limited hours. For such plants, their offer price at any hour must depend on whether they would be generating electricity at the other hours of the day.

---

[39]No firm would bid lower than its marginal cost, the cut-off price, which would be as high as the market-clearing price.

[40]The optimal bidding system in such markets remains a controversial issue, and there is much economic literature on the question. England pays on an as-bid system.

For such plants, bidding based on unit commitments—commitments of the unit to operate for long blocks of time—would be more appropriate and might result in lower bid prices. This issue was most likely to be relevant when market-clearing prices were near the costs of base-load plants and least likely to be relevant when market-clearing prices were near the costs of peaking units. Thus, this issue threatened to increase market-clearing prices during periods of relatively low prices but was likely to have little or no impact during periods of relatively high prices.

Given the alternative auction systems that could have been designed, the one chosen for the PX was reasonable, although not perfect. Since the system was necessarily untested, it could have been flawed in unpredictable ways. In fact, given the potential for strategic bidding or other means of exercising market power, any system designed for the PX could have been flawed. Any system that gave generators an incentive and ability to significantly increase the market-clearing price or the cut-off bid price had the potential to drive prices well above competitive levels. Any system that excluded bidding for long-term commitments could be awkward for some baseload generators. The possibility of such flaws was a major risk associated with restructuring the California electricity markets, indicating the importance of monitoring the system and adjusting when problems were identified.

THE CALIFORNIA INDEPENDENT SYSTEM OPERATOR (CAISO)

The system was even more complicated than has been suggested in the previous paragraphs, primarily because of the special characteristics of electricity:

- The amount of electricity used varies sharply over the course of the day as well as over the course of the year.
- The amount of electricity used at any instant cannot be perfectly predicted.
- The amount of electricity used cannot be controlled by CAISO or the utility. When an appliance, machine, computer, or light goes on, it draws electricity from the system. This is true even if insufficient electricity is available.
- Electricity cannot be stored. It is used at the instant it is generated. Therefore, electricity generation must be balanced against electricity use at every instant of time.

- When loads and electricity generation are spatially separated, electricity must be transmitted from the point of generation to the point of use. But transmission capacity is limited. Attempts to transmit too much electricity over a transmission path will result in the line shutting down to protect from permanent damage.

- If too little or too much electricity is generated in any location, relative to the use of electricity, the entire grid could become unstable and crash.

These characteristics necessitated the creation of an organization responsible for managing the transmission grid, providing resources to ensure safe operations of the grid, and maintaining sufficient quantities of electricity at all times. This organization was to be the California Independent System Operator.

Once markets cleared in the PX for a given hour, utilities and generators would have commitments to receive and to supply electricity. All utilities, in principle, would have balanced loads and resources; that is, the total load they expected would be equal to the electricity-generation resources committed.

However, those commitments could not ensure that the system would operate correctly. First, although each utility might have commitments to supply the total amount of electricity it needed, the individual commitments could well exceed the limitations of the transmission system to move electricity from points of generation to points of load. Some organization was needed to manage this transmission system. Second, although all loads and resources were to be balanced, in practice the participants in the market, even early in the day of actual delivery, could not perfectly project the electricity needs, if for no other reason, because the weather could not be predicted perfectly.

Figure 2.2, copied from the CAISO web site (http://www.caiso.com/SystemStatus.html), illustrates the issues of forecasting electricity usage. This graph shows actual and projected loads on a ten-minute-at-a-time basis on one normal Sunday in November 2001. The top line of the graph shows the available resources for each ten-minute interval during the day in green. For this day, the available generating resources are in the range of 30,000–32,000 MW.

The lower three curves show two projections of electricity consumption and actual consumption. The blue line shows the forecast

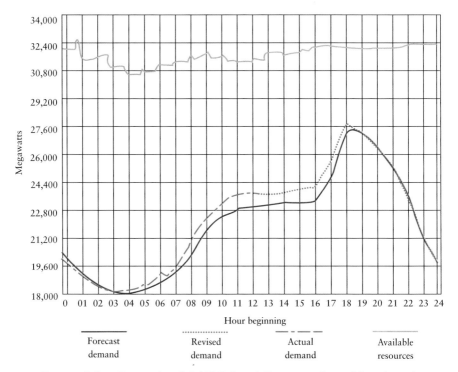

FIGURE 2.2:   Example of CAISO Load Forecast, Actual Load, and
Available Generating Resources: Sunday, November 4, 2001

electricity use completed once the previous day's electricity markets had closed. Note that, unlike the quantity of available resources, the forecast of actual load includes substantial variation over the course of the day. The broken red line shows the actual system demand (plus a 3 percent reserve margin) from midnight until noon, when the graph was generated. The dotted red line shows the "revised demand forecast," the forecast of the system demand expected for the remainder of the day. This forecast is revised by CAISO on an hourly basis to reflect changing conditions.

   In comparing the actual load with the forecast, one can see that although actual demand closely follows the forecast, at some moments demand is as much as 800 MW greater than the forecast. Even small variations of this type require responses from the system operator. Because the actual use of electricity exceeds the forecast, and because the forecast formed the basis for procurement of electricity, the system operator would be required to dispatch additional electricity on very short notice. The requirements to modify generation on short notice are even greater than suggested by Figure 2.2, since the graph illustrates only the variability across the entire control area. However, additional variability between Northern California and Southern California could require generation to be decreased at one location and increased at another.

Third, safe operation of the electricity system requires that operating reserves of generation capacity be made available to compensate for unexpected changes: a generator suddenly fails, a transmission line or transformer is damaged, electricity usage suddenly increases. Some organization was needed to obtain contractual assurance that electric generators could be brought on-line very quickly if needed. This function will be described more fully in the section "Ancillary Services."

CAISO Real-Time Markets

To perform these functions, the CAISO collected the schedules of electricity to be generated and of the electricity loads to be served by the investor-owned utilities, the municipal utilities, and a host of other entities on an hour-by-hour basis. Forty-some "scheduling coordinators" reported their schedules to CAISO; CAISO integrated these schedules and ensured that they did not collectively overload any parts of the transmission grid or were in any other ways not feasible.

Each scheduling coordinator was required to submit a balanced schedule in which the total loads and resources were equal to one another.[41] That is, the total projected use of electricity at each hour and the total generating resources to provide that electricity were required to be equal for each submission by every scheduling coordinator. Thus, in theory, the sum total of loads and resources would be balanced for the system, provided that individually submitted schedules did not create too much congestion on the transmission system, in which case CAISO was charged with rescheduling to keep the overall system operating appropriately.

However, as noted above, the participants in the market could not perfectly project the electricity needs, and the loads and resources could become unbalanced. To correct such imbalances, the CAISO was to run a real-time energy imbalance market, buying and selling electricity after the PX day-of market had closed. CAISO, therefore,

---

[41]More precisely, the sum of all loads and the sum of all generation submitted by a scheduling coordinator must be within 2 MW of each other.

had to monitor closely the actual use of electricity, comparing that to the quantities submitted by the scheduling coordinators, and had to use that evolving information to guide its purchases and sales of electricity in the real-time imbalance market. Purchases and sales could occur up to a few minutes before the electricity would be needed.

Deviations between predicted and actual supplies and demand would be corrected on this imbalance market. System designers expected these differences to be small, requiring only small purchases or sales. But the CAISO did not institute penalties for imbalances, even for extreme imbalances, although such penalties would be needed to ensure that scheduling coordinators did not deliberately misschedule whenever it was economically advantageous to do so. Thus, it should not have been a surprise that imbalances turned out to be large fractions of scheduled power.

The entity with the detailed minute-by-minute information was CAISO. Moreover, it was responsible for purchasing and selling electricity on behalf of the scheduling coordinators. Because it was engaged in these balancing transactions, its decision rules were central to the real-time market for electricity. These decision rules were encoded into CAISO software and were made publicly available as part of the published CAISO tariff. Thus, the market participants were fully aware of the rules and the operations of the market and could make their bidding decisions with full knowledge of how the markets would operate.

One rule was that the CAISO would acquire sufficient electricity to meet the loads it predicted. These predicted loads would not depend on the prices CAISO paid for the electricity and, in particular, CAISO would not reduce its electricity acquisitions even if the acquisition prices became very high, which allowed prices for electricity purchases on the imbalance market to become very high without the discipline of short-run demand reductions. A second rule was that CAISO would reject bids above some wholesale price cap level (to be discussed at a later point), which was, during different times, $250/MWh, $500/MWh, or $750/MWh. This rule put limits on wholesale prices in the imbalance market, but they were high limits.

CAISO Ancillary Services Markets

In order to manage the system, given the special characteristics of electricity, CAISO needed to obtain agreements with generators to provide generation reserves that could be called on at short notice to increase or decrease the total generation of electricity. These reserves, as well as additional resources or loads that can be controlled to keep the system stable, are referred to as "ancillary services."

Ancillary services (see box) include units whose output can be adjusted continuously and remotely by CAISO, units that can be brought up to full load within ten minutes, loads that can be reduced within ten minutes, and generation and loads available within one hour. Because CAISO balances the scheduled load and the actual load every ten minutes and adjusts its forecasts on an hourly basis, it acquires a portfolio of reserves that it can dispatch with different amounts of advance notice.

Sellers of ancillary services are paid by CAISO to make their generating units available should they be needed. If it turns out that these units are needed, the sellers are paid for the electricity generated.[42]

Every load-serving entity (typically an electric utility) is responsible for its proportional share of ancillary services. Each scheduling coordinator can choose whether to provide its share of ancillary services or to have these services purchased on its behalf by CAISO.

For those ancillary services not self-supplied by the scheduling coordinator, CAISO manages a single-price bidding system that operates in day-ahead and hour-ahead periods. The CAISO can obtain additional ancillary services through supplemental bids offered during the hour the reserves are needed.

Every generator selling ancillary services, by necessity, could generate electricity (although the converse is not true). Thus, the generation resources being bid into the ancillary services markets could have been used as resources to generate electricity, and many of the resources that were being bid into the real-time electricity market could be used as ancillary services. A single resource owner could submit bids to the CAISO to generate electricity and submit bids for each one of the ancillary services. However, the single resource could not be used simultaneously for the various purposes.

Thus, an additional complication for the CAISO was for its software to choose which bid to accept from a single generating resource, if any of its bids were to be accepted.

---

[42]Initially, this system was set up so that these units would be paid for the electricity plus paid for the ancillary services. However the FERC later required the CAISO to change the rules so that generators would be paid for either generating electricity or providing ancillary services, but not both.

TYPES OF ANCILLARY SERVICES:

Spinning reserve—Spare synchronized capacity that can be loaded to a specified amount within ten minutes and be sustained for at least two hours.

Non-Spinning Reserve (Generation)—Off-line capacity that is capable of starting up and ramping to the desired level within ten minutes and can be sustained for at least two hours.

Non-Spinning Reserve (Dispatchable Load)—Dispatchable loads that can be reduced within ten minutes and can sustain interruption for at least two hours.

Replacement Reserve (Generation)—Generation capacity secured in the day-ahead or hour-ahead market to cover forecast inaccuracies or system contingencies. Units are capable of starting and ramping up to the desired ouput within an hour.

Replacement Reserve (Dispatchable Load)—Dispatchable loads that can be reduced to a specified amount within an hour.

Regulation—Units controllable by ISO whose output is adjusted continuously by ISO to balance demand. Must be able to control with ISO AGC Package.

Black Start—Units that can start without an external source of power. Not currently running in auction via SI scheduling system.

Voltage Control—Units that contribute reactive support into the system to maintain system stability. Not currently running in auction via SI scheduling system.

SOURCE: "Scheduling and Bidding Guidelines. Market Operations," California ISO

RELATIONSHIP OF PX MARKET CLEARING AND
CAISO MARKET CLEARING

The electricity to be bought and sold on the CAISO real-time market was exactly the same electricity that could have been bought and sold under the PX in the day-ahead or day-of market. Thus, the PX markets and the CAISO imbalance market were simply alternative venues under which the same electricity purchases and sales could be arranged. Buyers could choose the markets where they wanted to make their purchase commitments just as sellers could choose the markets where they wanted to sell their electricity. The commitments to purchase and to sell through the PX were simply made up to a day earlier than the commitments to purchase and to sell through the PX real-time imbalance market. The PX and CAISO markets, therefore, were tightly linked to one another.

Moreover, the market participants understood that linkage. Therefore, prices on the two markets could be expected to be statistically very similar so long as firms were allowed to substitute freely between them. If generators expected the price on the real-time market to be higher than the price on the PX, they would avoid bidding into the PX and would choose to sell on the higher-priced real-time market. This would drive the prices up on the PX and down on the real-time market until the expected price difference disappeared. Similarly, if generators expected the imbalance market price to be lower, they would try to sell all of their electricity through the PX, thus lowering the PX price and raising the real-time price until the expected price difference disappeared. Incentives were equivalent for wholesale purchasers of electricity, who could schedule their purchases on the day-ahead or day-of PX markets or acquire their electricity through the CAISO real-time imbalance market. This process of adjusting on which market to bid would normally increase or decrease prices on the two markets until market participants expected the two prices would equate.

However, the rules established for the scheduling coordinators to some extent limited this free substitution between the markets and had the potential to increase market inefficiencies. In principle, the requirement that all submitted schedules be balanced might imply that firms would not be allowed to substitute completely between these two markets and that there would be relatively little electricity transacted on the imbalance market, except during those times when demand was unexpectedly large or small.

In practice, if utilities expected prices to be significantly lower on the real-time market, they would have a strong incentive to submit an unbalanced schedule, with scheduled resources well short of projected loads. However, the rules did not permit any-one to submit unbalanced schedules. This conflict between the incentives for unbalanced schedules and the requirement that the submitted schedules be balanced could easily be resolved through systematically biasing the projections of loads. A utility that sys-tematically and purposely underestimated loads could submit a schedule that would in fact be unbalanced but that appeared on paper to be balanced, thus meeting the letter, but not the spirit, of the requirement. Thus, the requirement that schedules be bal-anced did not substantially limit the ability of the electricity buy-ers and sellers to substitute between the two markets and did not lead to systematic price differentials between the PX markets and the CAISO real-time market.

In particular, the ability of the utilities to systematically under-estimate their loads implied that wholesale price caps in the CAISO real-time markets would translate to market prices in the PX limited by the same price caps, even though there were no for-mal price caps in the PX markets. If the wholesale market-clearing price would naturally exceed the CAISO price cap, utilities would under-schedule on the PX until the PX price was driven down to the CAISO price cap. The remaining transactions would occur on the CAISO real-time market, which was controlled by the price cap. Thus, the CAISO price cap would limit all PX prices.

When the price caps were controlling prices, there could be a shortage of electricity: the utilities might not be able to satisfy all remaining electricity demands through purchases on the CAISO. Normally, one would expect that the prospect of a shortage in the real-time market would cause utilities to bid above the price cap in the PX so that they would not be the ones to experience the consequences of the shortage. That is, if there were a $250/MWh real-time price control that was leading to shortages, one would expect a utility to be willing to bid $260/MWh or more in the PX to acquire all the electricity it needed. Normally, that would ensure that the utility's customers would not face required load shedding or blackouts (see discussion about energy emergencies in Chapter 4). However, California had established rules so that during a shortage all utilities would equally share the consequences, whether they had purchased enough electricity on the PX to cover their needs or not. Under these rules, bidding $260/MWh would cost the utility more but would provide no additional protection. Therefore, there was no incentive for any utilities to bid above the price cap on the PX, and the CAISO real-time price caps effectively controlled the maximum prices on the PX.[43]

When a utility consistently under-projected its loads, utility personnel would expect the schedule to be unbalanced and CAISO personnel would expect so as well. However, the submitted schedule would meet the formal requirement to be balanced. One unfortunate result was that the imbalance market would involve a much larger transaction volume than ever intended. In addition, operating rules that kept the CAISO separate from the PX restricted CAISO personnel from working to clear the imbalance market earlier than the hour during which the electricity was needed. This set of rules made the imbalance market unnecessarily chaotic and further created the inefficiencies that justified the role of energy traders.[44]

There is a second implication of allowing sellers and buyers to substitute between markets for their transactions. Not only would the market-clearing price be statistically the same under the PX

---

[43]It should be noted that had the situation been reversed—if price caps existed on the PX but not on the CAISO real-time market—the PX price caps would not have limited the wholesale price level. In the presence of such PX price caps, if market-clearing prices would normally exceed the price cap, utilities would try to schedule all of their loads on the PX, but the sellers would offer to sell only on the CAISO real-time market. There would be a shortage in the PX market: demand would exceed supply at the controlled price. But that shortage would have no particular relevance to the electricity system since no electricity was dispatched through the PX. The utilities, unable to purchase enough electricity on the PX, would need to purchase it on the CAISO real-time market; their electricity demands would simply become demands for purchases on the real-time market. With no price caps on the real-time market, prices would rise to market-clearing levels. The fundamental difference from the actual rules is not that the CAISO real-time market clears later than the PX markets, as some commentators have suggested, but that the electricity is dispatched through the CAISO and shortages there would have a real significance. Electricity was not dispatched through the PX and shortages there would create difficulties for the market managers and the participants but would have little or no real significance for the electricity system.

[44]It is not clear whether energy traders understood that the requirement for balanced loads would create further market opportunities for them or whether that was simply lucky from their perspective and unlucky from California's perspective. But it did predictably create many arbitrage activities.

and real-time markets; in addition, the price would depend on the total electricity supply and total electricity demand for each particular hour and not on the fractions of the electricity sold on the two markets. Therefore, for discussions of the overall wholesale price level, it will not be important to distinguish between sales on the PX market and sales on the CAISO real-time market.[45]

BIDDING STRATEGIES FOR ELECTRICITY GENERATORS

As discussed above, design of the markets operated by the PX and the CAISO was based on the theory that all bids to sell electricity or ancillary services would be priced at just the marginal cost. However, there are reasons that theory might be invalid. First, there was the possibility of exercising market power, and second, optimal bidding in competitive markets might require bidding above the marginal cost. Either reason would lead to bids that exceed the marginal cost of generating electricity or providing ancillary services.

The theory that a firm always bids to provide electricity or ancillary services at marginal cost depends on the assumption that a generator or marketer bids competitively, that is, bids taking into account the expected prices in the market and not attempting to change them. However, there would be an incentive for a firm to attempt to increase prices if it could do so and still sell its electricity. A generator could bid a high price, expecting it to be rejected. Rejection of the bid would move the market-clearing price up the merit order and might lead to a price increase. However, since the bid would be rejected, the generator's electricity would not be sold and that generating unit would earn less profit, not more.

If the generator had a portfolio of units, however, the high price, sure-to-be-rejected offer on one unit could sacrifice profits for that unit while potentially increasing prices on all other units. If the gain on the other units were great enough, then bidding a high price on only one unit could be a profitable strategy. If that were the case, the firm would have an incentive to bid above the marginal cost to increase the market-clearing or cut-off price.

If some bidding strategies were allowed, a generator would not even need a portfolio of generating units. If it were allowed to offer different bids for various portions of the capacity of a

---

[45]However, many issues of short-term risk bearing and market inefficiencies will still depend on understanding the differences between these two markets.

single unit, it would not need multiple units. A hypothetical example of the incentive to increase bids above marginal cost can be illustrated. Assume that a firm has 1,000 MW to offer for sale in a given hour, has a marginal cost of $35/MWh, and that the market-clearing price would be $40/MWh if the firm bid all 1,000 MW at its marginal cost. The firm would earn $5,000 during that hour.[46] The firm might choose as a bidding strategy to offer to sell only 900 MW during that hour at a price of $35/MWh and the last 100 MW at a price of $70/MWh. That bidding strategy would change the merit order; assume that the market-clearing price would rise to $41/MWh, a 2.5 percent increase. That firm would forgo the opportunity to sell the last 100 MW but would sell the first 900 MW at an increased price, obtaining a profit of $6/MWh on 900 MW sold for an hour. This profit would now be $5,400, an increase of $400. That firm would have a financial incentive to follow such a bidding strategy, increasing the bid price for some fraction of its capacity above its marginal cost, even though it would not be able to sell the last 10 percent of its potential output.[47]

The bidding strategy described above might be profitable for many firms, but whether it would be profitable was not known at the time of the restructuring and is not yet known with certainty even several years later. Putting the example in a California context, the generator had a capacity equal to only 2.5 percent of the total generation capacity,[48] a very small market share. Its bidding strategy reduced the amount of electricity offered for sale at market-clearing prices by 0.25 percent of the total and, as a result, increased the market-clearing price by 2.5 percent. Thus, the example assumes that the percentage increase in price is equal to ten times the percentage reduction in quantity offered for sale. This assumption might have been realistic when the California electricity system was operating near full capacity, the California retail price

---

[46]The firm would be selling 1,000 MW for one hour; the market-clearing price would exceed the marginal cost by $5/MWh.

[47]This example depends on the firm bidding high enough so that the high price bid is rejected. If the firm simply offers an increased bid but is able to sell its electricity on this market, it cannot increase its profit. In addition, this example assumes that the firm does not expect it might have to repay any overcharges it creates by utilizing this strategy.

[48]For this example, it will be assumed that at the original market-clearing 40,000 MW would be utilized.

caps were limiting retail responses, and there were few opportunities for importing additional electricity into California. In this example, under those assumptions, a firm having only a very small market share had the incentive to bid so as to raise the market-clearing price by 2.5 percent.

Under these assumptions, all firms with market shares of 2.5 percent or greater and marginal costs of $35/MWh or greater would have the same incentive as shown above, if such bidding strategies were allowable. If, for example, firms collectively having 50 percent of the market share would independently all follow the same strategy, then the market-clearing price could increase by around 50 percent, or to $60, in response to the 5 percent reduction in total quantity sold. At this higher wholesale price, a 2.5 percent market share firm would no longer have an incentive to follow this strategy, but a firm having 5 percent or more market share would.[49]

If any of the basic assumptions are relaxed (full capacity, retail price caps, little opportunity to import additional electricity, multiple bid levels allowed from one unit), then there would not be an incentive, or the incentive would be greatly reduced. The relaxation of any assumption (other than the fourth one) would reduce the impact of supply reductions on price. In that case, the incentive to bid above marginal cost would be sharply reduced and would be relevant only for firms with significantly greater market share.

For example, assume that under the same assumptions described above, the percentage increase in price would be twice as great as the percentage decrease in supply. If the firm offered to sell only 900 MW at marginal cost and the last 100 MW at a price above market-clearing , then the market-clearing price would rise to $40.20/MWh, a 0.5 percent increase. That firm would obtain a profit of $5.20/MWh on 900 MW sold for an hour: a profit of $4,680 and a decrease of

---

[49]With a market-clearing price of $60/MWh, the firm having only 1,000 MW of capacity would no longer have an incentive to bid high prices for 10 percent of its capacity. However, a firm with 2,000 MW, a 5 percent market share, would have such an incentive. That firm, if it bid all 2,000 MW at cost would obtain a profit of $50,000 for the hour. The firm reducing its sales to 1,800 MW could increase market-clearing price 5 percent to $63/MWh. This would increase the difference between price and marginal cost to $28/MWh and would increase profit to $50,400. Thus the incentive to offer a very high bid on a small fraction of the output would remain for firms with a 5 percent market share even though it would disappear for firms with only a 2.5 percent market share.

$320. That firm would not have a financial incentive to follow such a bidding strategy. Similarly, a 5 percent market share firm would not find such a strategy profitable.[50]

If the firm were restricted in its bidding so that a segmented bid would require 50 percent of its output to be offered at the higher price, the incentive would also disappear. Assume again that the percentage increase in price would be ten times greater than the percentage decrease in supply. If the firm offered to sell only 500 MW at marginal cost and the last 500 MW at a price above market clearing, then the market-clearing price would rise to $45/MWh, a 12.5 percent increase. That firm would sell the first 500 MW, obtaining a profit of $10/MWh on 500 MW sold for an hour. This profit would now be $5,000, neither increasing nor decreasing. That firm would not have a financial incentive to follow such a bidding strategy.

Thus, exercise of market power would be less likely if the system were well below capacity or when additional electricity could easily be imported into California. In addition, if demand for electricity were more responsive to price changes, then supply reductions would have only smaller impacts on prices and the incentives to bid above marginal cost would be much smaller than suggested in this example.

With California's restructuring there was a significant risk that firms could and would exercise market power in the manner described above or by following other bidding strategies. This created risks that the wholesale market prices would be too high. Moreover, the risk that firms might exercise market power did not depend on the particular auction system. The potential would have been as great for an as-bid auction system as it was for a market-clearing system. Thus, this was a risk of moving to almost any deregulated wholesale market.

In addition to the risk that generators could exercise market power was the possibility that competitive reasons would cause generators to offer bids to sell electricity or ancillary services at prices greater than marginal generation costs. These competitive

---

[50]If the firm offered to sell 1,800 MW at marginal cost and the last 200 MW at a price above market clearing, then the market-clearing price would rise to $40.40/MWh, a 1 percent increase. That firm would obtain a profit of $5.40/MWh on 1,800 MW sold for an hour, earning $9,720 rather than the $10,000 it could earn by bidding at marginal cost.

reasons would likewise lead to market-clearing prices higher than would be the case in their absence.

As indicated above, generators selling ancillary services could generate electricity and, for many firms, generators selling electricity could have used the capacity to sell ancillary services. Although a single resource owner could submit bids to CAISO to generate electricity and bids for each one of the ancillary services, the single resource could not be used simultaneously for the various purposes. The generator had to decide what prices to place on each of its bids, given its understanding about how the CAISO software would select among the various bids from a single generator. The generator bidding on the PX had to decide what prices to bid given its belief about the CAISO prices for real-time imbalance electricity and for ancillary services, markets into which it could bid, but only if it did not commit its electricity on the PX.

Given multiple opportunities, a firm bidding competitively—that is, not expecting to change any market-clearing prices—would not obtain the greatest profit by bidding at just its marginal cost. Such a profit-maximizing firm, when bidding to sell electricity on either the PX or CAISO markets, had a financial incentive to take into account its opportunity cost[51] of not being able to sell the capacity as ancillary services, which would lead to increases in the offer price at which it would bid to sell electricity. Similar considerations would hold for bidding into the ancillary services markets. A profit-maximizing firm, when bidding to sell its capacity as nonspinning reserve, must take into account its opportunity cost of not being able to sell the capacity as another ancillary service, such as regulation. Thus, the bid to sell as nonspinning reserve would be increased above marginal cost, adding in opportunity cost.

In general, optimal bidding will require the generator to estimate an opportunity cost based on the most profitable of the alternative uses for the generation capacity. This opportunity cost must be added to the marginal cost in order to determine optimal bids if the firm is operating competitively. Thus, firms bidding competitively can be expected to bid generation capacity at prices that are greater than marginal costs.

---

[51]The opportunity cost is the cost of having to forgo one opportunity to pursue another opportunity. Although opportunity cost is not easily measurable, it is a real economic cost often important for decision making.

The magnitude of the opportunity cost will depend on the expected market-clearing price for electricity or for ancillary services in the most profitable of the alternative uses. However, the generator does not typically know these market-clearing prices at the time it submits its bid and must guess them, instead. Thus, for a firm bidding competitively, the bid prices for each possible use of the generation capacity must take into account the bidder's best estimates of the market-clearing prices for each ancillary service and for electricity in addition to the bidder's estimates of its own marginal costs. Given the number of interacting markets, the problem of choosing the profit-maximizing bids would be very complex.[52] But no matter how complex the bidding problem, the optimal bids will normally be at prices greater than marginal cost.

The role of opportunity costs in raising prices can be difficult to evaluate quantitatively by an independent market observer because opportunity costs cannot be directly observed. Similarly, the role of market power in raising prices can be difficult for independent market observers to evaluate quantitatively since the exercise of market power may involve complex bidding strategies. These difficulties translate into monitoring problems, since the two issues are, at least on the surface, observationally equivalent. The simple observation that bid prices exceed marginal cost does not establish how much of the deviation is the product of market power and how much is the product of a purely competitive recognition of opportunity costs.

DIVESTITURE OF IOU-GENERATING ASSETS UNDER THE RESTRUCTURED SYSTEM

The degree of vertical integration in the industry was sharply reduced by AB 1890 and subsequent CPUC rulings. Although an investor-owned utility could still include the three separate functions—generation, transmission, and local distribution—the legislation

---

[52]Consider, for example, a firm bidding to sell electricity into the PX. It knows it could bid to sell the generating capacity as a reserve in an ancillary services market. It knows that if it makes the capacity available as a reserve, there would be some probability the capacity would be called upon to deliver electricity. Thus the opportunity cost would take into account the profits it would expect to earn being available as a reserve and the profits it would earn if it agreed to remain as a reserve but were called upon to generate electricity, with each term scaled by the probability of that event. Thus the firm would need to evaluate the expected prices for ancillary service and the prices it would be paid for electricity, as well as the probabilities of the various outcomes.

ensured that ownership of the three functions would not translate into coordinated decision making among these functions.

However, there was still a concern that common ownership of generation and retail functions would make it difficult to operate a competitive wholesale market and that utility ownership of a large market share of generating capacity would give the utilities market power, resulting in wholesale prices of electricity that would be too high. To address that concern, several options could have been implemented at the time of the restructuring.

First, the restructuring legislation could have allowed the utilities to continue acquiring electricity directly from their own generators, as well as buying it from nonutility generators, either through organized markets or through bilateral contracts. This option would have allowed the utilities to maintain some vertical integration. However, this could have posed incentive problems. First, it was recognized that acquisitions by the distribution component of the utility from the generating component would not be at arm's length, which would be true even if these functions were organized into two companies operating under the same corporate ownership, selling to one another. Prices would be set as intracorporate transfer prices and thus would not be truly arm's length. Therefore, intracorporate transfer pricing for financial regulation would not be dependable; there could well be incentives for increasing or decreasing the transfer price.

In addition, many people believed that a competitive wholesale market would not be possible without divestiture of generating assets. In particular, the local distribution component of the utility would choose to purchase from its own generating component even at a higher cost than electricity offered by new market entrants generating electricity. Once beyond the transition period, those high costs would simply be passed on to the consumers.[53] Since potential entrants in the wholesale market

_____

[53]Any utility that paid its own generating assets a higher-than-competitive price at the wholesale level of the market would increase its own average cost. A regulated utility would pass on these higher costs as higher prices to retail customers. If there were full retail competition, the increase in price of the regulated utility would give its competitors an advantage and the regulated utility would begin to lose market share. However, without such full retail competition one could not ensure that retail competition would fully discipline such wholesale transactions.

would understand these incentives, there would be only reduced incentives for new companies to invest in new generating assets. Existing electric utilities would then not face the market competition in their roles as electricity generators, which was the goal of the restructuring. The desirable benefits of a competitive system might not emerge.

Finally, this plan would not reduce the market power of the utilities in the wholesale markets. They would be net sellers of electricity as corporations. Although they faced average cost regulation for their retail sales, there still would be an incentive to exercise market power in wholesale markets if they were net sellers in those markets.

The CPUC ultimately implemented a two-fold solution. First, the CPUC required and/or strongly encouraged the utilities to divest themselves of their generating assets wherever possible. They were required to divest 50 percent of their generating assets and faced strong financial incentives to divest the remainder. Second, all remaining fossil-fired electricity generation owned by the utility could be sold only through the PX or the CAISO.[54] Together, those rules would ensure that the PX and the CAISO markets would include large volumes of transactions and that utilities would be precluded from any meaningful self-dealing between their wholesale and retail operations and would eliminate or sufficiently reduce their market power in the wholesale markets.

Divestiture would have one other regulatory advantage. Once the CTC was selected as a mechanism for recovering stranded costs, there still was the problem of appropriately measuring stranded costs. If the utilities continued to own the generating plants, there would not be a clean test of how large the stranded costs were. There would be the need for further hearings and possibly litigation to determine the values of the plants the utilities still owned. However, if they sold the plants, the economic loss could be measured easily as the difference between the remaining book value of the generating plant and its sales price. Thus, although this was at most a secondary reason, it did provide some motivation for encouraging the utilities to divest much of their fossil generation capacity.

---

[54]More precisely, no costs could be recovered for this generation unless the electricity were sold through the PX or the CAISO.

The incentives for divestiture were successful. As of 2000, only 29 percent of the electricity sold in the state was generated by the utilities and 44 percent was generated through plants that had been divested by the electric utilities and were then owned by nonutility generators. Details of the sales appear in Table 2.2, including which plants were sold to which firms, of what name-plate capacity, the book value, and the sales price.

When generation plants were sold at prices above their book value, the transaction would reduce the amount of stranded costs yet to be recovered through the CTC. Although some plants sold at prices below their book value—and thus were truly stranded costs—most plants sold at higher prices. On net, the divestiture of plants resulted in sales prices that exceeded the remaining book values by more than 70 percent, significantly reducing the amount of stranded costs yet to be recovered through the CTC.

Long- and Medium-Term Wholesale Contracts for Electricity

The divestiture required by the regulations created potential new problems associated with the accounting used to recover stranded costs. As the investor-owned utilities divested their generation assets, there could be incentives for the utilities to enter into long-term electricity purchase contracts with the company buying the generators. If there were linked agreement both to sell the generator and to purchase electricity under a long-term contract from that generator, there was a fear that the financial incentives could distort the selling price and the long-term sales price. Guarding against this potential would require more regulatory oversight.

In addition, there was a fear that long-term contracts could simply substitute for a utility ownership of the generators and a competitive market might not be created. Potential new entrants into the wholesale electricity market might be discouraged in the same way as would be the case absent divestiture of the assets. To ensure that the wholesale markets would not be too thin and there would be too little competition, there was a desire to limit the long-term contracts at the wholesale level.

However, this fear failed to recognize that with growth in electricity use would be growth in the needs for new electricity generation. There would be competition among the suppliers to provide for these new needs. That competition could be through spot markets or market competition for long-term contracts.

TABLE 2.2

Divestiture of IOU-Generating Assets in California

Power Plant	Purchaser	Nameplate Capacity MW	Book Value $million	Sale Price $million
Morro Bay, Moss Landing, Oakland	Duke Energy Corp.	2,881	390.2	501.0
Contra Costa, Pittsburg, Potrero	Southern Energy	3,166	318.3	801.0
Geysers (Sonoma & Lake Counties)	Calpine Corp.	1,353	273.1	212.8
	PG&E Subtotal	**7,401**	**981.6**	**1,514.8**
Alamitos, Huntington Beach, Redondo Beach	AES Corp.	4,706	224.1	781.0
Cool Water, Etiwanda, Ellwood, Mandalay, Ormond Beach	Houston Industries	4,019	288.3	277.0
El Segundo, Long Beach	NRG Energy and Destec	1,583	168.8	116.6
San Bernadino, Highgrove	Thermo Ecotek	300	(4.3)	9.5
	SCE Subtotal	**10,607**	**676.9**	**1,184.1**
Encina, Kearny, and other Peakers	NRG Energy and Dynegy	1,347	94.8	365.0
South Bay	San Diego Unified Port District	833	64.4	110.0
	SDG&E Subtotal	**2,180**	**159.2**	**475.0**
	Total	**20,187**	**1,818**	**3,174**

SOURCE: California Energy Commission, www.energy.ca.gov/electricity/divestiture.html

The competition to offer electricity on long-term contracts can be as intense as, or more intense than, spot market competition. Such competition for long-term contracts could allow a buyer of electricity and the seller of electricity to negotiate for a set of mutually satisfactory contractual terms, including appropriate distribution of risks and obligations. Because of the long-term significance of such a contract, the competing sellers tend to put much attention into their offers and the purchasers tend to evaluate the alternative offers very carefully.

Since long-term contracts can include mutually beneficial agreements on risk sharing, the average prices in these contracts could be lower than the expected prices when all competition is based on spot markets. A merchant generator facing the vagaries of water conditions, temperature, gas prices, and day-to-day fluctuations on spot markets may need a higher average market-clearing price to finance new generation than would a merchant generator with a long-term contract, having secure commitments to buy electricity at fixed prices or prices indexed to a reasonable set of external market conditions (such as the natural gas price).

Thus, the linked beliefs that (1) exclusive reliance on spot markets was necessary to assure competition and that (2) negotiated long-term contracts would limit competition were both fallacious. However, these beliefs, even if they were fallacious, seemed to motivate the CPUC in implementing AB 1890 to impose regulatory restrictions against the utilities entering long-term contracts.

To guard against the perceived problems of long-term contracts, once AB 1890 had been passed the CPUC restricted the ability of the investor-owned utilities to enter into any long-term or medium-term contracts. The CPUC required the utilities to acquire all their electricity not already under long-term contract through the PX or CAISO. This restriction went well beyond the long-term contracts. Since the PX and the CAISO originally did not have long-term or medium-term contracts, this requirement effectively prohibited the utilities from entering any long- or medium-term contracts.

The utilities tried as early as 1999 to gain the right to procure electricity on a longer-term basis. In March 1999, SCE filed an application for a pilot program under which it could enter traditional power purchase agreements for electricity and capacity. But the CPUC denied the application. In mid-1999 the PX applied to organize a block-forward market, the FERC approved the application, and the CPUC approved the request by the SCE and PG&E to participate in that market. But the block-forward market allowed contracts for no more than one year. More significantly, such markets, by necessity, offered a standardized contract and did not allow the wide range of contractual agreements that would be desirable for a utility to cover its purchases. But it was a step, albeit a small step, toward allowing the utilities to move away from exclusive reliance on spot markets to acquire electricity. However, until August 2000, the utilities had no right to enter bilateral contracts. The year 2000 events will be discussed in the following chapter.

Although there may have been a reason for discouraging long-term contracts during divestiture, once the divestiture was completed, there was no continuing need to regulate against such contracts. There was already much economic bias discouraging investor-owned utilities from committing to purchase very large quantities of electricity under long-term contracts.[55]

There remains debate about whether the CPUC decisions following AB 1890 were completely responsible for the investor-owned utilities' lack of long-term contracts or whether the utility executives should have entered these contracts with the stockholders bearing the asymmetric risk. Whatever the resolution of this debate, if it ever is resolved, the utilities had been relying dominantly on short-term spot markets for electricity when it became apparent that wholesale prices were rising rapidly. The financial risk was very great.

If investor-owned utilities had, after the restructuring, developed portfolios of contracts, some long-term, some medium-term, and some more flexible, they could have managed some of the risks inherent in the new system.

It is important to note that long-term contracts would not have been a panacea. Nor would they have ensured that the investor-owned utilities would have been able to buy wholesale electricity at lower prices than they could have with short-term contracts. Contracts, whether short-, medium-, or long-term, must have two parties. If the parties knew with significant certainty that the short-term prices would always be higher than the proposed long-term contract price, the rational electricity supplier would never

---

[55]This issue is discusses more fully in a later section, "Risk Bearing in the Restructured Retail Market."

be willing to offer such a long-term contract. Conversely, if the parties knew with significant certainty that the short-term prices would always be lower than the proposed long-term contract price, the rational electricity buyer would never be willing to accept such a long-term contract. For both parties to agree on a long-term contract price, they must assign a significant probability that short-term prices will be higher than the long-term contractual price and a significant probability they will be lower. Thus, it was never the case that entering into long-term contracts could have dependably reduced electricity acquisition prices from the spot prices.

However, entering such contracts could have substantially reduced the risk of large changes—up or down—in the acquisition cost of electricity. Utilities with such contracts thereby could have guarded against or at least limited the high risk of large fluctuations in the wholesale price of electricity. But that was not to be the case and thus the system was characterized by unnecessarily large risks.

Risk Bearing

Restructuring of wholesale markets created deep economic risks for investor-owned utilities. The wholesale market for electricity promised to be very volatile. Capacity limitations of electricity generators implied that if the system were to approach capacity, marginal cost would increase sharply. All spot sales of electricity would sell at a price equal to this marginal cost. Thus, small differences in requirements for electricity generation could lead to very large differences in the spot wholesale price. Moreover, the utilities were buying most of their electricity on these spot markets because they had divested most of their generating assets and had not entered long-term electricity supply contracts. Thus, total expenditures for acquiring electricity could increase sharply. Although this would not be an issue if the system never approached full capacity, continuing excess generation capacity could not be guaranteed.

The mix of generating facilities increased the risk that the system could approach capacity limitations or face volatile prices. Figure 2.3 shows the 1999 operational capacity of California's three investor-owned utilities in terms of the primary sources of energy used to generate electricity. Data are nameplate capacities.

Over half of the primary energy was natural gas. However, the infrastructure of pipelines to move natural gas in California was extremely limited, as was the capacity of pipelines to bring natural

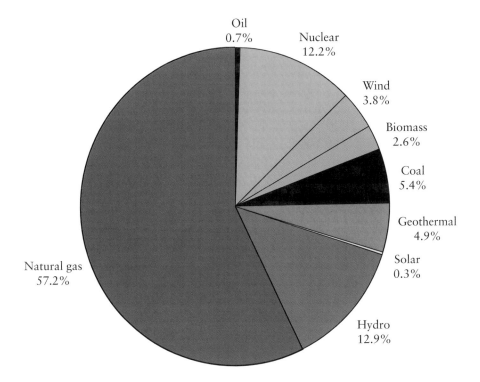

Figure 2.3:   1999 Operational Capacity of California's
Three Investor-Owned Utilities

NOTE: Some nuclear, all coal are out of state.

SOURCE: California Energy Commission, www.energy.ca.gov/electricity/operational_capacity.html

gas into California. Therefore, the risk stemming from the high volatility of natural gas prices and natural gas availability in the state was great. Utilities could, and did, sign long-term contracts to buy natural gas. However, such contracts, while reducing this risk, did not eliminate the risk entirely and would not assure that *additional* gas could be obtained when needed.

Another twenty percent of the electricity was generated through hydropower; however, the amount of available hydropower depended on the rainfall during the previous year. More significantly, much of the imports of electricity into California were derived from hydro-electric power in the Pacific Northwest; however, the availability of this electricity was also subject to much uncertainty. In addition, low rainfall in California might accompany those years of low rainfall in the Pacific Northwest. These risks were weakly correlated so that overall risk was increased.

Nuclear power had its own financial risks. In addition to cost and reliability variability, nuclear power faced the political risk that nuclear electric generating plants would be shut down for safety or other environmental reasons.

Divestiture had greatly increased the risk facing investor-owned utilities, although it did not change the inherent system risk. If the utilities had continued to own their generating capacity, they would have faced cost variations that changed with the average generation cost; but because they had divested the assets, they would face cost variations that changed with the marginal cost of electricity. Since the marginal cost is much more volatile than the average cost, divestiture led to far more cost volatility for the investor-owned utilities.

This risk could have been mitigated by long-term contracts, even long-term contracts whose prices were indexed to some measure of average cost of electricity generation—for example, contracts indexed to natural gas prices. However, the CPUC discouraged long-term contracts.

GENERATION CAPACITY RISK

Under both the old integrated system and the restructured competitive system there were inherent risks associated with decisions on how much new generation capacity to build, costs of operating existing capacity, and contractual commitments to buy or sell electricity. The fundamental risks associated with costs of fuel to generate electricity were the same under either system, as were the uncertainties about demand growth. If reserve capacity were the same under the two systems, then the risks of short supply of energy would have been the same as well. However, the incentives for capacity investment and utilization are very different under the restructured system than under the old system of vertically integrated utilities.

Under the old integrated system, if all utilities maintained enough reserve capacity to keep marginal generation costs very low, all could still earn sufficient financial returns on the capacity to justify the investment. Thus, utilities could continually invest in new generating capacity and the system could maintain equilibrium with adequate reserve capacity. The retail utility customers would continue paying the cost of the infrequently used capacity and electricity prices would remain systematically high and quite stable over time. Risks would be low because there would be adequate reserve capacity.

With competitive wholesale markets, if all merchant generators maintained enough reserve capacity to assure that marginal generation costs remained low, wholesale prices would remain low; however, most generators could not earn sufficient financial return on the capacity to justify the investment. Investment would be halted, leading to reductions in reserve capacity over time. As reserve capacity dropped, the frequency of price spikes and the average price of electricity would increase. As a result, the incentive to build new generation capacity would increase. If all went well, the system would approach a new equilibrium in which the average price of electricity would be equal to its average cost and the average over time of its marginal cost. In this equilibrium, the system would have less reserve capacity than it would under the old integrated system, causing the average cost and the average over time of price to be lower as well. However, prices would not be stable and risks would be larger because there would be only smaller amounts of reserve capacity.

However, in this new restructured system, reserve capacity might not smoothly approach a new equilibrium, especially if there are long lags from the decisions to invest in new generating capacity until the time that generating capacity goes on-line. It would be quite possible to have periodic times of inadequate reserve capacity and periodic times of excess reserve capacity, classic "boom and bust" cycles. During times of inadequate reserve capacity, wholesale prices would become very high, encouraging much new investment, particularly if investors did not have good information about future conditions; during times of excess reserve capacity, wholesale prices would be very low, discouraging investment. Unless investors could reasonably project future conditions, including the new electricity generation capacity to be constructed, each boom period would set the stage for the next bust; each bust would set the stage for the next boom. Risks would be further increased.

Such wholesale market fluctuations would be very disruptive even if they, on average, did not increase the wholesale electricity price, because they could create political pressures for price stabilization regimes at either the wholesale or the retail level. In addition, if, as was the case in California, retail price controls were already in place, such fluctuations (even short-term ones) would carry with them the possibility of financial crises.

In a competitive market system, encouraging the right amount of reserve capacity is very difficult and, to reduce the risks, careful policy development is needed. Several options can mitigate the risks of "boom and bust" cycles in competitive wholesale markets. First, good market information on projected demand growth, energy efficiency investments, and new capacity investments helps to reduce the cycles associated with myopic decision making. Markets for capacity in addition to markets for the electricity itself could help but have their own difficulties. Long-term contracts between generators and utilities can help match capabilities with needs and reduce the problem.

However, in the period after AB 1890 was signed, none of these options was adopted. The California Energy Commission reduced its role in creating forecasts of future electricity supply and demand conditions. No capacity markets were established, and long-term contracts were discouraged. Thus, the new system created the risk of severe long-term price fluctuations. State agencies did nothing to mitigate those risks.

WHOLESALE MARKETS: IN SUMMARY

The AB 1890 and CPUC rules created a complicated set of wholesale markets imperfectly coordinated with one another. These markets were given monopoly or near-monopoly status and thus utilities could not escape any problems associated directly with these markets. There remained, however, opportunities for exercise of market power by even those generators with small market share. Risk management options were taken from the investor-owned utilities through divestiture and through overreliance on spot wholesale markets, and volatility in the wholesale markets was nearly ensured. The risk of boom and bust cycles was created. The interplay of these various markets, the resulting bidding strategies of utility-buyers, generators of electricity, electricity marketers, and municipal utilities, and the responses of the CAISO and the PX personnel were all untested at the time of the restructuring.

The associated risks through the wholesale markets were natural implications of this particular system restructuring, and in fact would have been risks of any radical restructuring of the electricity system. The existence of risks does not imply that the undesirable outcomes *will* occur, but that they *may* occur. Risks suggest the need to monitor the wholesale markets and to be prepared to modify the system if the undesirable outcomes in fact come about, something that political leaders need to be willing to do.

RETAIL MARKETS UNDER THE RESTRUCTURED SYSTEM

Creating competitive retail markets was seen to be even more of a challenge, even though there had been extensive experience in other nations, such as Australia, New Zealand, and Great Britain. An ultimate goal was to set up a competitive retail market for electricity; however, at least two factors stood in the way: retail market power and risk management.

Although issues of retail market power and risk management could be, in principle, the same for investor-owned utilities, municipal utilities, and co-ops, the restructuring legislation treated investor-owned utilities differently than the others, if for no other reason than the CPUC had jurisdiction only over investor-owned utilities. Thus, the initial CPUC restructuring Order and AB 1890 applied only to investor-owned utilities, not to the municipal utilities or the co-ops. Since the rules for investor-owned utilities fundamentally changed and the rules for municipal utilities and co-ops did not, most of the following sections will discuss the investor-owned utilities and little attention will be paid to municipal utilities and co-ops.

Local distribution companies had a natural monopoly for the delivery services, the wires, the transformers, and the control systems. In addition, in the short-term they could be expected to have a significant degree of market power for the electricity itself, since electricity had always been sold as a commodity, bundled with the delivery services. Unless retail sales of electricity were unbundled from sales of delivery services, the issue of retail market power would remain.

The system established by the CPUC and AB 1890 therefore allowed delivery services to be decoupled from the retail sales of electricity. The delivery services would still be provided by the investor-owned utilities, operating as monopoly franchises, earning a regulated fee. The commodity itself could be sold by aggregators or generators, or utilities could sell electricity bundled with distribution services.

Investor-owned utilities would operate as regulated retail sellers of electricity subject to review and control by the CPUC, which communicated its intention to move to performance-based

regulation, a system whereby performance goals would be negotiated, including cost performance improvements. Nevertheless,
regardless of whether such a system was implemented, the investor-
owned utilities would remain as regulated firms.

As discussed above, during the transition period, AB 1890
imposed price caps for retail electricity sales by the incumbent utilities during a transition period. This price cap created a dilemma.
On one hand, the utilities were being required by AB 1890 to
reduce electricity prices for residential and small commercial customers. On the other hand, the CTC magnitude was to be chosen
so that all stranded costs would be recovered over a small number
of years. Thus with the CTC, the retail price of electricity would
be approximately equal to the recent historical electricity component of the bundled retail price, not 20 percent below that level.

The dilemma was resolved through a financial instrument.
The utilities were authorized during the transition period to issue
"rate reduction bonds" to finance the difference between their
cost for electricity (wholesale price plus CTC) and the price-
capped retail price, as well as to refinance some of their existing
capital equipment. These bonds would be repaid once all stranded
costs had been recovered and the CTC was no longer in operation. This plan implied that the retail electricity price reduction
that the ratepayers thought they were enjoying would be repaid
in later years.

RETAIL COMPETITION

The CPUC restructuring Order and Assembly Bill 1890 created
the opportunity for competition for retail electricity sales, in
principle allowing any customers to enter bilateral contracts with
electricity suppliers and therefore to bypass the electric utilities,
even though the CTC could not be bypassed. The investor-owned
utilities would be default sellers of electricity, available for everyone who wished to purchase their retail electricity from these
utilities. Their price-capped rates would be available for all customers, even those that switched to other retail suppliers but subsequently chose to return, implying an asymmetrical relationship
between the utility and the new competitors: the new competitors could choose whether to take new or returning customers,
but the utility could not.

Direct access and retail electricity competition for residential and
small commercial customers was made more difficult by the retail

price cap. For other electricity suppliers to be competitive on the basis of price, they would have to sell electricity at the investor-owned utility's capped price as well, after paying the CTC; they would have to sell electricity at prices lower than the sum of the wholesale price plus the CTC, losing more money the more electricity they sold.

New entrants could create a distinction in the minds of consumers about electricity delivered from different companies. For example, they could sell "green" electricity, advertised to be generated entirely or primarily by renewable sources. But this component of the market would necessarily be small, if for no other reason than most of the renewable forms of electricity were being sold under contract to the large electric utilities.

Entrants could bundle energy efficiency measures with electricity to help consumers reduce the overall cost of obtaining energy services (for example, warmth, lighting, cooking, clothes drying, refrigeration). The utilities themselves were offering some of these services using some of the public benefit charges included in delivery fees.

New entrants could compete on the basis of price if they marketed electricity primarily to those customers whose loads were less time-variant than typical loads. These could be industrial customers who used electricity at a roughly equal rate throughout the day or whose use of electricity did not vary across the year. For these customers, a new entrant could save money on the wholesale purchases of electricity and might be able to sell electricity at a lower retail price than did the incumbent utilities; however, the new entrant would have to pick its customers carefully.

In principle, some retailers could provide higher reliability of electricity for the industrial or commercial customers for whom reliability was essential or interruptible service for those customers willing to accept service interruptions in exchange for a lower overall bill. However, because electricity was being delivered by the same utility, no matter which firm was selling the electricity itself, it was not clear that an individual electricity retailer could economically offer such services without cooperation from the utility providing the delivery services.

These market opportunities existed for new entrants, but at least during the transition period, they were niche markets. Thus, it could be expected that during the transition period retail competition would be relatively limited.

RISK MANAGEMENT IN THE RESTRUCTURED RETAIL MARKET

Utilities had historically played the fundamental role of managing retail price risk for their customers, investing in a portfolio of electricity supply assets, some with costs that would vary with market conditions (for example, natural gas–fired units), some with costs that were predictable over time (for example, QF contracts or geothermal units), some with costs that remained low but had less predictable capacities (for example, hydroelectric), and some that provided energy services by using less electricity (for example, energy efficiency investments). For gas-fired units, whose cost could vary with market conditions, utilities would secure long-term contracts for natural gas to reduce the risk.

However, in competitive retail markets, risk management could be a challenge. As it turned out, California didn't come to grips with that challenge until it was too late.

Under the restructured system, management of retail price risk would be left entirely to the competitive marketplace. Given that the investor-owned utilities were required to divest most generation, buy their electricity on spot markets, and avoid long-term contracts, they had few instruments left for managing price risk. During the transition period, retail prices were expected to remain fixed, although the wholesale price of electricity and the CTC would both vary. Once the transition period was over, however, the retail customers could be expected to bear most of the risk of price fluctuations on the volatile wholesale market.

Retail customers remaining with the utilities and wishing for financial stability after the transition period would be expected to purchase financial hedges against fluctuations in wholesale prices. The expectation that many residential and small commercial customers would be willing to engage in sophisticated financial transactions in order to stay with the default utility seems improbable.[56] The more likely outcome, once the transition period was over and consumers began understanding the issues, would be for customers to accept the risk of price variations or to buy electricity from retailers that were willing to offer some assurances of price stability.

New electricity retailers could ensure price stability by providing risk management electricity sales contracts to attract customers

---

[56]See Ralph Cavanagh, "Revisiting 'the Genius of the Marketplace': Cures for the Western Electricity and Natural Gas Crises," *Electricity Journal* (June 2001).

and purchasing electricity under a mix of different contracts to manage the risk for their customers. Retail prices would vary with wholesale market conditions, but the variations would be greatly moderated.

If a variety of retail sellers emerged after the transition period, customers would be able to purchase retail electricity from retailers who hedged price risk in ways appropriate to their customers, which would require customers to be willing to leave the default utility.

The CPUC could have chosen an alternative wherein utilities could have operated as regulated monopolies, selling primarily to small residential and commercial customers and providing risk management for their customers. The utilities would negotiate a mix of short-, medium-, and long-term contracts to purchase electricity for resale, thus minimizing the risk of price variations.

However, the CPUC rules created strong incentives for default utilities to avoid great reliance on long-term contracts, even when such contracts would be in the interests of their customers. Under the CPUC rules, retail customers could choose to buy from competitors of the investor-owned utilities whenever those competitors offered electricity for sale at a price more attractive than that offered by the investor-owned utilities. However, those competitors were never obligated to sell electricity, nor were they regulated in the price at which they offered to sell. The investor-owned utilities, on the other hand, were obligated to serve all customers, including those who switched back from an unregulated competitor. Moreover, the retail price that they would charge would be based on the average cost of their acquisition of electricity, at least whenever there was no retail price cap.

These differences in obligation to serve and retail price-setting rules between the investor-owned utilities and the unregulated competitors created the incentive against the utilities relying heavily on long-term contracts. Consider what might happen if the regulated utilities did rely very heavily on long-term, fixed price contracts to purchase electricity.

If the spot prices turned out to be much lower than the prices in the long-term contracts, the unregulated firms could offer to sell electricity at a much lower price than could the regulated utilities, and large numbers of customers would shift their purchases to these firms and away from the regulated utilities. With fewer customers, the regulated utilities would purchase smaller quantities of electricity on spot markets; however, because the spot price of electricity would be lower than the contract price, reduced purchases on the spot market would increase the average cost and therefore the price charged to those customers remaining with the regulated utility. The price increase would cause even more customers to leave the regulated utility, thereby further increasing the price for those remaining. The greater the fraction of electricity the utility had contracted to purchase under long-term contracts, the more severe would be this "spiraling downward" process. If the purchases were dominantly long-term contracts, then the utility could end up obligated to purchase more electricity than they could sell.

If, on the other hand, spot prices turned out to be much higher than the average acquisition cost (including the cost of the long-term contracts), customers would abandon the unregulated competitors and would purchase electricity from the utilities. This, in fact, happened when the spot prices of electricity started rising in summer 2000. The increased retail sales would have required increased spot market purchases, thereby increasing the average cost and the regulated price.

But the unregulated retailers are not restricted in this manner. In particular, they need not allow their customers to ebb and flow this way. Retailers offering risk management contracts could choose to sell to only those customers willing to sign year-long or longer time period contracts. Thus, if spot prices were to drop sharply below the average acquisition price, these customers would be precluded from leaving. Moreover, they could base new contracts on their expectations of market conditions. If spot prices were to rise sharply above the average acquisition price, they need not take new customers or they could charge the new customers based on the prices for new wholesale contracts.[57]

This difficulty could be overcome. To do so, however, the incumbent utility would have to be allowed to impose contractual constraints on its existing customers,[58] stopping them from leaving

---

[57]In addition, the unregulated competitors could earn profits when the spot price was above the contractual price and would take losses when the spot price was below the contract price. But since long-term contracts typically have prices roughly equal to the expected average spot prices, then over time these unregulated firms would not be disadvantaged by long-term contracts in the same way as the regulated utilities would be.

[58]For example, all customers could be given a limited time (say, six months) to sign a one-year contract to purchase their electricity from the utility. If they do not do so, the utility would no longer be obligated to sell electricity to them. Similarly, if they switch to another provider, then they might be allowed to switch back to the utility only if they sign a one-year contract with a price designed such that their purchases from the utility will not increase prices facing the rest of the customers.

when spot prices dropped, and be allowed to limit the new customers it would serve, particularly when spot prices increased above average wholesale acquisition costs. But the CPUC did not provide these options to the investor-owned utilities.

Risk problems for the utilities would be especially threatening during the transition period because the price caps disabled a central adjustment mechanism. Typically, production costs are translated through wholesalers and retailers into consumer price increases, which motivate reductions in demand for electricity, in turn placing downward pressure on wholesale prices. During the transition period, however, the retail price caps would disable this process. Thus, the natural economic process limiting the magnitude of wholesale price increases would be missing and the risks associated with large wholesale price increases would be amplified.

In addition, during the transition period, since retail prices were capped, increases in wholesale prices would directly reduce retail margins, possibly resulting in a negative retail margin. Some retail risk would be hedged to the extent the utility generated electricity, but since each investor-owned utility divested most of its generation capacity, each would be a large net wholesale buyer and a large net retail seller of electricity. Thus, risk of wholesale price increases would be borne disproportionately by the utilities even if wholesale prices soared well above retail prices and utilities were losing money on every megawatt-hour of electricity sold.

Generally, however, a company losing money on everything it sold could sharply reduce or halt its sales. But the utilities were required to sell electricity to everyone who turned on their lights, appliances, machinery, or air conditioning. Thus, they were precluded from that normal adjustment process.

In summary, the restructured system put the utilities in an untenable risk-bearing posture, increasing risk during the transition period in three ways:

1. Wholesale price fluctuations would not be moderated by market forces.
2. Wholesale price increases would result directly in financial losses, since none could be passed on as retail price increases.
3. The utility could not reduce transactions when retail margins became negative. Worse yet, its obligation to take back customers implied that its transactions would increase when the loss per transaction became large.

Thus, during the transition period, investor-owned utilities, facing a profoundly high degree of risk, were precluded from most strategies for hedging or reducing risk. Traditionally "safe," blue chip investments, the investor-owned utilities were placed into a posture more risky than that facing most companies.

Although these were all important risks, at the time AB 1890 was passed, all participants anticipated that the cost of wholesale electricity would remain well below the retail price,[59] and the economic isolation between producers and consumers would not create a problem. However, no one could be sure this would be the case. The risks were large, although many of the participants in the process may have underestimated these risks.[60]

These risks could be viewed as merely theoretical, since anyone could have reasonably expected there to be one protection in the unlikely event of soaring wholesale prices. The newly restructured system was a politically designed process. The high risks were not inherent to the economic system but were the results of definable design flaws in the regulatory system. At the time of the restructuring, it would have been reasonable to believe that if the perfect storm descended on the state, the political system would adjust to the new reality. Unfortunately, as has become painfully apparent, this reasonable belief has proved to be disastrously wrong.

MUNICIPAL UTILITIES

California's many municipal utilities, serving 22 percent of California's customers, were allowed to continue operating as they had prior to the restructuring. Each municipal utility had a governing board, either appointed or elected within the municipality, responsible for managing the utility to benefit residents. Typically, municipal utilities were expected to cover their costs through sales of electricity. The governing boards retained the ability to increase retail prices at which the municipal utility sold electricity, if the need arose. These utilities typically purchased electricity using a

---

[59]More precisely, the cost of wholesale electricity would remain well below the retail price of the electricity itself, the retail price charged to customers minus the fixed costs of wires and other distribution services.

[60]The published analyses, including those done by the California Energy Commission and those published through the academic community, all forecast relatively low wholesale prices.

mix of short-, medium-, and long-term contracts so that they were hedged from rapidly changing wholesale prices.

Municipal utilities, therefore, differed sharply from the investor-owned utilities in that they retained all capabilities to manage their risks. As it would turn out, this ability to manage risk was fundamental in differentiating the impacts of the California electricity crisis on the municipal utilities from the impacts on the investor-owned utilities.

IN SUMMARY

California began the decade of the 1990s with a completely vertically integrated electricity system that had been working reasonably well as a regulated system. However, there were opportunities for improvement.

Some reasons for restructuring the system were good. The old system encouraged the investor-owned utilities to build too much capacity at too high a cost. It discouraged appropriate risk bearing on the part of the utilities and discouraged innovation. It included incentives for the utilities to favor their own generators and to avoid purchases from new competing alternatives.

Some other reasons were not good. The advocates of restructuring expected significant immediate cost reductions, pointing to the high average prices of California retail electricity. These high prices, however, were based primarily on the contracts to purchase electricity from qualifying facilities and on the high capital cost nuclear power plants. But the high-priced QF contracts had been forced by the CPUC. Moreover, at the time the nuclear power plants were initiated, it had been expected that they would provide low-cost power. A market restructuring would not eliminate the historical costs, no matter who was responsible for past decisions. Market traders expected that the particular California restructuring would create profit opportunities for their firms, a good reason from their perspective, but not a good reason from California's perspective.

Although some reasons that advocates advanced for restructuring were weak, there were sufficient good reasons to proceed. The process of analysis and debate from the early 1990s through the signing of the bill was remarkably open and allowed many opportunities for knowledgeable parties to participate in discussions. Many analysts, observers, and especially stakeholders joined the debate. In short, the process, through the signing of AB 1890, was remarkable for the debate that was encouraged and that influenced the final legislation. However, the broad participation may have resulted in a system designed by committee, with features beneficial to some participants, but harmful for the overall design.

Like all legislation, AB 1890 represented a series of compromises and included some mistaken judgments; however, it should not be judged as the final product. Rather it should be seen as a framework for further restructuring, since so many elements out of the system would require continued implementation and continued change.

Nevertheless, absent these additional changes, the restructured system left the investor-owned utilities and the state in a more risky situation than appropriate. From the perspective of those times, it was reasonable to believe that the state would pass through the transition period unscathed and would be able to move forward, once the stranded costs had been recovered, into a new era. However, even though not recognized, the risk was there from the very beginning that things could go wrong. And go wrong they did.

3

THE CHALLENGE

The year after AB 1890 was passed, a group of consumer advocates, led by Harvey Rosenfield, started the process of legally challenging the restructuring legislation. This group began collecting signatures to qualify what became Proposition 9, voted on in the 1998 statewide California ballot. Proposition 9 would have turned back the restructuring and reinforced a system of tightly regulated electricity transactions. It was not until the defeat of Proposition 9 in November 1998 that it was ensured AB 1890 would be allowed to operate.

Until its defeat, Proposition 9 created much uncertainty and reduced the incentives for private companies to invest in new electricity-generating facilities. By creating significant delays in the capital investment associated with investing in new generating plants, Proposition 9 increased the risks that were inherent in this newly restructured system.

Until early 2000, the new system seemed to be operating as intended in terms of the publicly visible goals. Wholesale prices remained below historical average costs and the utilities gained profits that they could apply to cover the stranded costs. By 1999, SDG&E had earned sufficient profits to cover all of its stranded costs and would no longer be subject to the retail price caps.

The divestiture of generating assets owned by the utilities was proceeding surprisingly well. Many old generating plants had been sold at prices that far exceeded the expected prices. These sales moved the electric utilities closer to the time when they would be able to leave the price control regime.

However, the high sales prices should have raised questions in the CPUC. It can be presumed that those plant buyers were not being irrational and that they believed future electricity wholesale prices would rise. These high selling prices thus should have suggested to CPUC members that there was a significant risk that future wholesale prices would increase dramatically. High prices also could have implied the need for long-term contracts or other methods for the utilities to protect themselves and the ratepayers from such risks.

Although the overall supply/demand balance had not yet improved in California or the western region, improvements were under way. In California, applications to construct many new electricity-generating units had been filed and approved; construction had begun for many thousands of MW of new capacity. Demand for electricity continued to grow but was growing at a relatively slow pace. Looking ahead, it was reasonable to project that the new electricity-generating plants would be on-line before growing demand surpassed the available supply of electricity.

One disappointment with operation of the new system seemed to be the lack of a competitive retail market for electricity. Several companies entered the market to sell consumers green electricity, advertised to be generated entirely by renewable sources; however, this component of the market was small. Other companies that tried to enter the market complained that the tightly regulated system gave them no opportunity to compete successfully.

Less publicly visible, however, were the operations of the PX and the CAISO. The market structure continued to prove unwieldy and the CAISO submitted to the FERC a sequence of proposed amendments to its tariff. After twenty-four amendments were filed, the FERC finally summarized its perceptions: "The problem facing the [California] ISO is that the existing congestion management approach is fundamentally flawed and needs to be overhauled or replaced."[1] This started a process of rethinking the market design that was never completed, since the events beginning in spring

---

[1]Federal Energy Regulatory Commission, "Order Accepting for Filing in Part and Rejecting in Part Proposed Tariff Amendment and Directing Reevaluation of Approach to Addressing Intrazonal Congestion," Docket ER00-555-000, 90 FERC 61, 000 (Washington, D.C., January 7, 2000), p. 9.

2000 overtook the process.[2] There were clearly continued problems with the market design and its detailed implementation. Personnel within the PX, CAISO, and FERC, as well as analysts studying electricity markets, were working to improve it.

By spring 2000, warning signs about the supply and demand imbalance throughout the western region had become obvious. Wholesale prices spiked upward in May 2000 and then again in June. There was insufficient electricity available in San Francisco on one day, causing a blackout. Lawsuits were filed to identify and hold accountable any companies responsible for the rapid price increases. The challenge had become apparent not just to technical specialists but also to the public and political leaders of the state.

In what follows, we analyze the changing circumstances that turned the risky situation into a challenge for the State of California. The challenge to California initially arose from changes in the supply and demand patterns throughout the western portion of the United States coupled with characteristics of electricity markets, which inherently made electricity wholesale prices highly volatile. Particular characteristics of California's restructuring combined with these additional changes to create the "perfect storm." This was the challenge that California faced in the year 2000.

THE NATURE OF THE CHALLENGE

The challenge grew in terms of two types of problems: (1) an electricity challenge associated with very tight wholesale markets for electricity in the West and California's management of its electricity markets, and (2) a financial crisis of California's investor-owned utilities associated with the State's regulatory control of these utilities.

The electricity challenge was primarily part of the challenge facing the western states as of mid-2000. Demands for electricity throughout the West had grown over the years, but supply had not. New generation capacity in California was under construction, but construction had not been completed. There were no direct

---

[2]For more discussion of the problems with the market system appearing before spring 2000, see William W. Hogan, "Electricity Market Restructuring: Reforms of Reforms" (Harvard University, May 25, 2001). Available at http://ksghome.harvard.edu/~.whogan.cbg.Ksg/.

incentives for consumers in California to reduce their demands for electricity because the State rigidly maintained retail price controls. Short-term supply reductions led to very tight markets and wholesale spot prices increased sharply in California and throughout the West.

The financial challenge was one facing the investor-owned electric utilities. As wholesale markets grew tighter, the investor-owned utilities, forced to rely to an inappropriately large extent on spot prices, faced the prospect of sharply escalating costs of acquiring electricity on wholesale markets. Yet the retail price controls, were they to be continued, would preclude the utilities from passing any of those costs on to their customers: the investor-owned utilities would be required to deeply subsidize electricity use by their customers.[3] The difference between acquisition cost and retail selling price was threatening to become great enough to deplete all their financial assets, absent relaxation of retail price controls. During this challenge period, two things were needed to avert a crisis: the retail price controls needed to be relaxed and the utilities needed to move away from spot wholesale markets and toward medium-term and long-term electricity supply contracts.

In what follows, these two challenges are discussed separately, with the electricity market challenge presented first.

ELECTRICITY SUPPLY AND DEMAND PATTERNS

REGIONAL MARKET LINKAGE

Contrary to many popular discussions, supply and demand conditions in California's electricity system are tightly linked to conditions throughout the western region of the United States; California's system is not isolated from electricity markets in the rest of the West. High-voltage transmission lines, across which electricity can be transmitted, connect adjacent states and adjacent regions within a state. Through this transmission system, the eleven western states, plus the Canadian provinces of British Columbia and Alberta, are electrically linked to one another. In principle, electricity generation in any part of the western region—more precisely, the Western Systems Coordinating

---

[3]The California municipal utilities were not so required and were free to increase their prices, based on decisions by their governing boards.

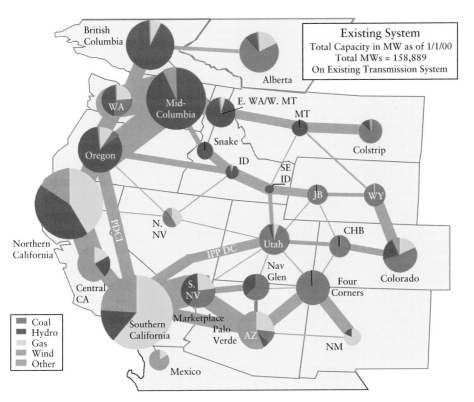

FIGURE 3.1:   Installed Capacity by Generation Type in the Western
Grid, as of January 2000

SOURCE: Western Governors' Association

Council[4] (WSCC)—could be used to satisfy electricity loads in any
other part of the western region, subject to transmission constraints.

Figure 3.1, created by the Western Governors' Association,[5] gives
an indication of the transmission capacity between the various states
and portions of states. The widths of the blue lines connecting the
circles are proportional to the relative transmission capacities.

---

[4]Eleven states are interconnected as part of the Western Systems Coordinating
Council (WSCC) area: Arizona, California, Colorado, Idaho, Montana, Nevada,
New Mexico, Oregon, Utah, Washington, and Wyoming. WSCC also includes
the provinces of Alberta, British Columbia, the northern portion of Baja
California, Mexico, and portions of several other states.

[5]Western Governors' Association, "Conceptual Plans for Electricity
Transmission in the West," August 2001.

Figure 3.1 shows that there is much transmission capacity between California and the Pacific Northwest and between California, Nevada, and Arizona. Thus, these parts of the western region are linked particularly closely and the greatest flows of electricity occur among these areas. California represents 42 percent of the generation and 51 percent of the consumption in this tightly linked portion of WSCC.

Given the possibility of transmitting electricity among states and given that federal regulations allowed open access to the transmission network,[6] utilities in the West had traded with one another either directly or through marketers well before California restructured its electricity markets. Significant quantities of electricity generated in one state have been routinely bought, sold, and transmitted between states. This was not the product of California's restructuring, which did allow the possibility of increased trade and increased electricity flow between states.

Thus, for the most part, in practice, electricity generation in any part of the West could be used to serve the electrical loads in any other part of the West, including California, subject to transmission constraints, which at some times could limit the amount of trade. Similarly, electricity loads in any part of the West could reduce the amount of electricity available to serve loads in any other part of the West, including California.

Since utilities and marketers can freely trade across state boundaries (subject to transmission constraints), spot prices tend to equate between any two adjacent regions whenever the transmission interconnections between the regions have excess capacity.[7] Any price difference would be an opportunity for traders to arbitrage the differences, buying in the low price area and selling in the high price area, thus eliminating price differences.

Because of the relative ease of electricity trade and the tendency toward price equality among the western states, changing supply and demand conditions anywhere in the interconnected western region have similar impacts on spot market prices throughout the entire region. A tight market in the Pacific Northwest can easily translate into a tight market in California, and vice versa. A tight market any place

---

[6]Particularly important were EPACT and FERC Order 888. See Chapter 2.

[7]Whenever the interconnections reach capacity, price differences can persist, just as there are price differences between the western region and the Midwest.

will typically lead to high spot wholesale prices everywhere in the West.

Although spot wholesale prices across the region tend to equalize quickly, long-term contractual arrangements reduce the amount available for sale on the spot markets at any moment of time. In most of the states other than California, the vast majority of electricity is generated by the utilities themselves or is contractually committed to the various publicly or privately owned utilities. Under such contracts, generators have committed to provide fixed quantities of electricity to particular utilities, or they have dedicated all electricity from particular generating plants to those utilities. Electricity so committed under firm contracts is generally not available for sale on the spot markets.

Spot market prices respond to the demand and supply for electricity transacted on the spot markets, not necessarily to the overall demand and supply in the region. In the short run, electricity loads and electricity supplies committed under long-term contracts are removed from transactions on the spot market, leaving a smaller spot market supply and an equivalently smaller spot market demand.

Residual quantities are not removed, however. Utilities operating under long-term wholesale contracts but with projected loads exceeding their committed generation are free to compete to purchase electricity on the spot market. Similarly, generators with supplies greater than their long-term contractual sales are free to offer to sell the surplus on the spot markets. Thus, supply and demand variations within the region translate directly into equivalent volume supply and demand variations in the spot markets.

Because long-term contracts reduce the total volumes available for transactions on the spot markets, a given magnitude of supply or demand variation represents a much larger percentage variation than would be the case absent the long-term contracts. This in turn implies that spot market prices are far more volatile than they would otherwise be. A given magnitude of supply reduction or demand increase leads to a much greater price increase on the spot markets than would be the case if there were no long-term contracts. Similarly, the large number of long-term contracts implies that supply increases or demand decreases have disproportionate impacts on spot market price reductions.

Thus, in the mixed system characterizing the West—most electricity sold on long-term contracts and a smaller amount sold on spot markets—spot market prices tend to vary sharply, whereas existing long- and medium-term contracts continue to operate at the contractually agreed prices.[8]

In the longer term (say, over a course of weeks or months), spot market conditions do influence the supplies and loads committed under long-term contracts. Buyers of electricity under long-term contracts may be able to reduce their use and sell the saved quantities into the spot markets when spot prices are significantly higher than long-term contractual prices. Alternatively, sellers and buyers may renegotiate long- and medium-term contracts to allow both to benefit from the opportunity to respond to high spot prices. The adjustment process under such long-term or medium-term contracts, however, is much slower than the adjustment in the spot markets.

Thus, in the mixed market system with most electricity sold on long-term contracts and a smaller amount sold on spot markets, those participants with long-term contracts are buffered from the changing market conditions. Because they are buffered, they need not respond as quickly or as greatly as those facing the more volatile spot markets. The diminished responses from those with long- and medium-term contracts have direct implications for the dynamics of the spot market. They imply that a greater response is called for from those participating primarily in spot markets and that spot market prices will be more volatile than would otherwise be the case.

Given the regionally linked electricity system and the mixed market system of term contracts and spot markets, supply and demand changes occurring either inside or outside of California could translate into very tight supply and demand conditions throughout the West, including slow supply and demand adjustment throughout the region and rapid and profound changes in wholesale spot market prices.

California's investor-owned utilities, after divesting most of their own generating capacity, and facing prohibitions against buffering themselves with long-term contracts, were forced to acquire much of their electricity on the very volatile spot markets.

---

[8]New long- and medium-term contracts, however, may reflect the volatility in the spot markets, since those contractual terms reflect the expectations of the buyers and sellers about the future expected spot market prices. In addition, if contract prices diverge greatly from current market prices for long periods, contracts can be renegotiated so as to benefit both contracting parties.

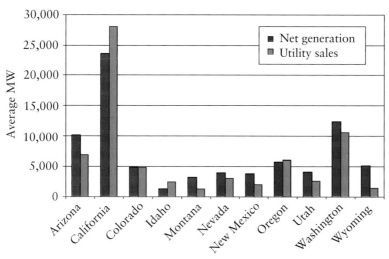

FIGURE 3.2:   Net Generation and Utility Sales, WSCC States, 2000

Thus, as a result of California's restructuring, California investor-owned utilities were cast unenviably as buyers participating primarily in spot markets, while most utilities throughout the West and most municipal utilities in California were well buffered by a mix of long- and medium-term contracts. The fury of the perfect storm would be concentrated on the California investor-owned utilities, amplified by the buffering the other utilities were enjoying.

WESTERN REGIONAL SUPPLY AND DEMAND BALANCES

Figure 3.2, using data from the U.S. Department of Energy, Energy Information Administration, shows yearly average rate of net generation[9] and the yearly average rate of utility sales in the eleven western states that are interconnected as part of WSCC for the year 2000. California's retail sales of electricity account for 40 percent of the total retail sales in these eleven states; California generation accounts for 30 percent of the total. Thus, although California is the largest single state, neither its generation nor its consumption represents a majority in the West.

The total electricity use in a state must be the sum of net generation plus net imports from other states, minus transmission and

---

[9]Net generation is generation net of the electricity used in the generating plant itself. Net generation is measured at the generating plant. Line losses and other distribution losses must be subtracted from net generation in order to determine the amount of electricity available for utility sales.

other losses. Therefore, whenever electricity sales in a state exceed net generation less losses, the difference is made up through electricity imports from other states or other countries (Canada and Mexico).

In a typical year, California generates 75 percent of its electricity in state, importing 25 percent from the Pacific Northwest and the U.S. Southwest. These are not simply one-way flows of electricity into California. In the summer, California imports much electricity from the Pacific Northwest. In the winter, California exports electricity to the Pacific Northwest. Figure 3.2 shows that California and Idaho are the only states that must import large portions of their electricity. Most of the other western states are nearly balanced or are net exporters of electricity.

In addition to information about transmission capacities, Figure 3.1 provides data on the primary sources of electricity generation in each state. The circles on the chart show the summer-installed generating capacity, by generation type, for each state or portion of a state. The sizes of the circles are proportional to the summer-installed capacities as of January 2000. Figure 3.1 shows that the primary energy source for electricity generation varies significantly across the western region. The Pacific Northwest relies primarily on hydropower, with some natural gas and coal. The mountain states, except Colorado, rely primarily on coal as an energy source for electricity generation. Colorado uses coal, hydropower, and natural gas. California relies on a diverse mix of energy sources, including natural gas and hydropower.

Although Figure 3.1 shows generation capacity in 2000, an analogous diagram for 1990 would look virtually the same. There had been very little growth in generating capacity throughout the western region in the decade prior to 2000.[10] However, there had been continuing growth in electricity use throughout the region. Thus, the amount of reserve capacity throughout the western region had been declining steadily for at least a decade before 2000. Tight supply and demand conditions had started to characterize most of the western region.

---

[10]A complete discussion of the long-term trends in California and the West appear in Jolanka V. Fisher and Timothy P. Duane, "Trends in Electricity Consumption, Peak Demand, and Generating Capacity in California and the Western Grid, 1977–2000" (Working paper from the University of California Energy Institute Program on Workable Energy Regulation [POWER], September 2001).

Throughout the region, most of the municipal utilities and investor-owned utilities had adjusted to this market tightening by ensuring their own supplies of electricity, either through their own generating units or through a combination of medium- and long-term contracts to purchase electricity. California investor-owned utilities had not been allowed to do so.

The generation capacity shown in Figure 3.1 could vary significantly with changes in the local conditions. In particular, the hydroelectric capacity represents the capacity of generators. But if the amount of available water were insufficient, some of that generated capacity must remain unused. Thus, low rainfall conditions in Northern California and in the Pacific Northwest can, and did, reduce the amount of hydropower that could be generated in those locations.

In addition, the electricity demand was notoriously time-dependent. A hot summer could greatly increase the demand for electricity in California or Arizona because of the large air conditioning loads; a cold winter could greatly increase the demand for electricity in the Pacific Northwest because of the large electric-resistance space-heating loads.

In spring 2000, then, California was part of a region that was tightly interconnected electrically. With California's particular regulatory environment, the dynamics of wholesale electricity market adjustments were skewed against California's investor-owned utilities. Most electricity either outside California or sold to California's municipal utilities was committed to long-term contracts. Most electricity purchased by California's investor-owned utilities was transacted on spot markets with supplies that could shrink rapidly in response to changing conditions either inside or outside of California. The markets for electricity had gradually become tighter and tighter throughout the region. Moreover, in spring 2000, rapidly changing conditions external and internal to California created for California the perfect storm.

The following sections focus more sharply on California and its changing supply and demand conditions, which can help explain why California was not prepared to weather the storm.

CALIFORNIA ELECTRICITY USE

California has been a relatively low user of electricity when measured on a per capita basis. The industrial structure, although intensely dependent on electricity, particularly for the high-tech

industries, is not a heavy electricity consumer relative to industry
in other states. The state is blessed with a temperate climate, and
thus air conditioning loads are relatively low. High prices for electricity, coupled with aggressive energy demand management programs, have kept consumption relatively low. California has had a
long tradition of efficiency incentives and services that have helped
to reduce California's electricity intensity in recent decades.

Table 3.1, using 1999 data from the U. S. Department of Energy,[11]
shows that the residential electricity consumption per customer was
37 percent below the U.S. average during that year. Thus, the challenge California was facing did not stem from California being a particularly large user of electricity on a per capita basis. Conversely,
that California had a lower per capita use of electricity than most
states did not allow California to avoid the challenge.

During the period from 1997 through 2000, the consumption of
electricity in California continued to grow slowly as it had for the
previous ten years. The California economy was remaining healthy
and population was continuing to grow steadily. Per capita electricity use grew modestly during that time. Figure 3.3 shows the net result. From 1990 to 2000, use of electricity increased from a 26,000
MW average consumption rate to one just above 30,000 MW, a
growth of 16 percent over ten years, or 1.4 percent per year. Growth
in energy consumption, however, was somewhat faster during the

TABLE 3.1

California versus All U.S. Residential Electricity Use
per Residential Customer

	California	All U.S.	California Relative to U.S.
Monthly Average Residential Consumption (MWh)	0.548 MWh	0.866 MWh	37% below National Average
Average Residential Consumption Rate (MW)	0.75 MW	1.19 MW	
Retail Average Revenues ($/MWh)	$107/MW	$82/MW	9th Highest

---

[11]Data in table are from http://www.eia.doe.gov/cneaf/electricity/esr/esrt14p4.
html. Data are based on the number of customers in the residential sector. This
figure corresponds closely to the number of households.

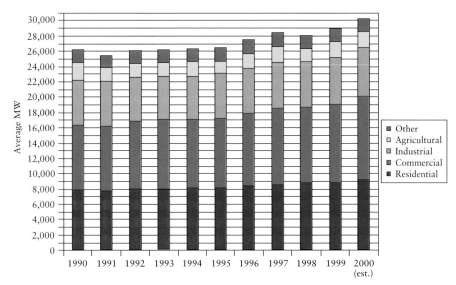

FIGURE 3.3:   California Energy Consumption Growth
SOURCE: California Energy Commission

1997–2000 period, increasing by almost 2,000 MW during the three years, or an average growth rate of 2.3 percent per year average. From 1999 to 2000, average consumption increased slightly more than 1,000 MW, almost 4 percent. Peak loads were growing at roughly the same rates.

Thus, although peak loads and total electricity consumption grew, growth was relatively slow. Taken alone, neither the absolute magnitude of electricity use nor the growth rate would have been likely to create a particularly significant challenge.

Some have argued that electricity demand in California has grown much more rapidly than expected, even if not particularly rapidly on an absolute scale. Although it is difficult to document the wide range of growth expectations, it is possible to compare actual growth to California's official forecasts of growth in electricity consumption and growth in peak loads.

Table 3.2 shows these forecasts of growth and actual growth over the five-year interval from 1995 to 2000, based on two California Energy Commission reports: the 1996 *Electricity Report* and the 1998 *Baseline Energy Outlook*. Since measured peak demand can be influenced strongly by curtailments, peak demand growth is shown first ignoring the curtailments and then adjusted for curtailments. Adjusting for curtailments, peak demand grew

13.4 percent from 1995 to 2000, in contrast to the 10.4 percent growth forecast in the California Energy Commission's 1996 *Electricity Report*.[12] Total consumption grew 14.5 percent from 1995 to 2000, in contrast to the 11.6 percent and 11.7 percent total growth in consumption forecast in the 1996 *Electricity Report* and the 1998 *Baseline Energy Outlook,* respectively.

Table 3.2 thus shows that electricity consumption and peak demand did grow somewhat faster than forecast by the California Energy Commission. Growth, measured by peak demand or by total electricity consumption, however, was no more than three percentage points greater than those forecasts. Therefore, the "electricity demand grew surprisingly fast" explanation can account for only a part of the tight market conditions.

TABLE 3.2

Official California Forecasts of Electricity Demand
and Consumption Growth versus Actual Growth

		Actual or Forecast Five-Year Growth	Underestimate of Five-Year Growth
Five-Year Growth in Peak Electricity Demand	Actual Growth Ignoring Voluntary Curtailments	9.2%	
	Actual Growth Adjusted for Voluntary Curtailments	13.4%	
	1996 *Electricity Report*	10.4%	3.0%
Five-Year Growth in Electricity Consumption	Actual Growth	14.5%	
	1996 *Electricity Report*	11.7%	2.8%
	1998 *Baseline Energy Outlook*	11.6%	2.9%

----

[12]The growth forecasts are based on noncoincident peaks since no forecast was available for coincident peaks. The actual peak growth is based on coincident peaks. The year 2000 coincident peak demand in the CAISO control area was 43,784 MW, but there were 1,710 MW of voluntary curtailments that day. No adjustment for curtailments was made for total electricity consumption since voluntary curtailments had a much greater percentage impact on peak demand than on total consumption during the year.

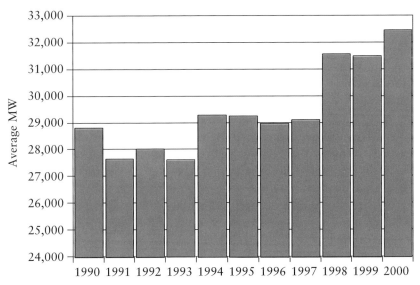

FIGURE 3.4: Electricity Generation Supporting California's Electricity Use

CALIFORNIA ELECTRICITY GENERATION AND IMPORTS

Total generation[13] required to support electricity consumption is shown in Figure 3.4, in which the vertical axis has a suppressed zero and which shows data for only the 1990 through 2000 period.[14] Note that total generation is slightly larger than use since there are losses in the transmission and distribution system.

From 1997 to 1998, total generation required to support California loads increased by 2,500 MW average and increased again by 1,000 MW in 2000. From 1990 to 2000, total generation required increased 12.6 percent over ten years, or 1.2 percent per year. Growth, however, was somewhat faster during the 1997 through 2000 period, increasing by 3.7 percent per year average. Measured in terms of electricity generation required to support California's electric loads, the growth rate was slightly faster than that measured by

---

[13]Data in this graph and the following graphs of California energy generation have been obtained from the California Energy Commission web site: http://www.energy.ca.gov/electricity/electricity_generation.html.

[14]Note that the consumption data and the generation data for 1997 seem inconsistent, with consumption shown as only 500 MW larger than generation in this year, in contrast to each other year. This is most likely an error in California Energy Commission data.

California data on electricity consumption. But under either measurement, growth was not particularly fast, and that growth alone would not have created a particularly significant challenge.

California had two generic sources of electricity to support the slowly growing electrical loads: electricity generated in California plus the net[15] imports of electricity into California. The two added together must be equal to the total use of electricity (consumption plus losses). Thus, if one of these two sources were to decline, the other had to increase more rapidly to satisfy the slow growth in use.

With tightening of electricity markets in the West, the amount of electricity available for sale on spot markets was shrinking, with that shrinkage occurring primarily outside of California. This resulted directly in an increase in the exports of electricity from California and a decrease in the imports of electricity into California: thus net imports into California declined.

Since 1990, imports had been averaging just above 5,000 MW, with, on average, equal quantities from the Pacific Northwest and the Pacific Southwest. In 2000, however, imports from the Pacific Northwest dropped with the extraordinarily low rainfall, following years of particularly high hydroelectric supply. Imports from the Pacific Southwest dropped sharply. The overall impact was a reduction in net imports to California of 2,200 MW (see Figure 3.5).

This measured reduction in net imports to California from surrounding regions underestimates the significance to the California energy crisis of the changes in the supply and demand balance in the remainder of the WSCC.[16] In response to the tight market conditions, spot market prices of electricity in these regions increased sharply during 2000. Increases in electricity prices reduced demand in these

---

[15]The net imports are the difference between imports into California and exports from California.

[16]This was pointed out by Jolanka V. Fisher and Timothy P. Duane (Fisher and Duane, "Trends in Electricity Consumption"), who reach similar conclusions: "Neither increases in California's annual consumption (or peak demand) nor decreases in California's historical share of WSCC-wide generating capacity is therefore at the heart of the state's supply and demand relationship from 1977 to 1998. Instead, the tightening of supplies throughout the WSCC during this period primarily reflects increases in consumption and peak demand in other states and a region-wide decline in new capacity additions relative to those increases in consumption. Above-average hydropower production (especially in the Pacific Northwest) from 1996 to 1999 masked this shift, then hydropower availability decreased significantly in 2000 (combined with significant increases in consumption in California and throughout the WSCC) to reveal apparent shortages."

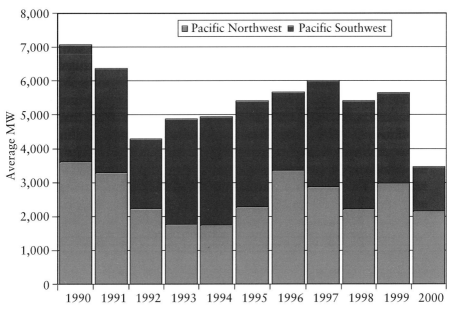

FIGURE 3.5:   Electricity Imports into California

regions and increased supply, making more electricity available for export to California. The data in Figure 3.5 reflect the *equilibrium* quantities of net imports from these regions once the market prices adjusted to the supply/demand conditions. The measured level of net imports into California during 2000 therefore overestimates the net imports that would have been available absent the sharp increases in spot market prices. The drop in measured imports underestimates the impact of changing import availability in reducing the supply function in 2000 for electricity in California.

The combination of the increase in California consumption and the reduction in available net imports implied that more electricity was needed from domestic sources. Figure 3.6 below shows that the total production of electricity from California sources[17] grew sharply since the electricity restructuring, with increases from 1997 to 1998 of 3,000 MW and from 1999 to 2000 of 3,100 MW, an increase of 12 percent in that year.

_____

[17]In this and the following figures, coal-fired units are included as California generation even though they are located outside of California. This coal-fired generation capacity is owned or controlled by California utilities.

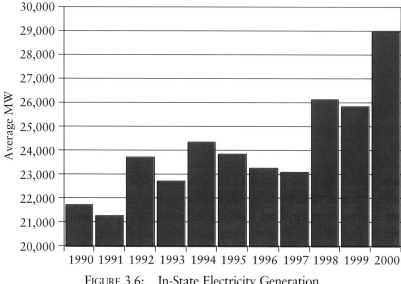

FIGURE 3.6:   In-State Electricity Generation

The pressure on California's electricity supply was even greater than suggested by those figures since, other than the natural gas- and oil-fired units, virtually all of the generating sources run at full available capacity.[18] Almost all of the oil-fired facilities have long ago been converted to natural gas, and thus virtually all of the generating facilities were capacity-limited, with the exception of natural gas-fired units. Figure 3.7 shows the production over time from these various sources, except for natural gas.

Hydroelectric power does vary from year to year, but variation is controlled by rainfall. Thus the hydropower output averaged over the year cannot adjust significantly to economic conditions.

The remaining supply of electricity came from natural gas–fired units. Figure 3.8 shows this total generation from gas-fired units over the last decade and that from 1999 to 2000, generation from these units increased 26 percent, reaching an all-time maximum production rate. During the decade from 1990 through 2000, however, 1,500 MW of gas-fired generation was retired. Thus, more gas-fired electricity generation was needed even though there were fewer gas-fired generating units left to generate that electricity.

---

[18]Available capacity for wind machines and solar generators is considerably less than nameplate capacity.

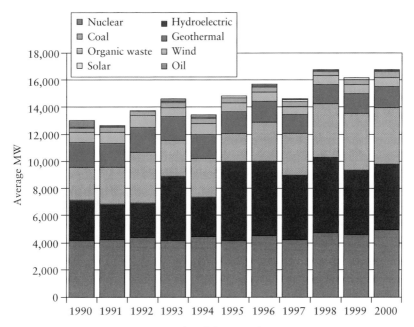

FIGURE 3.7: Sources of California Electricity Generation,
Other Than Natural Gas

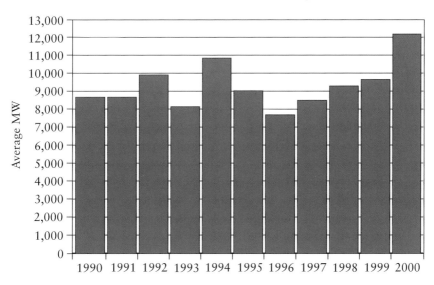

FIGURE 3.8: Gas-Fired Electricity Generation in California

This sudden increase in the generation from gas-fired units, coupled with the retirement of some existing units, could normally be expected to greatly increase the marginal cost of generating from the operating units and thus, under the market system, to increase the price of all wholesale electricity. Absent new construction, such a change would require the oldest and least efficient plants to be brought into service. Moreover, this change could be expected to increase the demand for natural gas in the state, thereby increasing its price and further increasing the marginal cost of generating electricity and thus further increasing the wholesale price. Each of these impacts, which would normally be expected, in fact occurred, as will be discussed later.

INVESTMENT IN NEW GENERATING UNITS IN CALIFORNIA

One of the reasons for the restructuring of the electricity system was that market forces were expected to call forth new supplies of electricity in California if needed; however, new supplies could be brought forth only if there were sufficient capacity to generate the electricity. For the private market to create additional generating capacity takes time, and the California process is particularly lengthy.

The sponsor of a new plant with more than 50 MW of nameplate capacity must bring an application to the California Energy Commission, proposing new plant construction. The California Energy Commission conducts an extensive review process, involving both in-house review and public hearing, often taking two or more years.[19] Once the plans for the plant are approved, construction can start. Other than for simple cycle peaker plants, construction can take one to two years.

Once the construction is complete, the plant is tested, first off-line and then in a low level of power output, before it is finally certified for operation. Until the last step is completed, the plant cannot supply electricity. The entire process from application to on-line status typically takes three to four years for large plants but can be reduced to less than one year for peaker plants.[20]

---

[19]In February 2001, Governor Gray Davis signed six Executive Orders to expedite the review and permitting of power-generating facilities in California.

[20]Peakers are simple, relatively low efficiency plants that generally are used only at times of peak need. Often these are simple cycle plants.

Thus, the issue of whether the restructuring was leading to greater supplies of electricity generated in California[21] was dependent on whether there was a significant change in the applications for new plants, their approvals, and the numbers subsequently under construction. It was unrealistic to expect that new capacity resulting from the restructuring would be on-line by summer 2000.

The following graph (Figure 3.9) provides the estimates of new applications, approvals, cancellations, construction, and subsequent operation of new generating plants in California, including the period before the restructuring, through 1996, and the period after restructuring, 1997 through 2001. Data are based on the year the application for certification was filed. The total height of each bar in the graph shows the number of applications made during a year. Data include utility-owned generation and QFs, including cogeneration plants and renewable energy.[22] Currently operational plants of capacity smaller than 50 MW are shown separately from plants with capacity of 50 MW or greater.

Figure 3.9 shows that in the 1980s annual applications to build new California electricity-generating capacity averaged about 1,000 MW per year. The majority of these were plants with capacity below 50 MW, which are not subject to California Energy Commission approval. But between 1990 and 1996, annual applications for certification averaged about 250 MW per year,[23] while annual retirements of generating capacity averaged about 450 MW per year,[24] decreasing generating capacity within California during those seven years by about 1,400 MW. Electricity use during that time continued to grow in California, as in the rest of the West. As opposed to the 1980s, when capacity was increasing by more than electricity use, California

---

[21]Electricity destined for the California market did not have to be generated in California. Merchant plants could be built just north of the California-Oregon border or just east of the California-Nevada or California-Arizona border without facing the slow approval processes in California. The following discussion, however, limits itself to generation plants in California.

[22]Application dates of plants of 50 MW capacity or greater are available from the California Energy Commission. For smaller plants data are available for the years the plants went on-line. In constructing this graph it was assumed that the smaller plants had a planning start date, equivalent to an application date, two years before they went on-line, except for the 2001 applications that were completed that year.

[23]New capacity growth was similarly very slow throughout WSCC.

[24]Source: California Energy Commission. www.energy.ca.gov/electricity/inactive_plants.html.

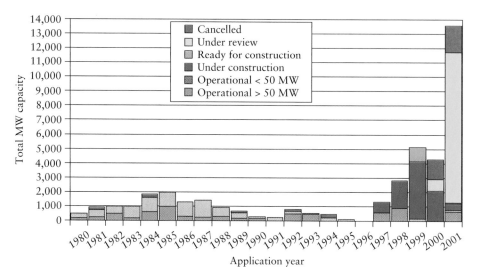

FIGURE 3.9:   Current Status of New Generating Plants, Applications Since 1980

was increasing its need for electricity generation while decreasing the capabilities to provide that electricity.

Figure 3.10 shows in more detail the composition of the new generation capacity in California coming on-line since 1978 (as opposed to Figure 3.9, which shows applications). The blue component of the bars shows the plants with nameplate capacity of

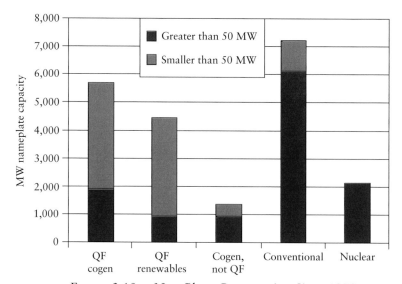

FIGURE 3.10:   New Plant Construction Since 1978

50 MW or greater; the red component of the bars shows plants with nameplate capacity smaller than 50 MW.

Figure 3.10 shows that the largest single source of new nameplate capacity was conventional generation, including both base-load facilities and peakers. About one-half of the total new nameplate capacity was QFs, either cogeneration or renewables.[25] The majority of the QF capacity was from small units (nameplate capacity smaller than 50 MW) and thus much of this capacity is often not highlighted in many public information sources.[26]

The restructuring marked a sharp turnaround in applications. In the years 1997 through 2000, applications averaged about 3,300 MW per year. All applications in the years 1997 and 1998 resulted in plants that are now either operational or under construction. Of the 1999 applications, all those approved are now either under construction or about to begin construction. One 1999 project, the Metcalf energy center in San Jose, has only recently been approved and is under construction.[27] The applications remained high in the year 2000 and jumped sharply in 2001, largely in response to the very high electricity prices. Therefore, in terms of the goal of calling forth increased supply, restructuring has been a complete success.

As of the end of the year 2000, none of this new supply was yet operational and, as of mid-2001, only 1,400 MW of this new capacity was on-line. Of the three plants now operational, one, a peaking plant with nameplate capacity of 320 MW, first went on-line in late June 2001, and two combined cycle plants with total nameplate capacity of 1,100 MW went on-line in early July 2001. In addition, 500 MW of peaker capacity, applications for which were filed in March 2001 or later, went on-line during summer or fall 2001. Table 3.3 provides basic data on those post-restructuring plants currently on-line, and Table 3.4 provides similar data for

---

[25]Delivered electricity from many renewables, particularly wind and solar, are significantly smaller than suggested by the nameplate capacity.

[26]For example, the California Energy Commission shows a graph that looks somewhat like Figure 3.9 on its web site, but with far less new capacity constructed in the 1980s. The difference is that the California Energy Commission graph excludes all nuclear power plants and small QFs.

[27]The approval was blocked for around two years by objections raised by Cisco Systems. Environmental groups, including the Sierra Club and the American Lung Association, endorsed this plant.

TABLE 3.3
Electricity-Generating Plants Going On-Line after Restructuring

Project	Applicant/ Host	Size (megawatts)	Project Type	Location	AFC Filing Date [1]	Date Deemed Data Adequate[2]	Date Approved	Construction Start Date	Date On-Line
Sunrise Power	Texaco Global Gas & Power	320 MW	Simple Cycle	Fellows, Kern County (Peaker)	Dec. 21, 1998	Feb. 1999	12/6/00	Dec. 2000	Jun. 27, 2001
Sutter Power	Calpine	540 MW	Combined Cycle	Yuba City area, Sutter County	Dec. 15, 1997	Jan. 1998	4/14/99	Jul. 1999	Jul. 2, 2001
Los Medanos Energy Center	Calpine	555 MW	Combined Cycle	Pittsburg, Contra Costa County	Jun. 15, 1998	Jul. 1998	8/17/99	Sept. 17, 1999	Jul. 9, 2001
Calpeak Border	Calpine	49.5 MW	Simple Cycle	Otay Mesa, San Diego County	Jun. 16, 2001	Jun. 18, 2001	7/11/01		Oct. 27, 2001
Calpeak Escondido	Calpine	49.5 MW	Simple Cycle	Escondido, San Diego County	May 8, 2001	May 16, 2001	6/6/01		Sept. 30, 2001

Alliance Century	Alliance Colton LLC	40 MW	Simple Cycle	Colton, San Bernardino County	Mar. 23, 2001	Apr. 5, 2001	4/25/01	Sept. 11, 2001
Alliance Drews	Alliance Colton LLC	40 MW	Simple Cycle	Colton, San Bernardino County	Mar. 23, 2001	Apr. 5, 2001	4/25/01	Aug.16, 2001
Hanford Energy Park Peaker	GWF Power Systems	95 MW	Simple Cycle	Hanford, Kings County	Apr. 5, 2001	Apr. 11, 2001	5/10/01	Sept. 3, 2001
Indigo Units 1, 2, and 3	Wildflower Energy LLP	135 MW	Simple Cycle	Palm Springs, Riverside County	Mar. 7, 2001	Mar. 16, 2001	4/4/01	Jul. 26, 2001 Unit 3, 9/1/01
Larkspur	Wildflower Energy LLP	90 MW	Simple Cycle	San Diego, San Diego County	Mar. 7, 2001	Mar. 16, 2001	4/4/01	Jul. 13, 2001

SOURCE: California Energy Commission; web site: www.energy.ca.gov/sitingcases/approved.html
(1) Applicant's filing date of Application for Certification (AFC).
(2) Formal process begins following Executive Director recommendation and Commission acceptance of Data Adequacy of the AFC.

TABLE 3.4

Electricity-Generating Plants, Greater Than 300 MW, Approved after Restructuring, Not Yet On-Line

Project	Applicant/ Host	Size	Project Type	Location	AFC Filing Date [1]	Date Deemed Data Adequate[2]	Date Approved	Construction Start Date % Completed	Estimated On-Line
Blythe Energy	Wisvest	520 MW	Combined Cycle	Blythe, Riverside County	Dec. 9, 1999	Mar. 2000	3/21/01	Apr. 27, 2001, 10% complete	Jul. 2004
Contra Costa Repower	Southern Energy	530 MW	Combined Cycle	Antioch, Contra Costa County	Jan. 31, 2000	May 2000	5/30/01	Aug. 1, 2001, 1% complete	Jun. 2003
Delta Energy Center	Calpine and Bechtel	880 MW	Combined Cycle	Pittsburg, Contra Costa County	Dec. 18, 1998	Feb. 1999	2/9/00	Apr. 2000, 58% complete	Apr. 2002
Elk Hills	Sempra/ OXY	500 MW	Combined Cycle	Elk Hills, Kern County	Feb. 24, 1999	Jun. 1999	12/6/00	May 7, 2001, 8% complete	Mar. 2003 (simple cycle 3/2002)
High Desert	Inland Group and Constellation Energy	720 MW	Combined Cycle	Victorville, San Bernardino County	Jun. 30, 1997	Dec. 1997	5/3/00	May 1, 2001, 11% complete	Jul. 2003
Huntington Beach Modernization	AES	450 MW	Combined Cycle	Huntington Beach, Orange County	Dec. 1, 2000	Feb. 7, 2001	5/10/01	May 1, 2001, 95% complete	Nov. 2001

Project	Developer	Capacity	Type	Location					
La Paloma	PG&E National Energy Group	1,048 MW	Combined Cycle	McKittrick area, Kern County	Aug. 12, 1998	Aug. 1998	10/6/99	Jan. 2000, 70% complete	4/02 turbine #1, 5/02 #2, #3, 6/02 #4
Metcalf Energy Center	Calpine and Bechtel	600 MW	Combined Cycle	San Jose, Santa Clara County	Apr. 30, 1999	Jun. 1999	9/24/01		
(Western) Midway-Sunset	ARCO Western Energy Company	500 MW	Combined Cycle	McKittrick, Kern County	Dec. 22, 1999	Mar. 2000	3/21/01	Mar. 2002	Jul. 2004
Moss Landing	Duke Energy	1,060 MW	Combined Cycle	Moss Landing, Monterey County	May 7, 1999	Aug. 1999	10/25/00	Nov. 2000, 40% complete	Jun. 2002
Mountain-view	Thermo Ecotek	1,056 MW	Combined Cycle	San Bernardino County	Feb. 1, 2000	May 2000	3/21/01	Aug. 21, 2001, 1% complete	Jun. 2003

TABLE 3.4 (continued)

Project	Applicant/Host	Size	Project Type	Location	AFC Filing Date [1]	Date Deemed Data Adequate[2]	Date Approved	Construction Start Date % Completed	Estimated On-Line
Otay Mesa	Otay Mesa Generating Company, LLC (Calpine Corporation)	510 MW	Combined Cycle	Otay Mesa area, San Diego County	Aug. 2, 1999	Oct. 1999	4/18/01	Aug. 24, 2001, 0% complete	Jul. 2003
Pastoria	Enron	750 MW	Combined Cycle	Tejon Ranch, Kern County	Nov. 30, 1999	Jan. 2000	12/20/00	Jun. 1, 2001, 1% complete	Jan. 2003
Three Mountain Power	Ogden Pacific Power	500 MW	Combined Cycle	Burney, Shasta County	Mar. 3, 1999	Jun. 1999	5/16/01	Sept. 2001, 0% complete	Jan. 2004

SOURCE: California Energy Commission; web site: www.energy.ca.gov/sitingcases/approved.html

those plants (300 MW or greater) that have been approved, but are not yet on-line.

SUPPLY AND DEMAND SUMMARY

As of May 2000, much new electricity generation capacity was under construction; however, approval of new plants remained slow and had been delayed by the abortive Proposition 9 campaign. Electricity use—both average and peak load—continued to grow. The entire western region was facing very tight electricity supplies. Electricity imports into California were reduced because of the needs in neighboring states. The amount of reserve generation capacity was shrinking rapidly. California's electricity system was facing a very severe challenge stemming from regional changes, not simply California changes.

WHOLESALE PRICE INCREASES

The growing challenge showed up temporarily in increased regional spot prices in May but had become readily apparent in June 2000, when wholesale electricity prices in all of the regional markets, including the California PX, reached[28] peaks above \$400/MWh. In July, peak prices soared even higher on all of the western markets, with all markets showing highest prices in excess of \$500/MWh during one week.

Figure 3.11 shows price ranges, estimated in *Western Price Survey,* on a weekly basis from April 1, 2000, through September 30, 2000. Data are present for three market centers—the California-Oregon Border[29] (COB), receipt points along the Columbia River (Mid-C), and the Palo Verde nuclear power plant switchyard, Arizona—and for exchanges on the PX. For each market, Figure 3.11 shows the lowest and highest prices estimated in *Western Price Survey* for each week.

---

[28]The Energy NewsData publication *Clearing Up* reported on June 16, 2000: "Markets throughout the region were drawn into price spikes. Power prices at Palo Verde/Four Corners and Mid-Columbia/COB moved upward in huge increments all week, with almost no overlap from day to day. At the peak of trading on Wednesday Palo Verde peak power was fetching 450 to 500 mills/KWh. COB and Mid-C had been over 400 mills/KWh."

[29]COB is located at the interconnection point at the California/Oregon border of the Pacific Northwest/Pacific Southwest AC Intertie. *Western Price Survey* is published by Energy NewsData Corporation of Seattle, Washington, www.newsdata.com.

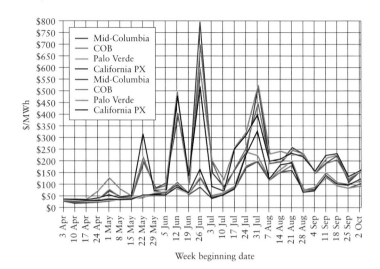

FIGURE 3.11:   Spot Wholesale Prices, Western Electricity Markets
through September 2000, Minimum and Maximum Prices

Figure 3.12 shows the off-peak and peak electricity spot prices
at the same four locations as in Figure 3.11. Here the data are the
average of the highest and the lowest peak prices estimated during the various weeks, as well as the average of the highest and
the lowest off-peak prices. The tight markets in the West led to

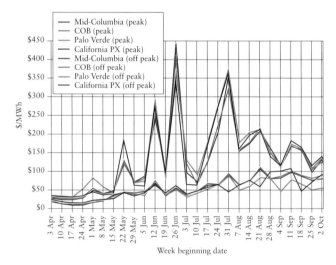

FIGURE 3.12:   Peak and Off-Peak Spot Wholesale Prices, Western
Electricity Markets through September 2000, Average of Minimum
and Maximum Prices

large percentage increases in not only the peak period wholesale prices but also the off-peak wholesale electricity prices.

Although those not carefully watching the electricity system might not have noticed the changes in supply and demand conditions described above, the dramatic changes in the wholesale price made the challenge obvious. Moreover, by that time, SDG&E had gone past the price control period and its retail prices increased correspondingly. Newspapers throughout the state covered the story. The first lawsuit was filed. The public had become aware that something dramatic was happening to the electricity system. There was a severe challenge to be overcome. Nevertheless, reasonable solutions were available and, at that point, the crisis could have been averted.

WHY DID WHOLESALE PRICES INCREASE SO MUCH?

The question of why wholesale prices increased so much in California and throughout the West is a subject of debate and of litigation. Some of the issues are inherent in the changes in supply and demand; others resulted from the restructured system; still others stemmed from the actions taken by various participants in the system, including manipulation of market rules.

Most fundamentally, the growth in demand with no growth in generation capacity led to a very tight market for electricity throughout the West. Peak loads and the system resources to meet these loads were almost equal to one another, so that there was very little unused generation capacity. In addition, the nature of the supply functions and the demand functions in this market implied that small variations in supply or demand for electricity could lead to disproportionately large variations in price. This characteristic—small quantity changes leading to very large price changes—is to be expected in wholesale electricity markets, absent sharp changes in their structure. California's retail price control made the matter worse. In addition, there was probably an increase in the degree to which merchant generators were able to exercise market power to raise wholesale prices. These issues will be discussed in the following sections.

SHORT-RUN SUPPLY FUNCTIONS FOR ELECTRICITY

On the supply side of the market, the essential feature is capacity limitation of generating facilities. Each generator is constrained by its physical capacity to produce electricity. The operator can choose to produce below capacity or to pursue maintenance and repair policies that influence the fraction of time that the plant operates, but cannot generate electricity from a plant at rates beyond its capacity. In California, many plants are quite similar to one another so that many would have similar marginal costs if they were operating significantly below capacity. For these reasons, the short-run supply curve for the system took on a "hockey stick" shape. For a wide range of system-wide outputs, the supply price increased gradually with increases in generation. However, as the system neared full capacity, larger fractions of the generating units operated at full capacity and more of the inefficient high-cost units were brought into service. At some point, even these very inefficient plants would be operating at full capacity. This physical capacity constraint leads to the hockey stick shape of the supply curve.[30]

Figure 3.13 illustrates this short-run supply function using data from the PX during July 1999. Each dot represents an observation

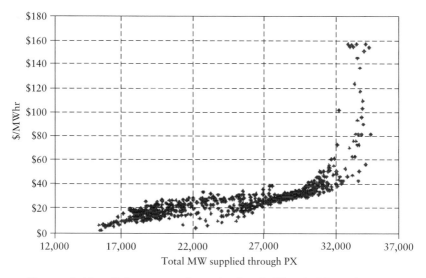

FIGURE 3.13:   Price versus Quantity for California PX, July 1999

SOURCE: California Energy Commission, www.energy.ca.gov/electricity/wepr

---

[30]Whether this curve is both a supply curve and a marginal cost curve depends on whether the generators at the margin were bidding their units at their marginal cost. If so, then this is both a marginal cost curve and a supply curve. If not, it is still a supply curve.

of an hourly price and quantity supplied during the month of July. The horizontal axis represents the MW of electricity committed through the PX for given hours during the month. As such, it includes both electricity generated in California and that imported to California. It excludes electricity purchased by municipal utilities under medium-term and long-term contracts, since that electricity was not exchanged on the PX. The vertical axis represents the market-clearing price for electricity for those hours. Under the assumption that the power exchange was operating as intended, the vertical axis is approximately equal to the highest marginal cost of generating facilities, given the total quantity sold.

The particular points were determined by market equilibria on different days of the month and during different times of the day. During the middle of the day, particularly on weekdays, the demand for electricity was high; during the night demand was low. A process through which the demand function has moved and the supply function has remained approximately stationary has generated these points. Thus, the set of dots traces out a short-run supply curve for electricity. If the sellers were bidding their particular quantities at their marginal costs, then this set of dots also traces out a marginal cost curve.

The hockey stick character of the short-run supply function is obvious. For quantities between 20,000 and 30,000 MW the price varied generally between $10 and $30 per MWh. However, for quantities around 34,000 MW the locus of points became nearly vertical.

This hockey stick shape of the short-run supply function is the result of the physical capacity limitations in the generating system, as discussed above, which would be inherent in this system regardless of the restructuring.

Contractual commitments throughout the rest of the West played a significant role in the shape of the short-run supply functions in California. Given the contractual commitments, available imports into California responded very little in the short run to changing prices in California. Had they been more responsive, the total quantity of electricity made available in California would not have had such a vertical section of the supply curve, since imports into California would have increased in response to price increases.

In the longer run—say over the course of several months— imports to California would be more responsive to the average price expected during a day.[31] Over this period, demand could adjust and contracts could be renegotiated. For example, in Washington, aluminum plants and other intense users of electricity shut down and eliminated their use of electricity altogether in response to the electricity price increases. A significant share of that electricity would then be available for exportation to California. Therefore, the medium-term supply curve can be expected to be somewhat less steeply sloped than the one in Figure 3.13.

The isolated nature of the west coast electricity market also played a role. Because there are only very limited interconnections between the western region of the United States and the rest of the nation, price differentials between the Pacific Coast and the Midwest could persist indefinitely without electricity being transmitted from the Midwest to the west coast. Thus, even in the long run, given that regional isolation, changing imports from the rest of the country would play little or no role in influencing the shape of the supply curve for electricity into California.

In what follows, I will abstractly represent the short-run supply curve by a line that generally has a shape as shown in Figure 3.13 but that has quantities more responsive to price. However, the electricity generated in California and the imports to California will be separated in order to clarify the analysis.

SHORT-RUN DEMAND FUNCTIONS FOR ELECTRICITY

The use of electricity declines in response to increases in the retail electricity price even over a period of months, although over a many-month period the demand declines by a far smaller percentage than the retail price increases. Using conventional estimates of the elasticity of demand[32] for electricity—the percentage reduction in demand motivated by a 1 percent increase in price—each average retail price increase of 10 percent could be expected to motivate a roughly 1–3 percent reduction in demand over the short run, perhaps over several months.

---

[31]This implies that analyses of the California electricity markets that use data on the intra-day adjustment of imports into California in order to estimate the slope of the import supply curve will systematically underestimate the impact of prices on supply to California.

[32]Here, and for other numerical examples, a short-run elasticity of demand for electricity will be approximated as 0.1–0.3. Long-run elasticities have typically been estimated to be as large as 1.0.

Therefore, to motivate a 4 percent reduction in demand, an amount that would roughly compensate for the demand increase from 1999 to 2000, would require a 13–40 percent increase in retail price. The average retail price of electricity[33] was about 12 cents/KWh (equivalent to $120/MWh) and the retail price would need to rise by between 1.6 cents/KWh and 4.8 cents/KWh to motivate that demand reduction, which would correspond to an increase of $16/MWh to $48/MWh.[34]

However, because of the retail price control in California, the increase in wholesale price did not lead to any increase in the retail price for most California customers. Therefore, when the wholesale market price increased, the average consumer of electricity in California did not face a direct economic motivation to reduce demand. In addition, the investor-owned utilities did not have the legal option to reduce their wholesale purchases[35] but were required to acquire as much electricity as their customers used. With this economic isolation between the wholesale price and the retail price, demand for electricity at the wholesale level in California was made very unresponsive to the wholesale price.

There were demand responses for customers of the municipal utilities in California or for industrial customers purchasing directly from generators or marketers. Most other utilities had sufficient medium-term and long-term contracts so that retail rate increases were not required, at least not immediately. Therefore, these demand responses were muted or eliminated. In fact, almost all utilities sell electricity at prices corresponding to the average cost of acquiring that electricity and acquire their electricity dominantly under long-term contracts. Therefore, the average cost— and thus the retail price—changes by far less than the spot wholesale price. Thus, even without retail price caps, spot wholesale price changes translate to far smaller changes in retail prices for most utilities.

---

[33]This is actually the bundled price of electricity and electricity delivery services. The conventional estimates of demand elasticity were based on this bundled combination.

[34]This amount is roughly the price increase that was allowed by the CPUC in January and March 2001, an average price increase of 4 cents/KWh.

[35]Utilities could choose to reduce their purchases through the PX by underscheduling the amount of electricity that they would need to satisfy their customers. If they underscheduled on the PX, they would be required to purchase additional electricity on the CAISO imbalance market. One way or the other, the utility had to acquire all electricity its customers used.

Some large industrial customers and state agencies, such as the California Department of Water Resources, had contracts to buy electricity at prices responsive to wholesale prices. And some had contracts to purchase a fixed quantity of electricity at a negotiated price. If this quantity could be resold, that user had an incentive to reduce electricity use when prices increased. In addition, some consumers chose to reduce electricity use because they understood that there was an "energy crisis" and they chose to help the state by reducing demand.

The net result is that short-run demand functions for electricity, when measured at the wholesale level of the market, tend to be almost vertical. That is, very large increases in wholesale spot prices lead to only small reductions in demand. Thus, I show demand functions as steeply sloping, only somewhat responsive to prices.

There were demand responses in other states for those utilities whose retail rates increased. Some companies—for example, those making aluminum in the Pacific Northwest—shut down all production, therefore completely eliminating their need for electricity; however, those responses would be reflected in the availability of net import supply of electricity to California. These demand (and supply) responses in other states would have the effect of making the supply curve for electricity more responsive to price than illustrated in Figure 3.13.

IMPACTS OF SUPPLY AND DEMAND CHANGES ON WHOLESALE PRICES

Figure 3.14 illustrates what the combined impact of increased California electricity demand and reduced supply of electricity imports would be on the spot wholesale price of electricity if the wholesale price increase had been allowed to translate to retail prices in California. The horizontal axis on this graph represents sales of electricity on the wholesale market for California use; the vertical axis represents the spot wholesale price of that electricity.

The upward-sloping hockey-stick-shaped lines together represent the supply function. The green line (the left-most of the three) represents the supply function for electricity generated in California. The two blue lines (the right-most lines) add the supply of electricity imports into California to the supply of electricity generated in California. The dashed blue line represents the 1999 situation with normal import availability; the solid blue

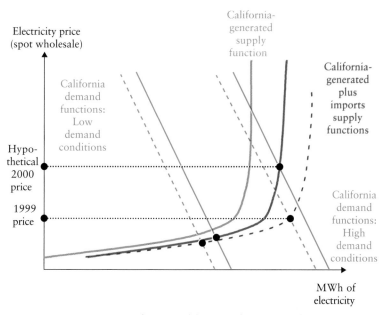

FIGURE 3.14:   Market Equilibria without Retail Price Control

line represents the 2000 situation with sharply reduced import availability.

There are four downward-sloping lines representing different California electricity demand functions, under the assumption that the increases in the average wholesale prices facing California investor-owned utilities were passed on to retail customers.[36] The right-most two represent the demand conditions in the years 1999 and 2000, with the dashed line representing 1999 and the solid line representing 2000. The left-most two represent low demand conditions and will be discussed at a later point.

Black dots are drawn at the 1999 and 2000 points of intersection between the California demand functions and the electricity supply functions (California-generated plus imports to California). Broken lines show the spot prices that would occur in the two years, under the counter-factual assumption that wholesale prices of electricity were passed on to retail customers. In response to increased retail prices, California consumers would find ways of reducing electricity use: turning off lights, unplugging spare

---

[36]If the entire spot market price increase were passed on to the retail customers, the demand functions would be less steep than shown here: there would be greater demand reductions in response to the price increases.

refrigerators, turning off air conditioners, or adjusting the thermostat. Even with the demand response plus the supply response to higher prices, the spot wholesale electricity price would have increased significantly, as shown in this graph.

Similarly, Figure 3.15 illustrates the impact of changed demand and supply on the wholesale price of electricity, given the reality of the retail price caps in California. The only difference between this graph and the graph of Figure 3.14 is that the demand functions are much steeper in Figure 3.15; price increases lead to much smaller reductions in demand. The demand functions are much steeper because California's retail price cap did not allow wholesale prices of electricity to be passed on to retail customers. Therefore there was not a direct economic incentive for California consumers to find ways of reducing electricity use.

Figure 3.15 shows that absent the demand response, the spot wholesale electricity price increased dramatically. Spot wholesale price increases were limited somewhat by the increased supply of California-generated electricity as prices increased and by the increase in imports to California in response to the price jumps (in-

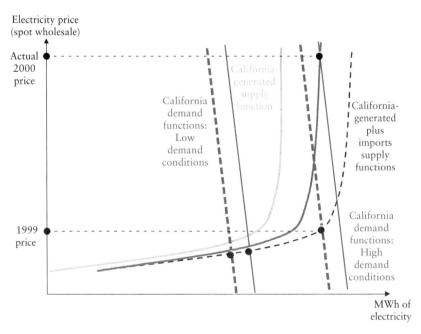

FIGURE 3.15:   Market Equilibria with Retail Price Control

creases relative to the downward shift in supply resulting from the reduced rainfall in the Pacific Northwest and the increased use in the Pacific Southwest). But absent demand reduction by consumers, spot wholesale prices jumped much more than they would have, had retail prices been allowed to increase along with the wholesale electricity prices.

In both of these graphs, in addition to the 1999 and 2000 demand functions, are two other, lower quantity demand functions. These left two demand functions represent the operation of the system during those times when there was sufficient excess capacity in the system. Modest increases in the demand function coupled with the decrease in import supply would lead to only small changes in price (the vertical positions of the two dots are very similar to one another). The response of electricity supply to prices, when there is adequate capacity, would serve to limit greatly the increases in wholesale prices resulting from demand increases, even if demand is very unresponsive to prices.

A comparison of Figure 3.14 to Figure 3.15 suggests that, had retail prices been allowed to move with wholesale prices in California, there still would have been a challenge and there still would have been wholesale price increases. However, because consumers would observe these price increases and be motivated to reduce demand, the wholesale price increases would have been much smaller than they in fact were. Thus California alone, with no changes in regulation from the neighboring states, could have sharply reduced the wholesale price increases that each of the states faced. But California political leaders chose not to take this action.

Figure 3.15 gives a primary explanation of why wholesale prices jumped greatly once the system neared capacity after having remained relatively stable for several years when there was adequate capacity.[37]

These figures also suggest that wholesale price volatility should not be viewed as an anomaly of the California situation but rather as inherent in electricity markets, as long as both the supply functions and the demand functions are very steep at the point of their intersection. The California price caps simply made a difficult situation much worse.

---

[37]See EMF Report 17, "Prices and Emissions in a Restructured Electricity Industry" (Energy Modeling Forum, Stanford University, May 2001) for a model-based analysis of the sensitivity of electricity prices to economic growth rates. This phenomenon is illustrated quantitatively by that study.

INCREASES IN ELECTRICITY GENERATION COSTS: NATURAL GAS PRICES

Increasing demand for natural gas, coupled with limitations on pipeline capacity into California and within California, led to increases in the natural gas price, increasing electricity generation costs. Figure 3.16 (data provided by Enerfax.com, publisher of *Enerfax Daily*, "North America's Free Natural Gas and Power Prices and News Information Source," www.enerfax.com) below shows increases in the California natural gas spot prices from April 1998 through October 2000. Note that in this period price more than doubled from $2.50 per million Btu to $6.00 per million Btu.

It is possible to estimate the impact of this natural gas price increase on the costs of operating a typical new combined-cycle plant or an inefficient unit.

Heat rates of a new combined-cycle power plant may be as low as 6.8 million Btu per MWh. For such a new combined-cycle power plant, when natural gas was selling for $2.50 per million Btu, the cost for natural gas alone would be roughly $17/MWh. When the natural gas price increased to $6 per million Btu, this cost of natural gas alone would increase to $41, a jump of $24/MWh, and the marginal cost of electricity generation would increase by $24/MWh. If these plants were at the high cost end of

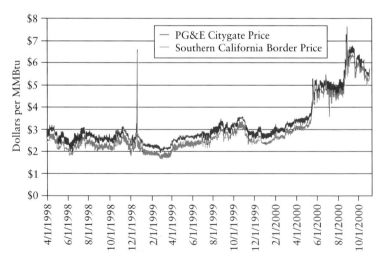

FIGURE 3.16:   Natural Gas Spot Prices in California: PG&E Citygate and Southern California Border

SOURCE: Enerfax.com

the merit order and thus determining the wholesale price, absent demand adjustment, wholesale price of electricity would increase by $24/MWh. In terms of Figure 3.15, the supply curve for California-generated electricity would shift upward by $24/MWh; the import supply component of the total supply function would not adjust; thus, the total supply function would shift upward by somewhat less than $24/MWh. With price controls in place, there would be only a small further adjustment of demand and the wholesale price of electricity could increase by almost $24/MWh.

The cost increase would be greater, however, for older, less efficient plants. Older plants may have twice the heat rate as the newer plants. For example, the SCE Highgrove 1 and 2 plants have heat rates estimated to be about 13.4 million Btu per MWh.[38] For these older plants, the marginal cost of the natural gas alone would be roughly $34/MWh when gas was selling for $2.50 per million Btu. However, when the natural gas price increased to $6, this marginal cost would increase to roughly $80/MWh, a jump of $46/MWh. In terms of Figure 3.15, the high-price portions of the nearly vertical section of the supply curve for California-generated electricity would shift upward by $46/MWh; the total supply function would shift upward by somewhat less than $46/MWh.

In times of excess capacity, the older inefficient plant would be rarely, if ever, used, but as total generation increased, the old inefficient plants became the source of the additional generation. Thus, the old inefficient plants, rather than the newer power plants, became the highest-cost units used and their operating costs determined the marginal cost of electricity generation. Therefore, two factors worked together to increase wholesale prices: the marginal electricity-generating units used to set the wholesale price shifted from efficient plants to old inefficient plants and the natural gas price used by these plants increased. These two factors together implied that the natural gas costs of the marginal electricity-generating unit increased from $17/MWh to $80/MWh, an increase of $63/MWh, which directly increased the wholesale price of electricity. In terms of Figure 3.15, this change represents a combination of the movement upward along the total supply function and a shift upward of that function together leading to the price change.

---

[38]Data estimated from Joel B. Klein, "The Use of Heat Rates in Production Cost Modeling and Market Modeling" (April 17, 1998, California Energy Commission).

In addition, as the system reaches full capacity and the use of natural gas increases, the quantity of natural gas needed exceeds the quantity purchased under long-term contracts. Therefore, the additional natural gas is purchased on the spot market. Thus, although long-term contract prices for natural gas may have influenced pricing behavior when the system was well below full capacity, at full capacity the spot market price of natural gas determines the marginal cost of electricity generation.

The simultaneous shift to use of the inefficient plants, the shift from contract natural gas to spot natural gas markets, and the overall increase in the natural gas price could account for a large share of the increase in the wholesale price of electricity occurring in this period. It should be recognized that these shifts did not *cause* the wholesale electricity price increase but rather were a response to the changing supply and demand conditions that were the primary cause of the wholesale price increases.

It should be noted that, because most of the electricity generated from gas-fired units is based on combined-cycle units, the average cost of electricity generation increased by far less than did the marginal cost. This increase in the natural gas price, therefore, led to increases in the profits of most electricity generators running gas-fired plants. If there had been long-term contracts in place, even contracts indexed for the price of natural gas, the cost that the utilities would have paid to acquire their electricity would have increased by far less than it actually did.

INCREASES IN ELECTRICITY GENERATION COSTS: RECLAIM CREDITS AND ANNUAL EMISSIONS CONSTRAINTS

A change in the price of an additional input was significant. In 1993 the South Coast Air Quality Management District instituted the REgional Clean Air Incentives Market (RECLAIM) to meet the target of NOx and SOx emissions. The RECLAIM program, a market-based approach to regulation, required emitters of NOx and SOx to acquire enough RECLAIM Trading Credit permits to match their actual emissions each year. Through 1998, there was an excess supply of permits in the market, primarily because the number of allocated permits exceeded the normal emissions levels. However, the number of allowed permits was decreasing sharply, and during 1999 the number of allocated permits had diminished to be equal to the total emissions. Through compliance year 1999, the price of NOx trading credits ranged from $1,500 to $3,000 per ton. For compliance year 2000, although permits had been selling for approximately $4,300 per ton in 1999, the prices for the first ten months of the year 2000 increased to an average of about $45,000 per ton.[39]

The significance of this price increase for electricity is related to the emissions characteristics of electricity-generating plants. A typical base-load gas-fired generating unit releases about 0.1 pounds of NOx per MWh of electricity generated. At a price of $2,000 per ton, or $1.00 per pound, the price of RECLAIM credits would add an insignificant amount (10 cents per MWh) to the marginal cost of such units. When the price soared to $45,000 per ton, or $22.50 per pound, this added about $2.25/MWh for a typical base-load gas-fired generating unit, an increase that still was small in comparison to the wholesale price increase. In terms of Figure 3.15, some of the flat, lower portions of the supply curve for California-generated electricity would shift upward by about $2.25/MWh, but this, itself, would have no impact on the high price equilibrium.

Old gas-fired turbines, however, may emit up to four pounds of NOx per MWh. For such units, the price of $2,000 per ton would add to the marginal cost of electricity generation about $4/MWh, still small but significant. However, when the price soared to $45,000 per ton, for the old turbine releasing four pounds of NOx per MWh of electricity generated, this increased the marginal cost by $90/MWh.

During times of energy emergencies, when all available generating units were operating, old gas-fired turbines, many of which were very inefficient, would set the marginal cost of generating electricity in California. For these plants, the incremental cost of natural gas could have been $80/MWh and the incremental cost of RECLAIM credits could have been $90/MWh. Adding these two costs together, in terms of Figure 3.15, the very highest-price portions of the nearly vertical section of the supply curve for California-generated electricity would shift upward by $170/MWh, resulting in much greater increases in wholesale prices for the very limited times in which the system was operating at that point.

Here too, it should be recognized that these shifts did not *cause* the wholesale electricity price increase but rather were a response to the changing supply and demand conditions that were

---

[39]"White Paper on Stabilization of NOx RTC Prices," South Coast Air Quality Management District, web site: http://www.aqmd.gov/hb/010123a.html.

the primary cause of the wholesale price increases. The significance of the increase in RECLAIM costs is that the uppermost part of the vertical section of the California electricity supply function was made more nearly vertical by the tight limitations on the RECLAIM market.

In addition, many plants, both inside and outside the South Coast Air Quality Management District, had annual emissions limits—in particular, annual NOx emissions limits. Absent retrofits to install new pollution control equipment, annual emissions limits translate directly to limits on the total MWh of electricity that can be generated from an individual unit in a given year.

Violation of those emissions limits was punishable by large fines and therefore, to avoid fines, generators had an incentive to reduce their electricity generation from those units. In one well-publicized case, the South Coast Air Quality Management District brought legal action against AES Corporation for exceeding its annual allowable emissions by about 600 tons. In December 2000, the District and AES reached a settlement in which AES agreed to pay a $17 million penalty, equivalent to about $28,000 per ton of NOx *in addition to* purchasing emissions credits to make up for the excess emissions, installing state-of-the-art air pollution controls on three of its power plants, and deducting the year 2000 excess emissions from its future year allocations. (Ironically, although AES was fined because it produced more electricity in 2000 than allowable within its annual emissions limits, California officials have accused AES of withholding generation in 2000— that is, of producing too little electricity.)

A power plant facing an annual emissions limit, and therefore able to generate only a limited number of annual MWh, incurs an opportunity cost in addition to the marginal cost of electricity generation. The opportunity cost exists because generating an additional MWh of electricity at one time eliminates the opportunity for the plant to generate an additional MWh of electricity at some other time. The cost to the plant owner of that eliminated opportunity—the "opportunity cost" of generation—is measured by the additional profit that could be earned at that other time from generating an additional MWh. More precisely, the "other time" must be where the firm expects not to operate at capacity and therefore when it could generate and sell another MWh. The opportunity cost is equal to the maximum additional profit that could be earned at such a time.

A profit-maximizing generator would not be willing to sell electricity unless the price it expected to receive were at least as great as its marginal cost *plus* opportunity cost. A firm bidding competitively thus would not offer a bid equal to its marginal cost but rather would offer one equal to its marginal cost *plus* opportunity cost. Therefore, annual emissions limits lead competitively bidding generators to increase bid prices above marginal cost and further reduce electricity generation. Bidding to sell electricity at a price equal to marginal cost *plus* opportunity cost is thus *not* an indicator that the firm is gaming the market or exercising market power but rather that the firm is bidding competitively, recognizing its annual emissions limits.

POSSIBLE EXERCISE OF MARKET POWER BY GENERATORS

A second possible explanation for the rapid increase in wholesale price is the exercise of market power by electricity generators selling into California markets. This explanation continues to have great political appeal, partly because, if true, it can be asserted that the challenge was not caused by flaws of the restructured system but rather by actions of corporations supplying electricity to California.

As discussed in Chapter 2, the theory underlying the operation of the California PX was that each generator of electricity would bid in its available supplies at its marginal cost. The quantities would be ranked in merit order from lowest cost to highest cost until sufficient quantities were available. The market-clearing price would be set equal to the marginal cost of the highest-cost unit needed to satisfy the demand for electricity on the wholesale market. Each supply that was bid into the market at a marginal cost below the market-clearing price would be able to sell its electricity at the market-clearing price. Any quantity bid at a higher marginal cost would not be sold. In this way, in theory, a price would be set for each hour such that all the electricity-generating units with marginal costs lower than that price would be called on to supply electricity and all the units with marginal costs higher than that price would not be called on.

That theory was based firmly on a belief that the price bids of the generators would always be equal to their marginal cost of generating electricity, which was itself dependent on an assumption that each generating unit was being bid independently of every other unit. However, for generators owning multiple units, it could be expected that the bidding would be coordinated among the various generating units;[40] the units would not be bidding independently of one another.

A company that owned several generators could choose to bid at prices higher than its marginal cost for some of its generating units (or to refrain from bidding at all). For those units whose bid was below the market-clearing price, such a bidding strategy would be irrelevant, since the payment would be based on the final market-clearing price. However, if a unit increased its bid sufficiently so that the bid became higher than the market-clearing price, the result would be the same as if that firm withheld from bidding entirely. The relevant portion of the supply curve—that below the new market-clearing price—would be moved to the left and the market-clearing price would be driven upward. As long as that firm had additional units that bid below the market-clearing price, it could make additional profits from those units.

In terms of Figure 3.15, the impact of such bidding would be to shift the California-generated and the total supply function toward the left, thereby increasing the equilibrium wholesale price. When the system was near full capacity, this reduction in supply would have increased the market-clearing price substantially. The firm could then make additional profits from the rest of its generating units, which would draw the higher price, but would have to trade those additional profits against the lost profits from the unit that increased its bid.

The success of these strategies was made more likely by the California retail price control and the resulting very steep demand curve, as can be seen by comparing the price responses to the fixed supply shift illustrated in Figures 3.14 and 3.15. Since in market clearing, as suggested by Figure 3.15, there would be little reduction in the observed generation of electricity, and since there would be an incentive for many of the generators to follow similar strategies, there might be little changes in the mix of electricity ultimately generated by the various companies. Thus, aggregate quantity data might not readily show the impacts of the strategy.

The incentive for firms to increase their bids in this way was intensified by the operations of the CAISO, whose mission was to

---

[40]Under the U.S. antitrust laws, companies are not prohibited from coordinating their price bids internally, that is, within one company. However, any coordination of price bids between two or more companies would generally be illegal under the Sherman Antitrust Act.

ensure that there would always be sufficient electricity available to avoid blackouts. In order to do this, the CAISO stood ready to purchase electricity on the imbalance market at any price up to some price cap, which varied over time (see the section "Wholesale Price Control Regimes"). Since this quantity to be purchased did not vary significantly with the prices of the electricity offered for sale at that time, the very short-run demand curve was very steep.

Generators understood this willingness, which would have provided a significant incentive for generators to alter their bidding into the PX. In particular, firms increasing their bids on electricity that they offered for sale could be expected to trade the possibility of increased profits against the risk that they would bid too high and not be able to sell their electricity at all. However, on most days the CAISO needed to acquire additional quantities of electricity on the real-time imbalance market the next day. Thus, firms that bid too much might not sell any electricity on the PX but could sell it the next day on the real-time market. Moreover, because there was an incentive for utilities to acquire significant quantities of electricity from CAISO real-time purchases,[41] the suppliers could have reasonable confidence there would be a demand for their electricity. Therefore, the dual market reduced the risk facing firms that were tempted to increase their bid prices greatly on the PX.

In addition, any incentive to withhold supplies to increase the price would be made stronger by the lack of long-term contracts for the utilities to buy electricity.[42] If a generator had a long-term fixed-price contract to sell its electricity, then even under the incentives described above, that generator would have no incentive to withhold its generation. Withholding would increase the market-clearing price, but that firm would reap no benefits from the increased price, given the fixed-price contractual sales of electricity. However, the deliberate public policy decision to discourage such long-term contracts ensured

---

[41]As will be discussed at a later point, the CAISO price caps provided an incentive for utilities to underschedule their electricity needs on the PX. Therefore they had to acquire significant quantities on the imbalance market.

[42]Some of the generators did have long-term contracts with marketers, not utilities. Such contracts would have reduced incentives to reduce electricity supply but would not have reduced the incentives on the marketers to exercise market power in ways described above.

that there would be strong incentives to withhold supply to drive prices upward.

Whether exercise of market power was important to the price jumps early in 2000 or whether the fundamental issue was the basic problems of supply and demand growth is still subject to disagreement.[43] Nevertheless, several issues do seem clear.

First, the restructured system included short-run incentives for firms operating fully within the regulations promulgated by the CPUC to submit bids above their marginal cost when the entire system was near capacity. When the system is near capacity, the hockey stick character of the supply function, in particular the nearly vertical section of the supply function, is relevant. In that situation, small changes in electricity supply could lead to large changes in price, or equivalently, large changes in price could be associated with only small changes in quantity supplied. Under those circumstances there is an incentive for firms to submit bids significantly in excess of their marginal cost if they believe those price bids can influence the revenues they receive for the electricity they sell.[44] However, the amount above marginal cost these firms could be expected to bid depends on several factors that have not been adequately quantified: the short-run and medium-run responsiveness to wholesale prices of electricity imports into California, the beliefs of generators about impacts of current price increases on future electricity demand reductions and consequently future profit reductions, the perceived risk of FERC-imposed

---

[43]For a more complete theoretical and empirical examination of the exercise of market power through September 1999, see Severin Borenstein, James Bushnell, and Frank Wolak, "Diagnosing Market Power in California's Deregulated Wholesale Electricity Market," University of California Energy Institute (August 2000). For analyses of market power during the summer of 2000, see P. Joskow and E. Kahn, "A Quantitative Analysis of Pricing Behavior in California's Wholesale Electricity Market During Summer 2000" (NBER Working Paper 8157, March 2001); Scott Harvey and William Hogan, "On the Exercise of Market Power Through Strategic Withholding in California" (April 2001), available at http://ksghome. harvard. edu/~.whogan.cbg.Ksg/; Paul Joskow and Edward Kahn, "Identifying the Exercise of Market Power: Refining the Estimates" (July 5, 2001), available at http://econ-www.mit.edu/faculty/pjoskow/papers.htm.

[44]Note that when the system is well below full capacity, there is some incentive for firms with multiple units to bid above the marginal cost, although the incentive is small and the optimal bid exceeds the marginal costs by only a small amount. This is because in that circumstance large reductions in supply result in only small price increases.

penalties for firms found to be bidding significantly above costs, and the supply and demand responses of the municipal utilities.

Second, pricing goods for sale anywhere in the economy exactly at marginal cost is probably the exception, not the rule. The issue is the degree of divergence between price and marginal cost. Non-marginal-cost pricing should not be a surprise.

Third, the requirement imposed on the utilities that they buy and sell all of their electricity on the PX or the CAISO precluded them from purchasing electricity through bilateral contracts or on other markets. To the extent that the state-chartered markets—the PX and the CAISO—had flawed rules that encouraged the exercise of market power, the ability to exit these markets would have been valuable to the utilities; however, the California rules prohibited that exit, giving the PX and CAISO monopoly positions.

There was a clear challenge to the state to the extent that firms were withholding supplies entirely or bidding well above their marginal costs. Market rules did provide opportunities for firms to increase their bids above their costs of operations perfectly legally. California public officials, however, were expressing outrage that the firms might have responded to incentives created by public policy. The challenge then, to the extent market power was a fundamental problem, was to change the behavior of the firms without changing the market rules, or to change the market rules. As will be discussed below, the state actions focused on trying to change the behavior of firms or to strengthen the price controls that had been imposed on the markets. The federal actions focused more on modifying the market structures.

CALIFORNIA-CONTROLLED
WHOLESALE PRICE CONTROLS

As the challenge became more severe, California officials began calling on the FERC to limit the increases in wholesale electricity prices in California through the imposition of wholesale price controls. However, price caps had been features of the California wholesale market from soon after the approval of the restructuring plans, and the management of those price caps was in the hands of California organizations.

In March 1998, the CAISO observed large increases in prices for some ancillary services and proposed price caps in the ancillary services markets and the imbalance market as the solution. In July

1998, the FERC responded, authorizing the CAISO to reject any bids to provide ancillary services whenever the CAISO believed those bids were higher than appropriate. The FERC explained that, because the CAISO had a responsibility as procurer of ancillary services, it had the discretion to reject bids that were too high.[45] With this decision, the FERC gave the State of California discretionary power over the price caps applicable to the CAISO.

Subsequently, the FERC authorized the CAISO to treat the real-time imbalance market similarly, allowing the CAISO to adopt price caps for its purchases in the imbalance (real-time) energy market. The FERC allowed the CAISO to set the purchase price at whatever level it deemed necessary and appropriate, thereby ceding a significant price control authority to a state institution. The FERC granted this authority until November 1999; however, the FERC offered the CAISO the opportunity to ask to extend the duration of its authority if the CAISO determined that there remained serious problems in the design of the markets.

The CAISO set an initial price cap of $250/MWh for its purchases in both the imbalance market and the ancillary services markets. In September 1999, the CAISO proposed to extend the price cap authority for one year, until November 2000. That same month the CAISO raised the price cap from $250 to $750/MWh, but indicated that it might lower the caps to $500 in June 2000 or to some unspecified amount if it determined that the markets were not workably competitive. The FERC accepted these proposals. In July 2000, the CAISO did lower the price cap to $500/MWh and in August 2000 further reduced the purchase price cap to $250/MWh. The CAISO applied the same price cap for ancillary services and for real-time electricity purchases.

Although the FERC authorized these price caps for the CAISO, the FERC never authorized formal price caps for sales on the PX. Nevertheless, as discussed in Chapter 2, because buyers could choose to purchase from either the PX or the CAISO, the CAISO price caps translated into price caps for the wholesale price in each of the markets.

Thus the price caps for the CAISO markets created incentives for sales and purchase transactions to be moved to the imbalance

---

[45]Subsequently the FERC ruled that the CAISO's maximum purchase price authority was acceptable because the CAISO did not have the authority to require sellers to bid into its markets and thus could not dictate the prices of those sellers.

market (or ancillary services markets), greatly increasing the transactions in the real-time market. However, the imbalance market had never been designed for large-volume transactions. Since these transactions were conducted in real time, there could never be an assurance that sufficient electricity would be available for the expected consumption. Therefore, the price-cap-induced movement of transactions from the day-ahead and day-of markets to the real-time imbalance market significantly increased the likelihood that there would be insufficient electricity to satisfy customer needs and therefore significantly increased the probability of blackouts, which fortunately did not occur during the period of growing challenge.

This incentive to move transactions to the CAISO imbalance market was so strong that by November the PX data no longer gave any indication of a conventional supply curve for electricity. Figure 3.17 shows the prices versus the quantities of electricity sold on the PX for November 2000, using the same data measured in the same way as Figure 3.13. Figure 3.17 is based on observations of prices and quantities of electricity transacted on the PX in November 2000, whereas Figure 3.13 provides information for July 1999.

The wide spread of prices for any given quantity primarily resulted from transactions moving away from the PX and toward

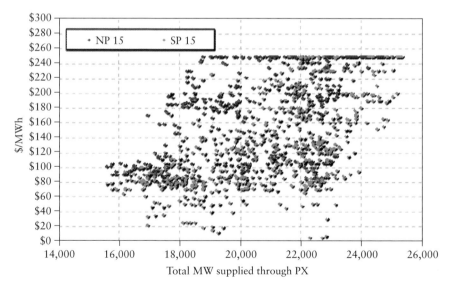

FIGURE 3.17:   Price versus Quantity for California PX, November 2000

SOURCE: California Energy Commission, www.energy.ca.gov/electricity/wepr

the CAISO imbalance market. By November 2000, as much as 30 percent of the electricity (10,000 MW) was sometimes bought and sold on the imbalance market, not going through the PX at all. In Figure 3.13, the supply curve became almost vertical for total transactions of about 34,000 MW through the PX. Because so much electricity was being transacted directly on the imbalance market, the maximum quantities being bought and sold on the PX during November never exceeded 26,000 MW, even though the peak load most weekdays was between 32,000 MW and 34,000 MW.

Figure 3.17 also shows the direct result on the PX prices of the CAISO price caps, with all PX prices remaining at or below $250/MWh.

In addition, price controls themselves created incentives for California suppliers to sell their electricity out of state whenever the out-of-state prices exceeded the California price caps. For example, in the final week of June 2000 the Bonneville Power Administration and utilities and the Pacific Northwest outbid California for electricity, reportedly paying as much as $1400/MWh.

Single-state price caps in a regionally interconnected market proved, not surprisingly, to be a recipe for creating shortages. Fortunately, however, the shortages were relatively mild during the period of growing challenge and did not escalate to blackouts.

Governor Gray Davis seemed to understand these facts but placed blame on the generators, not on the state market structure. Looking back on the period of growing crisis, Governor Davis, in his January 2001 State of the State speech, asserted:

> On many days, 10 to 12 percent of the electricity generated in California leaves our state in search of even more exorbitant prices elsewhere. On some occasions, the merchant generators have brought the State to the very brink of blackouts by refusing to sell us back our own power because they could find higher prices elsewhere.

Although the governor was aware that price caps in California were creating problems, he continued to advocate even greater price control authority.

Given that price caps on the CAISO imbalance market, absent explicit price caps on the PX, were creating more difficulties than would coordinated CAISO price caps, there were at least two possible policy directions: eliminate the price caps on the imbalance market or increase the scope of price controls, imposing price controls on the PX as well.

California political leaders chose the latter strategy. In August 2000, after being encouraged by Governor Davis, the PX proposed to the FERC that it be allowed to change from implicit price caps to explicit price caps. It proposed to impose maximum prices on demand and supply bids for the day-ahead and the day-of markets to be equal to $350/MWh, a figure calculated as the sum of the $250 price cap on CAISO purchases of imbalance energy plus a $100/MWh estimate of the cost the CAISO at that time was paying for replacement reserves.[46]

Soon thereafter, in September 2000, also after urging by Governor Davis, the CAISO proposed to the FERC that it be allowed to further extend the termination date of CAISO purchase price cap authority beyond November 2000. In October, the three investor-owned utilities and The Utility Reform Network (TURN) filed a request to the FERC that would impose a price cap of $100/MWh for all electricity sales. The CPUC filed a motion requesting the $100/MWh price cap but with a set of defined exceptions.

California's electricity organizations were lining up behind price controls rather than correcting the fundamental flaws in its markets, a pattern that would continue beyond the challenge period and into the crisis period. As will be discussed in the following section, this strategy of continued pressure on the FERC for wholesale price controls was consistent with Gray Davis's challenge period policy framework.

In November 2000, the FERC took decisive steps to remove price cap authority from California organizations, denying the PX

---

[46]Price caps on the ancillary services markets, combined with the price caps on the imbalance market, could impose an effective limit on PX prices. Under CAISO procedures, offering electricity as replacement reserves could be a particularly profitable strategy whenever the generators believed the total supplies of electricity would not be adequate to meet the demands without drawing on the replacement reserves. A supplier could offer its capacity into the replacement reserves market and would receive $100/MWh of capacity each hour. If that electricity were sold, the supplier would receive an additional payment of $250/MWh, for a total payment of $350/MWh. If the probability of selling electricity were high, then that strategy would be as profitable as selling the same electricity on the PX for almost $350/MWh. In this case, the market-clearing price on the PX would be almost $350. The PX proposal was designed to set an explicit price cap equal to this implicit cap.

request for its price control authority and announcing that it was removing the CAISO price cap authority in sixty days. In the interim, it removed the authority from the CAISO to modify the price caps, freezing the CAISO price cap at the then current level of $250 for sixty days, until the price cap authority would disappear. The era of California-managed wholesale price controls was about to end.

In place of California-managed wholesale price controls, the FERC ordered that at the end of the sixty days the CAISO and PX auctions be changed to a "soft price cap" system that would limit market-clearing prices to $150/MWh but would allow market participants to submit bids over $150/MWh with appropriate cost verification. Such bids above $150/MWh could be paid "as bid," but they would not set the market-clearing price.

But before the end of the sixty days, the CAISO markets were on the edge of collapse. The CAISO was forced to declare Stage 2 emergencies for four days in a row and saw no end to the shortage. Blackouts were imminent. The electricity challenge was turning into a full-blown crisis. On December 8, 2000, Terry Winter, chief executive officer of the CAISO, asked the FERC to allow the CAISO to replace its $250/MWh price cap with a soft price cap system similar to the one scheduled for the end of the sixty days but with the interim break point set at $250/MWh. The FERC agreed immediately and California could then purchase electricity to avoid blackouts. Predictably, Governor Davis and the California legislature vilified Mr. Winter for that action, but his actions probably saved California from wide-scale blackouts during December. These FERC-controlled changes in price caps are discussed more fully in the following chapter.

THE FINANCIAL CHALLENGE

The high wholesale prices, the lack of long-term contracts, the divestiture of utility generation assets, and the retail price controls together created a tremendous financial challenge for the utilities, one that urgently needed to be addressed during the challenge period. In early 2000 the utilities had seen that there would be pressures on supply and demand for electricity and knew they faced a fundamental challenge, a challenge they could not surmount absent action by the governor, legislature, or the CPUC.

By the time the challenge became apparent, they had divested about 60 percent of their generating assets. Divestiture itself would not have been particularly harmful if the utilities had re-placed these generating assets with long-term contracts to acquire the electricity, perhaps at prices indexed to natural gas prices.[47] But they had not been allowed to do so.

As of mid-2000, the utilities could have reduced, but not elimi-nated, the risk of wholesale price increases if they had been able to enter long-term contracts to purchase electricity at fixed prices. In early spring, these contracts were being offered to the utilities. For example, in June and July several of the larger generators were of-fering to sell significant amounts of capacity with opening offer prices of about $50/MWh.[48] Prices were likely to have been lower than $50/MWh earlier in 2000. Both PG&E and SCE made requests of the CPUC and appealed to Governor Davis to allow them to enter such contracts. The initial response was quite negative.

On June 22, 2000, the CPUC decided, in a narrowly split vote, to allow the utilities to buy power outside the CAISO and the PX markets. However, the California Legislature subsequently over-rode the decision, requesting that the CPUC demonstrate that al-lowing utilities to purchase energy from outside of the CAISO and the PX was in the public interest, a demonstration that the CPUC never provided. Thus the utilities were forced to continue purchasing and selling all electricity on these two markets.

However, in August, once prices had jumped sharply, the CPUC did file an order allowing the utilities to enter limited numbers of bilateral contracts. Even then, any purchases other than from the PX would either need preapproval or face an after-the-fact reasonableness review, whereas all purchases from the PX were considered per se reasonable. And without clear guide-lines about the CPUC vision of reasonableness, utilities faced the prospect of being severely penalized if, retrospectively, their long-term contracting decisions turned out to be economically unat-tractive, but they could not expect to be rewarded if, retrospectively, their decisions turned out to be economically at-tractive. Throughout the challenge period—in fact, throughout the electricity crisis—the CPUC never adopted any guidelines and did not preapprove any contracts. These strong asymmetric

---

[47]In fact many municipal utilities had no generating assets at all. But they maintained portfolios of medium-term and long-term contracts under which they acquired electricity.

[48]Private communication from Robert Weisenmiller, based on his polling of many of the larger generators.

economic incentives gave the investor-owned utilities a significant incentive to rely on the PX and not enter into longer-term forward contracts to buy electricity. Thus, even this limited concession did not reasonably encourage long-term contracts.

This failure to encourage long-term contracts and the resultant overreliance on spot markets helped establish the financial challenge. The overreliance on spot markets ensured that when wholesale prices began to soar, the utilities would pay these high prices for almost half of the electricity they would need to serve their loads. This lack of reasonable risk management options was central to the financial challenge.

By fall 2000, the challenge was hitting the electric utilities with a tremendous force.[49] The restructured system left them selling electricity to their customers at an average price of about $65/MWh for the electricity (plus another $60/MWh for transmission, distribution, and other delivery services), yet the wholesale price of electricity ranged from $150/MWh to $1000/MWh for half of the electricity they were selling (see Figure 3.11). Almost one-half of the remainder from the QFs was already being purchased at high prices. Generation from their own hydroelectric assets and nuclear power plants accounted for only 30 percent of their electricity, thanks to the divestiture.

The accumulations into the transition accounts to pay for stranded costs quickly reversed, with large *negative* competition transition charges. Thus, the more electricity they sold, the more money they lost. But, unlike most other businesses, they were not allowed to tell their customers that, because the cost of the product was too high, they would not supply it. Not only were the utilities subsidizing all industrial, commercial, and residential customers, they were forced to continue doing so.

The utilities could readily project forward to the time when all of their financial assets would be spent and their credit would be gone. The option of medium- and long-term contracts was no longer helpful because the pricing being offered for medium- and long-term contracts had risen along with the spot wholesale prices.

During the challenge period the political institutions—the governor, the legislature, and the CPUC—needed to allow the wholesale price increases to be translated into retail prices. Without

[49]An excellent timeline of these events, compiled by Southern California Edison, appears on the web: www.sce.com/SC3/005_regul_info/ 005g_market/005g2_chronology.shtml.

reductions of the wholesale prices or corresponding increases of the retail prices, the utilities could project their own insolvency.

Once the financial imbalance became obvious, each of the utilities requested increases in retail rates to cover the average cost of the electricity they were selling. Even though there were price controls on the electricity sales, these price controls had been established to allow the utilities to accumulate sufficient revenues to pay for the stranded costs. Thus, it was perfectly logical that if the pricing structure were no longer serving the goal for which it was established—enabling the utilities to accumulate financial assets to pay for the stranded costs—it should not have been continued, especially since it was operating in exactly the opposite direction, reducing the financial assets available to pay for stranded costs.

The requests for retail price increases (often referred to as "rate relief") were made primarily to the CPUC and secondarily to Governor Davis. Through the challenge period, absolutely no rate relief was made available to the utilities. In fact, SDG&E, the only one of the three major investor-owned utilities that under AB 1890 would no longer be subject to retail price controls, remained free of the controls only for a limited time. The California Legislature voted to reimpose those controls.

With the political institutions—the CPUC, the governor, and the legislature—turning their backs on the legitimate requests of the utilities, PG&E and SCE sued the CPUC in Federal District Court. The utilities relied on the federal "filed rate doctrine," which requires states to pass the costs of electricity purchased subject to federal tariffs on to utility customers. The utilities interpreted federal tariffs to include FERC-approved tariffs.

In addition, utilities argued, "the CPUC's rulings also are unlawful in that they violate the Commerce, Takings, and Due Processes Clauses of the Constitution."

In particular, the Takings Clause requires the State to set retail rates that are not confiscatory. Rates are confiscatory if they fail to provide the utility a reasonable opportunity to recover its prudent costs of service and a fair rate of return commensurate with the risks undertaken. Confiscatory rates unlawfully interfere with reasonable investment-backed expectations.[50]

---

[50]Both quotations from *Southern California Edison Company v. Loretta M. Lynch et al.*, Complaint for Injunctive and Declaratory Relief, November 13, 2000.

However, legal proceedings seldom proceed quickly, and this was no exception. The lawsuit remained in progress through the challenge period and the crisis, until SCE finally settled its suit in October 2001. The PG&E case is still proceeding in U.S. District Court.[51]

Although the challenge facing the investor-owned utilities could have been solved by early action from the governor, the CPUC, or the legislature, by the end of the November 2000 none of the appropriate policy responses had been forthcoming. Thus, by the end of the challenge period, they were facing a near-certain financial crisis, absent an abrupt state policy shift.

STATE POLICY RESPONSES DURING THE CHALLENGE PERIOD

On June 15, 2000, soon after the June price spikes, Governor Davis requested that Michael Kahn, Chairman of the Electricity Oversight Board, and Loretta Lynch, President of the CPUC, examine the causes of the blackout that had occurred in the San Francisco Bay Area and the associated wholesale price increases. Ms. Lynch and Mr. Kahn duly responded to Governor Davis's request and issued a report, which they forwarded to Governor Davis and posted on the CPUC web site.[52] The cover letter of the report, dated August 2, 2000, began:

Dear Governor Davis:
In response to your letter of June 15th, included as
Attachment 1, the attached report analyzes the electricity
conditions facing California, including the Bay Area
black-outs of June 14th and the circumstances giving rise
to forced outages and related pricing problems. Your

---

[51]On May 2, 2001, U.S. District Judge Ronald Lew dismissed as premature the PG&E lawsuit that sought to overrule decisions by the CPUC that PG&E was not entitled to recover money it had spent to buy electricity for its customers during the crisis. The judge ruled that the CPUC orders were not yet final, but were only interim orders. Judge Lew stated that PG&E could refile its suit when the CPUC orders were finalized. PG&E has done so.

[52]*California's Electricity Options And Challenges: Report To Governor Gray Davis.* The report is available on-line through the California Public Utilities Commission: http://www.cpuc.ca.gov/published/report/Table%20of%20Contents.htm.

concerns have proved well-founded in light of recent retail price escalations in San Diego and the state-wide wholesale price upsurges. The Bay Area outages and the San Diego price increases are only the first manifestations of problems in our electricity system.

The first paragraph of the executive summary of the report stated:

California is experiencing major problems with electricity supply and pricing caused by policies and procedures adopted over the past ten years. This summer, California has seen both electricity price volatility—exemplified by huge increases in wholesale electric prices and increases in retail prices in San Diego—and supply and delivery system instability—culminating in unprecedented black-outs in the Bay Area. These serious, but thus far isolated, examples represent a precursor of what lies ahead for California's economy over the next 30 months. California's reliability deficits and retail price volatility may not improve in that time without a mid-course correction.

Thus, very early in the process, Governor Davis was aware that there were important challenges facing California. Moreover, two of his appointees gave him broad advice and a set of specific recommendations designed to address the problems they had identified. But even after that report, California policy responses during the period of growing electricity challenges were surprisingly limited, relying almost entirely on efforts to establish or strengthen price controls at both the retail and wholesale levels.

One policy framework, articulated by Governor Davis, provided the guidance for California's response to the challenge. Price controls at both the wholesale and the retail level seemed to be the one and only goal of the State's policy framework during the challenge period. The State could enforce and expand retail price controls, which they did very aggressively, though they could not unilaterally impose wholesale price controls since the federal government, and particularly the FERC, had the primary jurisdiction over wholesale markets. Thus, Governor Davis orchestrated a broad campaign to urge the FERC to maintain and expand wholesale price controls.

Governor Davis articulated his overall strategy in a series of letters dated July 27, 2000, and summarized that strategy in a press release issued that day. Portions of that press release follow:[53]

> *SACRAMENTO—Governor Gray Davis today called on federal and state regulators to take swift action to extend the caps on wholesale electric rates in California and provide San Diego ratepayers with millions of dollars in refunds. . . .*
>
> *In letters to two state regulatory agencies and two California-based panels charged with overseeing California's power market, Governor Davis called for a coordinated state effort to urge federal regulators to take strong measures to reduce power rates in both the short- and long-term.*
>
> *The legislation signed into law in 1996 by Governor Pete Wilson to deregulate California's investor-owned electric utilities left state agencies and the Governor with limited options to regulate prices, Governor Davis noted. However, today's initiatives are designed to maximize the leverage of California's regulatory agencies with the Federal Energy Regulatory Commission. . . .*
>
> *In letters released today, Governor Davis:*
>
> - *Called on the California Independent Systems Operator . . . to immediately apply to FERC for extension of its authority to establish price caps for wholesale power. . . . Governor Davis also requested the ISO to reduce the "wholesale price cap to the lowest reasonable level". . .*
> - *Urged the California Public Utilities Commission (PUC) . . . to "take all actions necessary to assure that electricity supplies are adequate and that prices paid by California consumers are just and reasonable." He called on the Commission to file a petition with federal regulators next week to support extending wholesale price caps. He also urged the PUC to ask FERC to declare that no competitive market for energy currently exists in California—action that would support wholesale price caps.*

---

[53]This and other press releases can be reached through Governor Davis's home page: http://www. governor.ca.gov/state/govsite/gov_homepage.jsp.

- *Requested the Electricity Oversight Board . . . to take three actions at its August 1, 2000 meeting. They include: urging the ISO to petition FERC for continued authority to impose wholesale price caps; establish price caps at the lowest reasonable level; and file a petition with FERC requesting a finding that no competitive market exists in California. . . .*
- *Called on the California Power Exchange . . . to apply for caps on the price bid for wholesale electricity in the day-ahead and day-of "spot markets" that it operates. . . .*

In a separate letter to the PUC President Loretta Lynch, Governor Davis requested the PUC at its August 3, 2000 meeting to authorize the return of $100 million in refunds from the California Power Exchange to San Diego Gas & Electric ratepayers.

As discussed above, the PX and the CAISO both complied with the governor's request, submitting requests to the FERC to establish or extend their price control authority.

In addition, although the California Legislature took only very limited actions, they were consistent with the governor's overall strategy. Several bills were introduced, but never passed, to urge the FERC to impose price controls on the wholesale market. Assembly Joint Resolution No. 77, a joint resolution of the California Senate and Assembly, did gather sufficient votes to pass. It reiterated the wholesale price control strategy, resolving:

That the Electricity Oversight Board, working with the Public Utilities Commission, shall petition FERC to modify the Independent System Operator (ISO) tariffs to require that the prices in the energy and ancillary services markets are just and reasonable whether they result from the operation of these markets or other mechanisms.

It further resolved:

The Electricity Oversight Board shall direct the Independent System Operator to show cause why the price caps in the ancillary services and real-time energy markets should not be lowered to $100 per megawatt-hour immediately and continue until at least March 31, 2001.

In September, the California Legislature reestablished retail price controls in San Diego. Assembly Bill 265, authored by Assemblywoman Susan Davis (D–San Diego) and Senator Deirdre Alpert (D–Coronado), imposed retail price controls on electricity for consumers and small businesses in San Diego at $65/MWh (6.5 cents/KWh). The price control regime, slated to continue through December 2003, was made retroactive from June 1, 2000. This reduction of electricity prices could be expected to increase electricity demand and to exacerbate the electricity problems.

Gray Davis's policy framework, focusing entirely on price control, thus was fundamental to almost all the steps the State took during the challenge period. The State continued to force the investor-owned utilities to rely on wholesale spot markets, and thus the utilities were not able to begin to manage the wholesale price risks they faced. In addition to the reestablishment of retail price controls in San Diego, such controls were not relaxed for PG&E and SCE. No significant steps were taken to guard against the possibility of energy emergencies.

Only very limited positive steps were taken within California to go beyond Governor Davis's policy framework, namely, those taken to increase electricity supplies and decrease electricity demands. Governor Davis signed an executive order that directed "all California agencies involved in building new energy facilities to streamline the review process for siting new power plants without compromising environmental laws or public health and safety protections." The order required that "all state agencies involved in permitting new facilities must submit their review and findings within 100 days of receiving a completed application." That order could be expected to speed new construction but would have no impact on electricity supply during the challenge period or during the crisis. In September, Senate Bill 1388, authored by Senator Steve Peace (D–San Diego), was passed, speeding the approval process for new power plants.

State-owned buildings were directed to reduce their use of electricity, but only during serious energy emergencies.[54] Senate Bill 1194, authored by Senator Byron Sher (D–Palo Alto), and AB 995,

---

[54]The order was applicable only to Stage 2 and Stage 3 emergencies. See Chapter 4 for a discussion of these emergencies.

authored by Assemblyman Rod Wright (D–South Central Los Angeles), were signed into law. These extended in time the existing AB 1890 requirement of a separate electricity rate component, collected as a bypassable charge, to fund energy efficiency and conservation activities, public interest research and development, and development of renewable resources technology.

In short, other than imposing or urging others to impose electricity price controls, the State governmental bodies took remarkably few significant policy steps to avert the coming electricity crisis. Moreover, the State took no positive steps to avert the coming financial crisis, but rather, by reimposing price controls in San Diego, threatened to exacerbate the problems.

IN SUMMARY

Between 1997 and the autumn of 2000, the risk embedded in the restructured system, although perhaps not apparent to all participants in that system, had become a reality. California consumption of electricity grew slightly faster than historically, available imports in California dropped sharply as markets became much tighter throughout the West, new California generation capacity was being constructed but was not yet operational, virtually all California electricity generation units other than natural gas–fired were at full capacity, and as a result, production in California from existing gas-fired units increased sharply. The increase in use of gas-fired units implied not only that the efficient ones were on-line, but that the old inefficient plants were brought on-line as well. The inefficient ones used more natural gas and emitted more NOx and SOx than the newer, more efficient units, thereby increasing the marginal cost of generating electricity. The increase in the use of natural gas pushed up its price. The RECLAIM market experienced a massive jump in the price of emissions credits as the available supply of credits decreased. These factors together would contribute to the challenge.

During the summer and fall of 2000, the severe challenge demanded leadership and wisdom from California's political leaders. Mastering the challenge would not be easy after wholesale electricity prices had jumped during the summer of 2000. By that time, all meaningful solutions were likely to involve short-term economic sacrifices by many, including the voters in California. Yet, as of the summer of 2000, there were important policy actions still possible that would have avoided a California electricity crisis and a financial crisis. However, California's political leaders never rose to the challenge. This failure of political leadership turned the challenge into a crisis.

4

THROUGH CRISIS

By December 2000 and January 2001, there was no question that California was in the midst of a crisis. Yet even then, statewide policy actions were available to avoid the long-term consequences of that crisis, although perhaps it was too late to avoid the short-term consequences. However, the failure of leadership persisted. And the crisis deepened.

This chapter examines the growth and subsequent remission of California's energy crisis and the evolution of state and federal policy during that crisis.

THE NATURE OF THE CRISIS

The California "energy crisis," like the challenge, can be seen as two crises—a western electricity crisis and a financial crisis of the investor-owned utilities that turned into a state budgetary crisis. Once the challenge reached crisis proportions, these two crises exacerbated one another. Conceptually, the two crises were separable from one another. There could have been a western electricity crisis that did not lead to a financial crisis,[1] and there could have

---

[1] In fact, in the Pacific Northwest, as well as the remainder of the eleven western states, there was the same electricity crisis, but it did not turn into a financial crisis primarily because the utilities did not face the same risky posture as the California investor-owned utilities. Most of the utilities in the West were protected through long-term contracts for most of their electricity aquisitions.

been a financial crisis without an electricity crisis. However, these two crises fed on one another during late 2000 and early 2001, spiraling California deeper into the dual crises.

The electricity crisis grew directly from the electricity challenge that was facing the western states because the basic problem—the increase in demand for electricity coupled with the decreases in electricity supply—was managed poorly by the State of California. The financial crisis started primarily as a crisis for the investor-owned electric utilities and turned into a crisis for the State budget. That the financial challenge turned into a financial crisis was the direct result of State regulatory, administrative, and legislative action or, more precisely, inaction.

Not only did the electricity crisis lead to the financial crisis but also the financial crisis made the electricity crisis substantially worse. Since the investor-owned utilities did not receive adequate revenue to pay their suppliers, the utilities began delaying their payments, promising to pay later, which created significant uncertainty among suppliers, who could not be sure they would ever be paid. The uncertainty of future payments would lead a rational supplier to increase the price at which it was offering to sell the supplies into the California market, therefore increasing the wholesale prices further. In addition, because the investor-owned utilities were delaying their payments to suppliers, some suppliers were not financially able to continue generating electricity. For the smaller companies, cash flow problems could be severe. In particular, many QFs were owned by relatively small companies that were not able to continue generating electricity without being paid. Therefore, some of these generators went off-line and stopped delivering electricity, thus further reducing electricity supply and exacerbating the electricity crisis, which in turn made the financial crisis worse.

In what follows, these two crises are discussed separately, even though they were tightly interrelated. Some policies are integrated into discussion of the crises; however, some crosscutting policy issues are discussed in separate sections.

THE ELECTRICITY CRISIS

By December 2000, the challenge had grown into a crisis, with even greater increases in the wholesale electricity prices and frequent energy emergencies. The crisis remained severe all winter.

Not until late spring 2001 did the electricity crisis start to disappear, with wholesale prices falling, electricity consumption declining, and the frequency of energy emergencies falling. During the peak of the crisis, the standard belief was that summer 2001 would be even worse than December and January had been, since summer is California's period of peak electricity use. However, by summer 2001, the energy crisis had mostly subsided. By that time, new generating plants, whose applications for certification were filed in 1997 or 1998 (see Table 3.3), were first coming on-line, and electricity demand had declined relative to 2000. Wholesale prices had declined sharply from their peaks, and the energy crisis had all but disappeared. By fall 2001, wholesale prices had declined to typical historical levels and energy emergencies had disappeared entirely. The crisis had passed.

The California energy crisis was a short-term event—of only seven months' duration—though intensely painful. Large amounts of the new generation capacity, mostly initiated in the first few years after AB 1890 was passed, are projected to come on-line during the next few years. Thus, it is unlikely that the electricity crisis will return soon, if at all, unless California policies chill the investment climate enough that many plants currently planned or under construction are canceled.

WHOLESALE PRICES

Monthly average data for electricity sales on the day-ahead PX market through December 2000 are shown in Figure 4.1 with data shown separately for Southern California (SP15) and Northern California (NP15).[2] The average spot wholesale price of electricity reached a short-term peak in August 2000, declining during the next two months as the days grew cooler and the demand for electricity decreased. However, even the $100/MWh price in October was several times higher than normal. November and December showed new increases in the electricity prices. In December, the average PX price for electricity in Northern California slightly exceeded $300/MWh, while in Southern California that price was roughly $225/MWh. Daily peaks were much higher than either of these figures in December for both Northern and Southern California, where

---

[2]Comparable data for subsequent months are not available because the PX was shut down in January. The PX ultimately declared bankruptcy in March 2001.

$/MWh

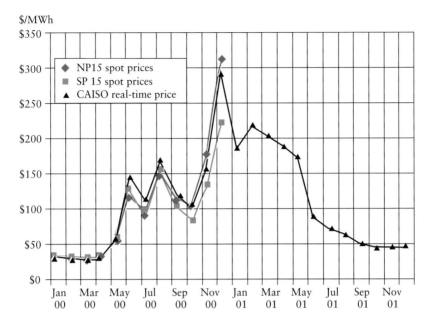

FIGURE 4.1:   Spot Wholesale Prices, California PX (Day-Ahead),
CAISO Real-Time

the maximum December price on the PX was slightly above $1,000/MWh. The *minimum* price of electricity sold on the PX for any one hour throughout the month of December in Northern California was $132/MWh!

The longer series in Figure 4.1, the "CAISO real-time price," is the weighted average of prices paid for all wholesale real-time purchases of electricity scheduled through the CAISO. This includes electricity sold under the price cap (whenever a price cap existed), electricity transactions based on bids accepted over the price cap, and out-of-market purchases scheduled in real time.[3]

These two price series differ in that the "CAISO real-time price" includes out-of-market purchases, which come from entities that are not in the CAISO control area, such as out-of-state generators or municipal utilities, for example, the LADWP. These out-of-market

---

[3]Source: Data from a sequence of CAISO monthly memos entitled "Market Analysis Report for . . . ." The most recent available is "Market Analysis Report for December 2001," a memo from Anjali Sheffrin, Director of Market Analysis, CAISO, to ISO Board of Governors. www.caiso.com/docs/09003a6080/12/50/09003a6080125047.PDF.

purchases never went through the PX but were negotiated in real time. Whenever the price caps were in effect, the out-of-market purchases generally carried a higher price than those purchases transacted on the PX. Thus, the exclusion of these observations generally biases the PX prices downward, as can be seen in Figure 4.1.

To the extent data are available, prices were similar among the western markets most of the time, with the exception of two weeks in December 2000 (the week of December 11 and the week of December 18). During those weeks, the maximum prices during the peak period were $5,000/MWh at Mid-Columbia and $4,000/MWh at the California-Oregon Border, while the maximum prices recorded on the PX were $1,400 and $950. Figure 4.2 shows the same type of data that were displayed in Figure 3.12, the average of the high and low prices during peak periods on a week-by-week basis for the various market centers, although for a longer time period. Data are shown from April 1, 2000, to October 1, 2001. The top pane of the chart shows the full range of prices; the bottom pane is truncated at $500/MWh.

As Figure 4.1 illustrates, the wholesale price paid for electricity reached the maximum monthly average in December 2000, stayed high through May 2001, and has been falling ever since.

The sharp decrease in wholesale electricity prices had not generally been anticipated much in advance of the actual reductions. Expectations of future prices can be measured by observation of the futures prices prevailing at different times. Figure 4.3 shows the published futures prices for electricity averaged over the two markets centers, Palo Verde and the COB, relevant for imports and exports of California electricity. This figure shows that on May 4, the futures price for electricity to be delivered in August was $550/MWh. Prices were near $400/MWh for delivery in June, July, and September. However, by June 8, the August futures price had declined to $240/MWh and prices for adjacent months had gone down to below $200/MWh. By July 16, all futures prices had declined to below $100/MWh.

These figures reflect very sharp changes in beliefs, occurring between early May and early June, about the prices electricity would command in wholesale markets. In addition, the beliefs seem to have continued to evolve downward through July and into August, consistent with the actual reductions in prices.

One can use either the time that wholesale prices sharply decreased or the time that beliefs about future prices sharply decreased in order

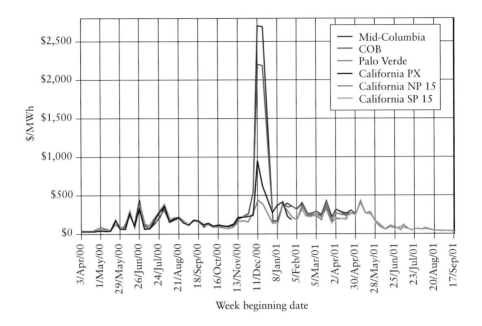

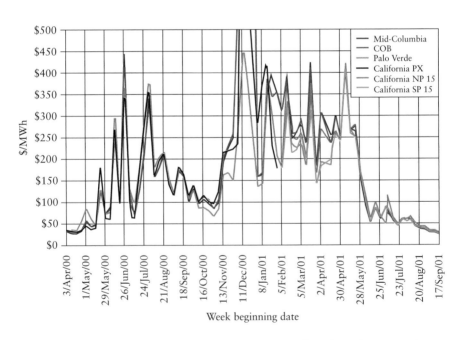

FIGURE 4.2:   Spot Power Prices: Average of High and Low Peak
Prices, Various Western Markets

SOURCE: *Western Price Survey*, www.newsdata.com

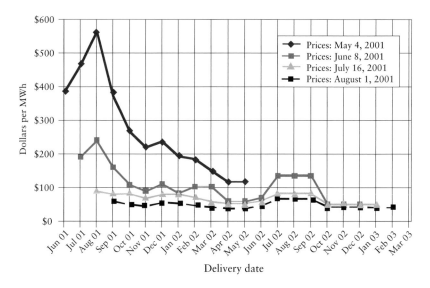

FIGURE 4.3:   California Electricity Futures Prices at
Several Different Times

to define the end of the California electricity crisis. Using those crite-
ria, the crisis can be seen as beginning in late November 2000 and
ending in June 2001, a seven-month event: short, but painful.

ELECTRICITY SUPPLY AND DEMAND

The basic economic forces underlying the price increases and
their subsequent declines throughout the West were the same
forces of electricity demand (particularly peak demand), available generating capacity, electricity-generation costs, and possible market power described in the previous chapter. None of
the difficulties had been overcome by the end of the challenge
period and some became worse as a result of the California financial crisis. This section describes only those factors that
changed in important ways from the challenge period and during the crisis.

Electricity Imports and Exports

What at first might have seemed surprising was that prices were so
high in winter, since demand for electricity in California typically
peaks in summer and declines in the winter. However, Pacific
Northwest utilities peak in the winter and decline in the summer.

During the winter, when California typically needs less electricity and the Pacific Northwest needs more, California exports electricity to the Pacific Northwest.

During 2000, the low rainfall in the Pacific Northwest reduced the availability of water for hydropower generation and that reduction continued to reduce the available generation of electricity in the Pacific Northwest. Thus, the demands for exports of electricity from California during winter 2001 increased.

In terms of Figure 3.15, California's demand for electricity is reduced during the winter—the demand curve shifts leftward—but the import supply curve is also reduced and also shifts leftward.

Natural Gas Prices

Contributing to the increase in electricity prices during the crisis were even more dramatic increases in the natural gas price than had occurred earlier in 2000. In December, the California natural gas price jumped to above $50 per million Btu, a factor of ten higher than it had been. Although this price peak lasted for only two weeks, the spot natural gas prices in California remained above $10 per million Btu until June 2001 (see Figure 4.4). These high prices did not result from limitations in the availability of natural gas at the wellhead or at market centers. Prices of natural gas at Henry Hub, Louisiana, the major market center, remained below $10 per million Btu, whereas the California price exceeded $50. Rather the price spike resulted directly from the large demand for natural gas to fuel electric generators during the winter, when the demand for natural gas naturally peaks, coupled by limitations in the pipeline capacity to transport natural gas within the state[4] and the absence of natural gas held in storage from previous months.

The sharp increase in natural gas prices, coming just when investor-owned utilities were not paying generators for electricity they sold, provided strong incentives for generators either to stop producing electricity or to bid very high prices to sell the electricity they did generate. Thus, these natural gas prices probably con-

---

[4]The CPUC, SCE, and PG&E brought suit in the FERC against El Paso Corp., a Texas pipeline company, charging that it had withheld capacity so as to cause a gas shortage that would increase prices. In October 2001, the chief administrative law judge of the FERC ruled in favor of El Paso, concluding that the California parties failed to prove the contention that El Paso had withheld capacity.

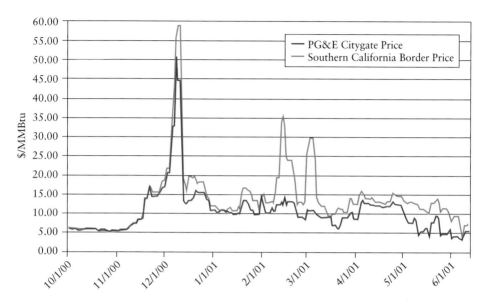

FIGURE 4.4:   Natural Gas Spot Market Prices: PG&E Citygate and
Southern California Border

SOURCE: Enerfax.com

tributed substantially to the wholesale electricity price increases
during the crisis, particularly to the December electricity price
spikes.

Risk Created by the Financial Crisis

Because of the financial crisis, which will be discussed in a subsequent section of this chapter, the utilities began delaying their payments to electricity generators, promising to pay later. However, it
was becoming clear that unless the state took appropriate policy
measures, the utilities were unlikely to become capable of paying
for the electricity in a timely manner, if at all, creating significant
uncertainty among suppliers. And most suppliers would be able to
sell their electricity out-of-state or to the municipal utilities in
California if they were not compelled to sell to California's investor-
owned utilities.

Uncertainty of future payments would lead a rational supplier
to increase the price at which it was offering to sell supplies into
the California market, thereby increasing the wholesale prices
further. For example, if a supplier believed that there was only
a 70 percent probability of receiving $100/MWh for electricity

and 30 percent probability of never being paid at all, then the sale of that electricity would be worth no more than $70/MWh to the supplier. If the cost to that supplier of generating the electricity were $77/MWh, that supplier would not be willing to sell the electricity for a promised price of $100/MWh. A bid of $110/MWh[5] would represent a bid at exactly the expected value of the cost of generating the electricity. The uncertainty of payment alone would have had the direct effect of increasing the bid prices and thus the market-clearing prices in the wholesale market.

This increase in bids to account for market risk would appear exactly as if the generator were trying to exercise market power to increase the wholesale price of electricity. Determining whether such bidding was based on an attempt to exercise market power or a competitive response to the financial risk is very difficult, since it depends on the generator's assessment of the probability it would be paid.

This phenomenon was particularly obvious in the November 2000 through January 2001 period, when the utilities were not paying for the electricity they were receiving and their credit ratings were declining sharply. In January, however, the State of California stepped in as the creditworthy buyer, seemingly guaranteeing the payment for all electricity purchased on behalf of the utilities. Instead, California refused, despite repeated FERC orders, to pay its own spot market wholesale power bills. Until November 2001, the DWR did not even allow itself to be billed by CAISO for its purchases. The investor-owned utilities still have not paid for wholesale electricity purchased before January 2000. During 2001, continuing nonpayment caused some suppliers to drop off-line, and continuing risk of nonpayment caused others to include a credit premium in their bids. The FERC subsequently approved a 10 percent credit premium to compensate for continuing financial risks for sales to California. Thus, even though the State had seemed to guarantee payment for all electricity, the state-created financial crisis continued through 2001 to reduce supplies and to place upward pressures on wholesale prices. A subsequent section, "Policies Impacting Risk to Electricity Suppliers," further discusses this continued risk.

---

[5]$110/MWh multiplied by 0.7 equals $77/MWh.

Possible Exercise of Market Power

As will be discussed in a later section, in mid-January 2001 the governor ordered the DWR to start purchasing wholesale electricity on behalf of the electric utilities, since they were no longer considered creditworthy buyers. Other than electricity self-generated or purchased through preexisting contracts, the investor-owned utilities no longer acquired electricity other than through the DWR. This change fundamentally altered the market structure in California, shifting market power toward the State. Instead of several competing buyers of electricity buying on an organized market, for all practical purposes, the DWR became the dominant buyer of electricity in California. The DWR was able to choose how much of the electricity it should purchase ahead of time and how much it should acquire on the real-time CAISO market; thus, if DWR chose, it could acquire almost all its electricity through bilateral contracts outside the CAISO.

As the dominant buyer, the DWR was not able to change the total electricity consumption or the timing of that consumption, which were passively determined by the load. Nevertheless, the DWR could negotiate short-, medium-, and long-term contracts with the various sellers. The DWR was not required to pay the same price to each seller or to disclose the prices it paid for any particular transactions:[6] it had the ability to price-discriminate for purchases other than those on the real-time market.

Figure 4.5, based on data released by the DWR, illustrates both the large numbers of entities from which the DWR was buying electricity and the wide range of prices it was paying. Each bar on the chart represents a private sector or public sector entity selling electricity to the DWR during the first six months of 2001. Blue bars represent public entities: Powerex (a subsidiary of BC Hydro), LADWP, DWR, BPA, SMUD, and the City of Burbank. Red bars represent private entities: Mirant, Dynergy, Williams, AES, and Duke Energy. Sellers are shown in order of their total electricity sales to the DWR, with those selling the most electricity furthest to the left. The height of the bars shows the cumulative fraction of electricity purchased, that is, the fraction of purchases represented

---

[6]Data on purchase prices ultimately had to be released, but the releases came long enough after the time of transactions that the information would have little or no value to the generators trying to defend against discriminatory pricing by the state.

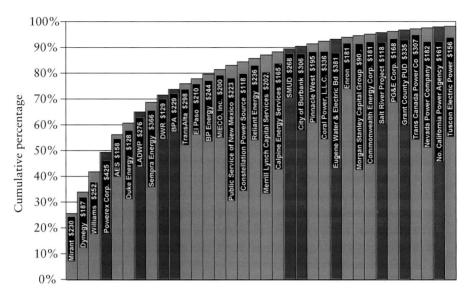

FIGURE 4.5:   DWR Electricity Purchases, January through June 2001

by that seller and all larger sellers. Mirant supplied 26 percent of the DWR purchases. Dynergy supplied 8 percent; thus the cumulative supply for dynergy and Mirant is 34 percent. Williams sold another 8 percent, and thus the cumulative percentage is shown as 42 percent. The graph shows that four sellers accounted for almost 50 percent of the purchases by the DWR, eleven sellers accounted for 75 percent, and twenty-one sellers together accounted for 90 percent. Thus the market structure was one in which a single dominant buyer, the DWR, was purchasing electricity from very many competing sellers.

The average prices of electricity sold to the DWR are shown above the names of the sellers. Figure 4.5 shows that the prices negotiated by the DWR varied widely across the sellers. Of the four largest sellers, the DWR paid Mirant an average price of $230/MWh, Dynergy an average price of $187/MWh, Williams $252/MWh, and Powerex $425/MWh. The highest price in the group was more than twice the lowest. Among the sellers accounting for 90 percent of the transactions, the DWR paid prices ranging from $128/MWh (Duke Energy) to $425/MWh (Powerex Corporation), a difference of greater than three-to-one. Monthly data show the same pattern of price discrimination by the DWR among the sellers for each of the six months.

A skillful, price-discriminating dominant buyer purchasing from a group of competing sellers should always be able to reduce the total acquisition cost, even without reducing the total amount of electricity purchased, although it could not reduce the acquisition price below the prices at which the generators could sell electricity out of state, where there were competing buyers.

The DWR's ability to price-discriminate in its purchases reduced the incentives, if they existed, for sellers to attempt to exercise market power in the ways described in previous sections. For with the DWR as the dominant buyer, if a firm offered a small portion of its output at a high price and the rest at a low price, the DWR could simply choose to buy the low-price portions at the bid price, reject the high-price offer, and purchase that quantity from another supplier instead. Although a seller would have incentives to increase the price at which it offered the bulk of its product, as would be the case in an as-bid auction, the seller's lack of information about the cut-off price created incentives against price increases. If it suspected that a seller was trying to manipulate market prices, the DWR could purchase from other sellers, even those offering electricity at higher prices, to discipline sellers it suspected were attempting to manipulate market prices. This possibility of strategic purchasing by the DWR implied that as of late January, any generator market power could be exercised only (1) for sales through the CAISO real-time market and ancillary services markets or (2) through actual reductions of generation, say by taking plants off-line. Even if the DWR chose not to operate in a proactive manner to exercise its new market power, at the minimum the DWR had the power to block any maneuvers by suppliers attempting to manipulate markets.

Thus, to the extent that suppliers were exercising market power, that market power disappeared during the last half of January 2001, to be replaced by DWR market power as the dominant buyer. Therefore, if market power was an important force for increasing prices during the challenge period and into December and early January, it is unlikely to have been an important force for keeping prices high in February through May.

Generators Off-Line

A fundamental driving force for the supply reductions, and hence the wholesale price increases, during winter 2001 was the reduction in availability of electricity generated in California. Large numbers of generators went off-line during late fall 2000 and winter 2001. Historically, between 1,000 and 6,000 MW average daily generating capacity would normally be off-line in a month. However in the period between October 2000 and May 2001, a monthly average of 12,000 MW generating capacity was off-line, reaching a peak of 15,000 MW in April 2001. Figure 4.6 shows these data.

This large amount of off-line generating capacity resulted from a combination of causes, but the greatest fraction of generators was reportedly off-line for repairs or maintenance. However, whether the maintenance and repairs were forced upon the generators, were part of a competitive cost-minimizing solution, or were designed to increase wholesale prices has not been fully resolved. This empirical matter probably cannot be resolved without careful in-depth assessment of facts that currently are not publicly available.

It is reasonable to believe that all or most of the generators were shut down for legitimate maintenance and repair needs. Many of the gas-fired units were old and had deteriorated with age. California had just gone through a summer in which generators were being operated more intensively than they had been in many years, and many had been cycled on and off, adding to the stress on

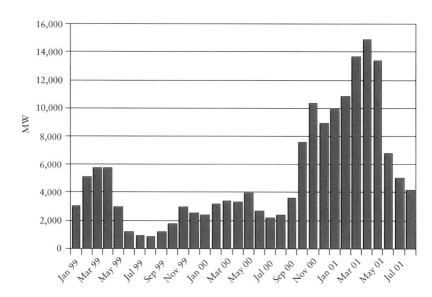

FIGURE 4.6:   Average Generating Capacity Off-Line

SOURCE: California Energy Commission

these old plants. The firms operating the generators have asserted that a larger than average need for repairs resulted from running the plants at full capacity for the entire summer and that plants had been forced off-line for needed repairs. One such outage has been very well documented: an accident at SCE's San Onofre nuclear power plant in February 2001 took over 1,000 MW off-line for several months. Since SCE was a buyer of electricity, it had an intense incentive to bring that plant back to operation as soon as possible.

It is also reasonable to believe that shutting down some plants was largely a matter of choice, not of necessity. Whether some old plants can still be run while in need of repairs is a matter of engineering and operational judgment. There were economic incentives to shut down some of the plants. Firms that owned a portfolio of generators had an incentive to withhold one of their plants from generating electricity in order to increase the wholesale price of electricity sold by the remaining plants. Such an opportunity to exercise market power would be a financial motivation to take one plant off-line for repairs, even though the plant could have continued to operate if the owner had so chosen.

In response to the concern that the large number of plants off-line could have been the result of deliberate withholding, the FERC initiated an investigation. In February 2001, the FERC issued a report on the causes of the outages with the following conclusion, based on its field and office observations:

> *The telephone audits and the on-site inspections disclosed that the outages occurred at generating plants that were 30 to 40 years old. These generating facilities were operated at a significantly higher rate in 2000 than in previous years. Most of the generating facilities were out-of-service because of tube leaks and casing problems, turbine seal leaks and turbine blade wear, valve failure, pump, and pump motor failures.*
>
> *Staff did not discover any evidence suggesting that the audited companies were scheduling maintenance or incurring outages in an effort to influence prices. Rather, the companies appeared to have taken whatever steps were necessary to bring the generating facilities back on-line as soon as possible by accelerating maintenance and incurring additional expenses. Also, the outages did*

not necessarily correlate to the movement of prices on a given day.[7]

Other observers argue that these telephone audits could not have detected plants that were shut down for manipulating market prices. In addition, even field audits may not detect actions to slow down repairs. The GAO reviewed the FERC analysis and concluded:

FERC's study was not thorough enough to support its overall conclusion that audited generators were not physically withholding electricity supply to influence prices. FERC's study was largely focussed on determining whether or not the outages that occurred were caused by actual physical problems—such as leaks in cooling tubes—requiring maintenance or repairs. However, it is practically impossible to accurately determine whether such outages are orchestrated or not because plants frequently run with physical problems and the timing of repairs and maintenance is often a judgment call on the part of plant owners or operators.[8]

Neither the FERC study nor the GAO was able to assess quantitatively and definitively the genesis of the plant outages. The FERC "did not discover any evidence" of strategic manipulation of outages but did not claim to have proved there were no strategic manipulations. The GAO concluded that "FERC's study was not thorough enough" but did not claim to have evidence that there was strategic manipulation. Absent litigation, with discovery of internal documents and testimony under oath—and possibly even with a litigation—it is unlikely that we will ever know definitively whether these outages were uncontrollable or whether they resulted from strategic manipulation.

A smaller but significant number of the off-line plants—perhaps up to 3,000 MW—were not the old gas-fired units but rather

---

[7]FERC, "Report on Plant Outages in the State of California." Prepared by Office of the General Counsel, Market Oversight & Enforcement, Office of Markets, Tariffs and Rates Division of Energy Markets, February 1, 2001.

[8]USGAO, "Energy Markets: Results of Studies Assessing High Electricity Prices in California" (June 2001). USGAO, "Energy Markets: Results of FERC Outage Study and Other Market Power Studies," Statement of Jim Wells, Director Natural Resources and Environment (Thursday, August 2, 2001).

were the QFs whose operators were not being paid for the electricity they were selling the investor-owned utilities.[9] Thus, some portion of the reductions in capacity, but far from a majority, was the direct result of the uncertainty imposed on the QFs and the reduction in their cash flow, which was a direct result of the financial crisis.

Figure 4.6 shows that May 2001 was the last month for which such a large amount of generating capacity was off-line: in May almost 14,000 MW were off-line, whereas in June that figure dropped to 7,000 MW. The 7,000 MW increase in available supply of electricity was a very important component to loosening the market and driving wholesale prices down toward more normal levels in June.

The reasons for the sudden change in available supply are not altogether clear. As discussed in the subsequent section on FERC rulemaking, the FERC May and June Orders included "must offer" provisions. These Orders may have had a significant impact. In addition, by June, QFs were being paid for the electricity they sold and had, for the most part, come back on-line. Natural gas prices had dropped substantially and the costs of running the less efficient units had decreased substantially, thus making it more attractive for them to be kept operational.

New Generation Capacity

During the challenge period small amounts of new generation capacity became available. In May through July 2000, approximately 1,000 MW of new generation capacity had come on-line in Colorado, Nevada, and New Mexico. A 250 MW cogeneration plant went on-line in British Columbia at the beginning of October 2000.

However, during the last half of the crisis, new generation capacity was rapidly becoming operational throughout the West, including California. A very small amount became operational in March 2001, but starting in late April, new plants came on-line at the rate of around 1,000 MW per month for the next six

---

[9]On March 20, 2001, the *Los Angeles Times* reported, in a story entitled "Small Power Firms' Cutbacks Contribute to Blackouts": "Monday, about 3,000 megawatts of qualified-facilities generation went offline because the companies that operate the power plants can no longer afford to buy natural gas used to fuel the plants due to the utilities' failure to pay money owed to the companies, said Jim Detmer, vice president of operations for the state's Independent System Operator."

months. By June 1, 2001, almost 2,000 MW had become operational; by August 1, over 5,000 MW had become operational; and by October 1, almost 7,000 MW were on-line. Figure 4.7 shows the cumulative new generation coming on-line after August 2000, with data from ten western states plus British Columbia.[10] Additional capacity was completed in the Mexican portions of WSCC, but these data are not included in that figure.

Figure 4.7 shows that about 800 MW of new capacity came on-line in British Columbia and Arizona around the beginning of May 2001 and that over 1,000 more went on-line by June 1. The additions were primarily in Arizona, but smaller amounts also went on-line in Colorado and Wyoming. These increases in new generation capacity combined with the June reductions in the number of plants off-line placed significant downward pressure on spot wholesale prices, which declined sharply around June 1.

In California, as of the beginning of the crisis, no new generation capacity had yet come on-line, although much was in the construction pipeline. Not until late June and July 2001, *after* the sharp decline in wholesale prices, did any new generation capacity become operational. These new plants, Sunrise Power, Sutter Power, and the

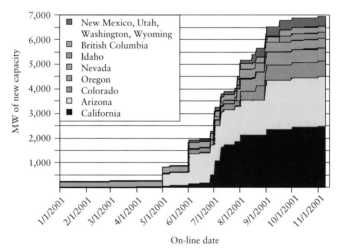

FIGURE 4.7:   New Electric Generation Capacity On-Line in WSCC
(excluding Mexico)

[10]These data were compiled from many different publicly available sources, including the California Energy Commission for plants in California.

Los Medanos Energy Center, contributing 1,400 MW of capacity, had been initiated between December 1997 and December 1998, shortly after the restructuring legislation. However, they were completed slightly too late to have had any impact on electricity prices until after the crisis had ended.

Figure 4.7 shows that as of November 2001, of the new capacity in the West, 36 percent was in California, which is comparable to California's 40 percent of the electricity consumption. And California's new capacity came on-line after the first new capacity in Arizona and British Columbia. These data thus do not support a claim that California State governmental actions successfully brought a disproportionate number of plants on-line nor that the State's actions were particularly successful in speeding up the construction process for those plants already under construction.

The new generation capacity under construction in California and the rest of the West can be expected to insure against a near-term repeat of the electricity crisis. Figure 4.8 provides estimates, published by the California Energy Commission, of the new California-only generation capacity projected to come on-line before the end of 2004. These data are based on electricity-generating plants currently under construction. Figure 4.8 shows the capacity additions both from large plants (greater than 300 MW) and from

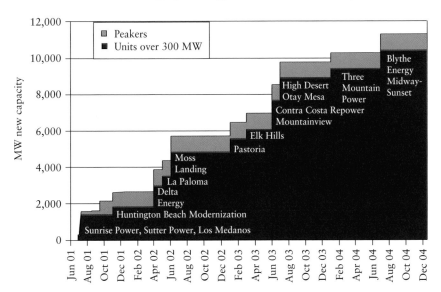

FIGURE 4.8: Expected New Generating Capacity in California from Plants under Construction

peaking units currently under construction.[11] Figure 4.8 shows that by the beginning of summer 2002 there can be expected to be roughly 4,000 MW of new capacity on-line and almost 6,000 MW by the end of summer 2002.

Energy Conservation

Electricity demand, measured both in terms of peak demands and total megawatt hours, declined from 2000 to 2001. During spring and summer 2001, these significant reductions in the consumption of electricity and the peak demands for electricity started becoming apparent, thereby taking pressure off the tight electricity market. The reductions continued at least through the end of 2001.

Figure 4.9 shows the reduction in average electricity consumption and in peak demand based on California Energy Commission data.[12] The bars show the peak demand reductions on a month-by-month basis from 2000 to 2001; the lines show the reductions in average electricity use. The monthly peak electricity demand was reduced, on average, by 1,900 MW (4.4 percent), and the monthly average use was reduced by 1,200 MW (4.3 percent). Although this demand reduction was substantially smaller than variations in the capacity of plants off-line, it was comparable in magnitude to the new generation capacity on-line by the end of the period. Demand reductions, which generally can occur more rapidly than new construction, have been important in putting downward pressure on wholesale prices.

Some of the month-to-month variability was the result of differences in weather conditions between 2000 and 2001. The California Energy Commission has estimated that weather-adjusted peak demand, averaged over the months from January through November, declined by 7.4 percent and that the weather-adjusted average electricity consumption declined by 5.2 percent, figures somewhat larger than the unadjusted changes.

In addition, there were reductions in electricity use throughout the West. In the Pacific Northwest, in particular, there were significant numbers of industrial shutdowns, including in the aluminum industry, which together reduced the demand for electricity in the West.

---

[11]Because the construction time for peaking units is so short, there may be more peaking units on-line during this time horizon, if needed, based on plants for whom no application has yet been filed.

[12]Data are published by the California Energy Commission on its web page.

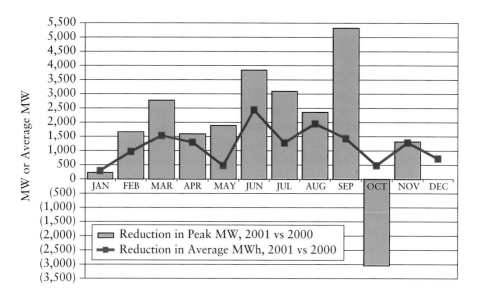

FIGURE 4.9:   Reductions in Electricity Use, 2001 versus 2000,
                MW Peak and Average MW

SOURCE: California Energy Commission

These demand reductions stem from a combination of factors—
expectations of increased electricity prices, high retail natural gas
prices,[13] the energy demand management programs, energy efficiency and conservation programs, publicity about electricity
problems, and the decline in the California economy. Subsequent
empirical work will be needed to assess the quantitative significance of these various factors.

Some of the demand reductions can be expected to be transient;
for example, the significantly reduced lighting levels in large stores

---

[13]Many customers, particularly in Northern California, received one single
bill for natural gas and electricity purchases. When the natural gas prices increased, newspapers carried stories about consumers whose energy bills had increased and who were finding ways of reducing their electricity consumption
in response. Although a reduction in electricity use in response to an increase
in the natural gas price is not what economists normally predict, it seemed to
be occurring in California. Perhaps subsequent empirical work will be able to
examine whether this phenomenon in fact occurred in significant amounts. But
the requisite empirical work has not yet been completed, or at least not yet
been published.

or parking lots in shopping centers or the changes in temperature settings of air conditioners. In addition, the demand reductions associated with the decline in the California economy will be reversed as the economy recovers and again starts to grow.

However, many of the demand reductions will be permanent.[14] The reduction in public sector use through the substitution of light-emitting diodes in traffic lights rather than conventional lightbulbs will not be reversed. Buildings have been reroofed with light-colored materials, thereby reflecting radiant energy rather than absorbing it, reducing the air-conditioning load. Consumers and firms that have substituted compact fluorescent lights for conventional incandescent lights are unlikely to go back. The utilities are again promoting energy efficiency programs, and these, too, can be expected to result in permanent reductions in electricity use.

California could still face electricity problems in the winter of 2002 if many generating plants again go off-line, or if a cold winter leads to large demand in the Pacific Northwest.[15] As time goes on, however, the probability of continuing problems declines. With the large amount of new capacity scheduled to come on-line within the next several years and continuing demand reductions, supplies of electricity are likely to remain adequate, unless California policies chill the investment climate enough that many plants currently planned or under construction are canceled.

ENERGY EMERGENCIES AND ROLLING BLACKOUTS

The electricity crisis was marked by energy emergencies and fear of rolling blackouts. Crises resulted from supply and demand imbalances: electricity supply was not sufficient to satisfy all electricity demand and keep a safe margin of operational reserves. Blackouts occurred when supply was so small that groups of customers had to be "blacked out" to avoid instability in the grid. Although blackouts came to symbolize the electricity crisis, energy emergencies were the norm during the crisis and blackouts were the exception.

---

[14]These reductions will be permanent, relative to the level of economic activity and to the population. But a growing population and growing economy will increase the overall level of electricity use even with these permanent reductions.

[15]Particularly in Washington, electricity is used for space heating in many homes. Cold weather can greatly increase the space-heating loads.

Figure 4.10 diagrams the various stages of energy emergencies and the demand responses, alerts, and warnings issued by the CAISO at the various stages of energy emergencies. Blackouts occur only when the CAISO has declared that a Stage 3 emergency exists, that is, when operating reserves decline below 1.5 percent. During some Stage 3 emergencies, rolling blackouts, although threatened, are not ultimately required.

As Figure 4.10 indicates, in anticipation that Stage 3 emergencies might occur, several options would be taken in turn. First, during a Stage 1 emergency, when operating reserves were projected to fall below 7 percent, public alerts were issued with calls for people to reduce their use of electricity during the energy emergency, particularly during peak times. Commercial establishments would be encouraged to reduce "unnecessary" lighting and to curtail use of air conditioning or other heavy uses of electricity.

During a Stage 2 emergency, when operating reserves were projected to fall below 5 percent, more severe measures were taken. Utilities had contracts with large users, particularly large

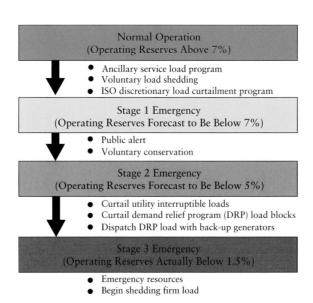

FIGURE 4.10:   Electricity System Emergency Levels

SOURCE: *CAISO 2001 Summer Assessment,* March 22, 2001, California Independent System Operator

industrial users,[16] to reduce use of electricity significantly during Stage 2 emergencies. The loads for these large users could be interrupted during energy emergencies, although such contracts included a provision limiting the number of such required interruptions. Since these users had each voluntarily agreed to such contracts, this load shedding would be concentrated on firms whose operations would not be severely damaged by an interruption of electricity service. In addition, the CAISO established a demand relief program (DRP) under which energy aggregators agreed to reduce their aggregate demand when so ordered by CAISO. Under this program, load aggregators develop and market programs to those end-use customers willing to reduce electricity use in response to a CAISO curtailment order, which could be issued during a Stage 2 emergency, up to a limited number of curtailment hours in each month for a given participant.

These curtailments sometimes were not sufficient to avoid moving to a Stage 3 emergency, during which the CAISO called on emergency generating resources and ordered utilities to begin shedding firm load; that is, it ordered blackouts. In rolling blackouts, shortages were allocated to the utilities. The utilities had been required to identify electricity "blocks," or areas that could be blacked out simultaneously. During the emergency, utilities were required to shut down all electricity in those blocks for a limited time, typically one to two hours. If the shortage continued, other blocks would be blacked out in sufficient quantities to ensure that the entire grid did not crash.

Alternatively, the CAISO could have been willing to pay higher prices to obtain additional supplies, either from the generators participating in the California market or from out-of-market purchases. While the price caps were in effect, this option had been foreclosed. Upon the lifting of the price caps, however, such high-price purchases were possible, to a limited extent.

The separation of the PX and the CAISO, and the resulting restrictions embedded in the CAISO tariff, made this process of ac-

---

[16]Other large users could have such interruptible service. For example, the Claremont Colleges had interruptible electricity contracts and experienced such contractual blackouts.

quiring electricity to avoid Stage 3 energy emergencies far more difficult than it needed to be. As discussed above, when the PX and CAISO were established, the PX was given responsibility for all trading on the day-ahead and the day-of markets. The CAISO was not allowed to buy or sell on those markets; that is, the CAISO was restricted to real-time purchases and sales of electricity. "Real-time" has been interpreted as during the hour that the electricity is needed. Thus, because of the early decisions to separate the PX and the CAISO, the CAISO tariff precludes it from acquiring electricity to meet emergency conditions earlier than during the hour that electricity is needed.

This restriction was in effect even when CAISO personnel were confident ahead of time that the electricity would be needed. Moreover, as discussed at another point, the utilities were typically greatly underscheduling their loads, sometimes by as much as 35 percent. All underscheduled loads had to be covered by CAISO purchases with purchases occurring *during the hour that the electricity was needed,* thereby making the process far more hurried than it needed to be.

Organizations other than the CAISO could make contractual commitments to purchase electricity well in advance of the time it would be used. Thus, when electricity supplies were short throughout the western states, the CAISO, because of limitations in its tariff, would be the last entity to be able to acquire supplies to avoid energy emergencies. That restriction thus increased the likelihood that the blackouts would be concentrated in California.

Figure 4.11 plots the energy emergencies declared by CAISO during the challenge and the crisis periods. Data are presented on a daily basis; each major division on the horizontal axis represents two weeks. Stage 1, 2, and 3 emergencies are indicated by the 1, 2, and 3 on the vertical axis. Rolling blackouts are shown as one level higher.

The first energy emergency was declared on June 14. This one-day Stage 1 emergency resulted from the heat wave hitting California and surrounding states while supplies were tight. During mid-July through August, Stage 1 and Stage 2 emergencies, including multiday emergencies, became common. Mid-September saw a brief return of energy emergencies. With the cooler autumn weather, there were no more energy emergencies until November.

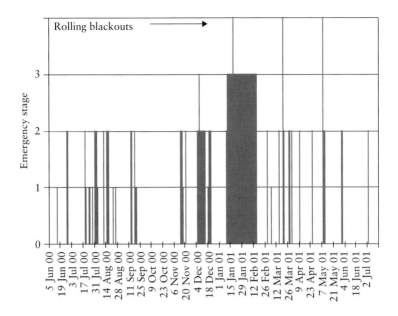

FIGURE 4.11:   Energy Emergencies and Blackouts in California

Stage 2 energy emergencies returned in mid-November. However, in December and January energy emergencies became the norm. December 4 began an eleven-day period of Stage 2 emergencies, during which the CAISO first declared a Stage 3 emergency. The emergencies seemed to take a break for the holidays at the end of the year—a time of generally reduced commercial activities. After the first week of January, the CAISO declared energy emergencies for thirty-two consecutive days. The first rolling blackouts occurred January 17 and 18.

Once the coldest part of the winter had passed and the heating loads in the Pacific Northwest had subsided, energy emergencies became less common. Stage 2 emergencies, however, continued to recur, including two episodes of rolling blackouts, each two days long.

Although everyone in California was asked to conserve energy during each energy emergency, none of the demand reductions was mandatory unless a Stage 2 or Stage 3 emergency was called. During a Stage 2 emergency, conservation or load shedding was mandatory, but only for those organizations that had entered contracts allowing for such mandatory load shedding. Only when Stage 3 emergencies were severe enough to require rolling blackouts did the shedding of loads extend to individuals or organizations that had not agreed to allow such curtailments.

Blackouts came to symbolize the electricity crisis in California. Nevertheless, although blackouts were the symbol, and the threat of blackouts was frequent, actual blackouts were very rare. The CAISO ordered blackouts in fact on only six separate days, as shown in Figure 4.11 and in Table 4.1. Moreover, blackouts were called for only a small fraction of the load at any time, as shown in Table 4.1. The most severe was on January 18, in which 1,000 MW of load was curtailed, accounting for 3.2 percent of the peak demand that day. Other rolling blackouts ranged from 300 MW to 500 MW, or 0.9 to 1.7 percent of the peak load.

Perhaps blackouts came to symbolize the electricity crisis in California because, for several months, the threat of blackouts was always real. Initially almost everyone was vulnerable to such interruptions, with the exception of hospitals and other emergency locations. Blackouts hitting industrial plants on only short notice could and did lead to very high costs. Blackouts covering areas of street lighting and traffic lights raised the risk of traffic accidents. The fear of blackouts was expressed frequently in newspaper stories, editorial cartoons, and letters to editors. Thus, although there were many instances of very large costs incurred, particularly by industrial facilities, the fear of blackouts may have generally been greater than the direct consequences of the blackouts themselves.

The last rolling blackout was ordered on May 8; the last energy emergency was declared on July 3 during a heat wave. Since that day, the CAISO has not declared any energy emergency.

TABLE 4.1
Rolling Blackouts in California

Date (All 2001)	Curtailment Ordered (MW)	% of Peak
January 17	500	1.6
January 18	1,000	3.2
March 19	500	1.7
March 20	500	1.7
May 7	300	0.9
May 8	400	1.1

THE FINANCIAL CRISIS

As of December 2000, the financial challenge had become a crisis that ultimately resulted in PG&E declaring bankruptcy and SCE teetering on the brink of bankruptcy for a month. Once the financial limits of the utilities had been reached, this crisis moved to a hemorrhaging state budget. At this time, the state budgetary issues have yet to be fully resolved.

That the financial challenge turned into a financial crisis was the direct result of state regulatory, administrative, and legislative action. The state could have averted the financial crisis during the challenge period if it had stopped forcing investor-owned utilities to deeply subsidize electricity use by their customers.[17]

Had the state relaxed its price controls, the utilities would not have faced a financial crisis and the state budget would have retained a sizable surplus. Consumers and businesses would have faced higher electricity prices but not of crisis proportions. Thus, the financial crisis was caused simply by the unwillingness of the state regulatory authorities, under the leadership of the governor, to allow retail electricity prices to rise sufficiently to cover the cost of acquiring that electricity, or even most of the cost.

The significance of the regulatory controls is apparent from a comparison of the impacts on the investor-owned utilities with the impacts on the municipal and investor-owned utilities throughout the other ten western states and on the municipal utilities in California. During both the challenge period and the crisis, the increases in spot wholesale prices were very similar throughout the eleven western states. Therefore, other than electricity purchased under long- or medium-term contracts, wholesale electricity prices increased by roughly the same amount for investor-owned and municipal utilities throughout the entire eleven-state region.

Yet only California, and only the investor-owned utilities of California, faced a fundamental financial crisis. Some investor-owned utilities in other states and some municipal utilities in California faced difficult financial problems, but none was brought to the brink of bankruptcy, as were the investor-owned utilities in California.

---

[17]As noted previously, California municipal utilities were not so required and were free to increase their prices based on decisions by their governing boards.

There are two fundamental differences between California's investor-owned utilities and all the other entities. All the other entities acquired the vast bulk of their electricity through either their own generation or a mix of medium- and long-term contracts, and faced regulatory bodies that could have increased the retail prices if needed to keep them creditworthy, although in many cases these bodies did not increase retail price by as much as wholesale price increased. Only the California investor-owned utilities faced the western electricity crisis with a requirement to purchase most of their electricity on spot markets and with a regulatory body that refused to raise retail electricity rates until it was too late. Therefore, only the California investor-owned utilities faced the devastating financial crisis.

The financial crisis did not end even when all financial assets of the utilities were depleted. The state took over from the investor-owned utilities the obligation to purchase sufficient electricity to satisfy electricity demand. As a result, over the course of roughly six months, this decision decimated the State budgetary surplus. In essence, the State of California had put itself in the place of the investor-owned utilities as the only entity facing the western electricity crisis without long-term contracts to purchase electricity and with price controls limiting the price at which the electricity was sold to its customers. Thus, the State of California started facing the same financial crisis that the CPUC and Governor Davis had imposed on the investor-owned utilities. However, as will be discussed at a later point, the CPUC had the power to raise retail electricity rates and the state had the power to enter medium- and long-term contracts to purchase electricity. When needed to reduce the impact on the California State Treasury during the crisis, the CPUC and the state ultimately took the actions they had precluded the utilities from taking.

THE FINANCIAL CRISIS AND THE UTILITIES

Until January 2001, no retail rate increase was forthcoming and the investor-owned utilities remained trapped between soaring wholesale prices and the retail price controls rigidly enforced by the CPUC and strongly endorsed by the governor.

A loud and clear warning came from the financial community on December 20, 2000, when Standard & Poor's warned that utilities would not be able to finance wholesale power purchases without clear and definitive action from California's regulators to ensure that costs could be repaid. Citing the likelihood of default, Standard & Poor's asserted that unless such clear and definitive actions were taken within twenty-four to forty-eight hours, there would be a downgrade of credit ratings of the utilities to "deeply speculative" levels.

In a classic "too little, too late" move, on January 3 the CPUC proposed, and on January 4 agreed, to allow SCE and PG&E to raise rates by a mere 1 cent/KWh ($10/MWh). The increase was too small by a factor of at least 3 to begin to compensate for average wholesale cost increases of over $100/MWh. Moreover, the CPUC made it clear that the rate increase would be a *temporary* surcharge, to be in effect for ninety days and subject to refund. The CPUC promised to investigate the rate issue further during the ninety-day period, stating, "we do not yet have the facts to evaluate the utilities' claims of their dire circumstances." By that decision, the CPUC clearly signaled that they were willing to drive the utilities to bankruptcy.

The governor only grudgingly accepted any price increase at all, stating in a press release: "If I had my way there would be no rate increase to consumers. But given the colossal failure of California's deregulation scheme, the PUC's decision was unfortunately necessary."

However, four days later, Governor Davis did offer the investor-owned utilities some hope. In his "State of the State" address on January 8, 2001, he stated unequivocally:

> *To utilities and the financial community, let me say this: I reject the irresponsible notion that we can afford to allow our major utilities to go bankrupt. Our fate is tied to their fate. Bankruptcy would mean that millions of Californians would be subject to electricity blackouts. Public safety would be jeopardized. Businesses would close. Jobs would be lost. Investment would flee the state. And our economy would suffer a devastating blow.*

Yet even with those dramatic, although overstated, comments, the governor remained opposed to the single most important action that he could take to solve the financial crisis—a meaningful retail price increase consistent with the cost increases the utilities were facing. And, as it turned out, Governor Davis did nothing to back up his words with actions.

To keep buying electricity, both PG&E and SCE used their available cash and credit to pay for the massive financial shortfalls. However, the rate of net outflow was staggering. For example, the costs that PG&E faced exceeded their revenues by roughly $1 billion per month. By PG&E estimates, the cumulative shortfall was $3.4 billion by October 2000, $4.5 billion by November, and $6.7 billion by year-end 2000. By the end of the first quarter of 2001, the cumulative shortfall amounted to about $9 billion. Similarly, SCE, by the end of the process, had incurred liabilities and indebtedness from procuring electricity, totaling approximately $6 billion. Any company, including PG&E and SCE, faces limits on its financial reserves and its borrowing capacity. By January, SCE had reached those limits. PG&E reached its limits in a similar timeframe.

On January 16, SCE formally notified the U.S. Securities and Exchange Commission (SEC) that it had suspended payment of some power purchase and debt obligations. Its public filing stated that the utility's cash reserves of approximately $1.2 billion as of January 15 would be exhausted by February 2 if it met all its financial obligations. This default meant that debtors would be entitled to exercise legal remedies to collect. Standard & Poor's and Moody's Investors Service subsequently downgraded SCE's bonds to below investment grade. No longer would SCE be treated as a creditworthy buyer of electricity.

On January 19, Standard & Poor's downgraded the ratings on PG&E's bonds to below investment grade, reflecting PG&E's defaults on January 17. Therefore, PG&E would no longer be treated as a creditworthy buyer. On February 1, 2001, PG&E announced that it could not make full payment to the CAISO and QFs for November CAISO energy purchases and December QF electricity deliveries. Of the somewhat more than $1 billion due, it would make partial payments of $161 million.

Before that time, the utilities had been able to purchase electricity even though they were delaying payment for it, because they were creditworthy. Some QFs with contracts to sell electricity to the utilities had attempted to break the contracts, citing that the utilities were not paying for the electricity, but the attempts usually had been rebuffed in court. As long as a utility was deemed creditworthy, suppliers were obligated to continue supplying electricity.

Once a utility was not creditworthy, however, sellers had a legal right to abrogate their electricity sales contracts with that utility. Moreover, there was strong motivation for these suppliers to break the contracts, because the spot prices of electricity at that time had so far exceeded the fixed prices in the long-term contracts and the seller could no longer be assured it would be paid. The motivation coupled with the legal right to break the contracts made it clear that all the contracts were vulnerable.

The FERC chair, apparently anguished by the growing disaster, clearly communicated to the policymakers of California on January 18:

This year, energy is costlier in most regions of the country, but in California a cavalcade of misjudgments and bad luck have caused a genuine economic and social crisis. The situation has deteriorated further since early January. Negotiations over long term contracts have reached impasse, notwithstanding many hours of tough talk in Washington and the herculean (but ultimately inadequate) efforts of state legislators to buttress sagging utility creditworthiness and to find a sustainable retail rate compromise. California's reserves have evaporated this winter as recurrent plant outages continue and weather forced valuable units off line. Yesterday, the ISO had no choice but to order rolling blackouts in northern and central California in order to prevent a system collapse. So, to the financial crisis, we now add a serious threat to human welfare. With consumer rates frozen below cost (and below 1996 levels), with generators wary of making sales to entities probably unable to pay for power generated at unseasonably (and even historically) high cost, and with no plan to amortize existing utility arrearage, Southern California Edison and Pacific Gas & Electric stand at the brink of insolvency. For following the state's restructuring law, they may go bankrupt. Moreover, with only minimal forward contracting and utilities still subjected to high PX spot market prices for their "net short" position, the Commission's plan to diminish and discipline the spot market remains unrealized. Amidst a severe power shortage, conspiracy theories, resistance to more realistic rates, and calls for palliative price caps continue to obscure the issues and delay solutions.

Perhaps bankruptcy can be averted. . . .

Urgency is a must. I am persuaded that California's utilities can still be withdrawn from the brink. But their descent into Chapter 11 does not materially alter the need to act to devise a coordinated plan of action. We have reached this stage of growing crisis through a series of acts of short-term thinking and now the desperation is palpable. We cannot, however, keep moving from one failure to the next, with no agreed-upon objectives. The Governor's stated plans are unrealistic and ours cannot be fully implemented without his help. Time to put down the guns.[18]

By mid-January the governor had delivered reassuring words for public consumption but had taken no action to support those words; the CPUC had granted merely a temporary rate increase that was far too small; the legislature had taken no meaningful actions to solve the financial crisis; wholesale prices remained well above the retail prices; utilities were rapidly running out of financial assets and borrowing capacity; utility bond ratings had been downgraded to junk bond levels; and electricity suppliers arguably were no longer legally required to sell electricity to the two utilities. The plight of the utilities was desperate and the governor's "irresponsible notion" was promising to become a reality.

Then, and only then, was the governor forced to begin to address the financial crisis, since absence of action could have resulted in large regions of the state without electricity, a condition that surely would have destroyed the governor's chances for reelection. Several options remained at that time.

First, the state could stand by and allow the utilities to file for bankruptcy protection. The implications of this alternative were not completely known but various scenarios could be envisioned. Bankruptcy would put the future of the utilities under the control of a federal judge who would have very strong powers. The judge could not force suppliers to continue selling electricity to the utilities unless the utilities could ensure that those new obligations would be paid. Alternatively, the judge could order the generating assets to be sold to the highest bidders. However, if market power was being exercised, it was likely that the highest bidder would be the one most

---

[18]FERC Chairman Hoecker, "Addendum to remarks of January 4, 2001" (January 18, 2001).
http://www.ferc.gov/electric/bulkpower/Furtherconcurrence_Jan_18.PDF.

able to increase the value of the generating asset through the exercise of market power. One way or the other, a bankruptcy judge would be expected to ensure that the utility's selling price for electricity would be no less than its purchase price. Therefore, the judge would have the power to require that the retail prices of electricity be raised to cover the ongoing costs of purchasing electricity.

Alternatively, the judge could allow the utilities to stop supplying electricity to those customers whose prices were below costs for new purchases. However, it would have been highly unlikely for any judge to take such a harsh action; it would have such devastating consequences for all of California. Thus, absent reduction in the wholesale price of electricity, it was reasonable to expect that retail customers would face greatly increased electricity prices one way or the other, if the governor simply allowed the utilities to go bankrupt.

The second option would have been to allow what so many people had been urging: to increase the retail price of electricity for both consumers and businesses. The CPUC could have entered such an order. However, based on CPUC normal procedures, that would have been a slow process. Moreover, the CPUC had just affirmed that they were not willing to provide a rate increase of more than $10/MWh. Thus, by the time the growing crisis forced the governor into action, it was too late to depend entirely upon the CPUC, at least for the short-term solution.

However, the governor of California does have almost unlimited powers conferred by the State Government Code, including the ability to suspend both statutes and regulations. Explicitly included in the code are almost unlimited powers to deal with sudden and severe shortages of electrical energy. Governor Davis could have used this emergency power unilaterally, without approval by the legislature, to suspend retail price controls and unilaterally increase electricity prices. Then, while retail price controls were suspended, the governor could have worked with the legislature to modify the law and with the CPUC to set the basis for the appropriate retail price increases. The personal risk to the governor would have been that voters, knowing that he had raised electricity rates contrary to his previous public statements, might not support his reelection. He chose not to take that course of action.

Instead, on January 17, immediately after the credit rating downgrade implied that the utilities were no longer creditworthy buyers, Governor Davis chose to use his emergency powers another way. He issued a Proclamation that a "state of emergency" existed within California, allowing him to take unilateral action. Governor Davis ordered the DWR to assume responsibility for procurement of wholesale electricity for customers of California's three major IOUs and to start purchasing electricity on behalf of the electric utilities. Subsequent legislation[19] extended and broadened the authority available to the governor once he had declared the state of emergency.

Under the governor's plan, the state would purchase the electricity on behalf of the utilities' customers and the utilities would sell the electricity on behalf of the state and reimburse the DWR based on the retail rates at which the electricity was sold. Essentially, the DWR would sell the electricity it purchased to the utilities, charging a price equivalent to the utilities' retail prices. This plan allowed the state to avoid the consequences of power suppliers refusing to sell electricity to the California utilities.

In addition, the DWR would ask the CPUC to increase retail rates to allow the utilities to begin fully reimbursing the DWR for its electricity purchase costs. Apparently, the governor saw rate increases as acceptable if implemented on behalf of the State Treasury.

Adding injury to insult, on January 19 the CPUC confirmed that, no matter how much the utilities were paying to buy electricity in the wholesale market relative to the regulated selling price of electricity, and no matter whether they were creditworthy, they were obligated to continue buying sufficient electricity to fully serve all their customers. The temporary restraining order issued by the CPUC stated in part:

> *In this interim decision, we are issuing a temporary restraining order (TRO) preventing Pacific Gas and Electric Company (PG&E) and Southern California Edison Company (Edison) from refusing to provide adequate service to all of their customers. . . . We affirm that regulated California utilities must serve their customers. This requirement, known as the "obligation to serve," is mandated by state law.*

---

[19]On January 19, 2001, he signed SB 7, which directed DWR to procure electricity for the next twelve days and appropriated initial funds for this purpose. On February 1, 2001, the Legislature enacted AB 1X, which, among other provisions, authorized the DWR to continue purchasing electricity through December 31, 2002.

> *A bankruptcy filing or the threat of insolvency has no
> bearing on this aspect of state law. Even utilities that file
> for reorganization must serve their customers.*[20]

On January 23, the U.S. Department of Energy extended for two
weeks an emergency federal order directing electricity producers to
sell to SCE and PG&E, even though they were not creditworthy. In
doing so, however, Energy Secretary Spencer Abraham warned that
there would probably be no further extensions.

STATE PAYMENTS TO BUY ELECTRICITY

Under Governor Davis's order that the DWR purchase electricity
on behalf of the utilities, the retail prices would remain low and
the high cost of wholesale power purchases would be borne initially by the State Treasury. The state would issue long-term revenue bonds to reimburse the State Treasury. Repayment of
interest and principal of these bonds would be a surcharge on
retail electricity prices and thus ultimately the ratepayers would
pay all of these costs. Although meant as a temporary measure
until the utilities again became creditworthy purchasers, this was
the first of several steps taken by the government to interject the
state squarely into the middle of the electricity system.

Once the state became the primary buyer of electricity, there
were no longer any transactions on the PX, and that institution
had no way of raising money to pay its costs. The process of dis-
mantling the PX began. The PX ultimately declared bankruptcy
in March, thus eliminating one of the two market institutions established by AB 1890.

Governor Davis continued to assert that increases in the retail
electricity price to meet the cost of electricity would not be in the
interests of the consumers of electricity. However, his assertions
failed to acknowledge that the people of California would in fact
pay the entire wholesale price of the electricity even though the retail prices would be kept low during the crisis. The high wholesale price of electricity represented the cost to the State of
California, whatever the retail price. The entire cost would be
paid by a combination of consumers, businesses, and taxpayers in
California. The price of retail electricity determined *which* of

---

[20]The entire text is available at http://www.cpuc.ca.gov/PUBLISHED/
FINAL_DECISION/4653.htm.

these entities would be paying what fractions of the total cost, not whether the cost would be paid. Low prices to consumers would save those consumers money as purchasers of electricity but cost the taxpayers of the state the same amount saved by consumers. Low retail prices of electricity to businesses would save those businesses money in their role as buyers of electricity but cost the taxpayers of the state the same amount saved by the businesses. If the state issued bonds to pay the costs, as had been announced by Governor Davis, then future ratepayers would be responsible for paying the entire cost of current electricity purchases. None of that difference would be paid by the electric utilities, because they had no financial assets left. Therefore, at best, low retail pricing was a zero-sum game among businesses, residential consumers, and taxpayers, many of whom, of course, were the same people.

However, the failure to raise retail prices did more than simply move the burden of payments from Californians as buyers of electricity to Californians as taxpayers or from current ratepayers to future ratepayers. The low prices eliminated the natural market incentives to respond to those high prices by reducing electricity use, which would have lowered the wholesale price and therefore reduced the cost to California. So more than simply reallocating the high wholesale cost, the failure to raise retail prices greatly increased that cost. After all, why would corporations and individuals choose to go through the cost and difficulties of reducing their use of electricity to save costs for the state if people other than the firm or consumer reducing the use would capture much of the savings?

As of the beginning of 2001, it was generally projected that California would have an $8 billion budgetary surplus during the year. This projected surplus was largely the result of a healthy California economy; however, Governor Davis's commitment for the state to become the wholesale purchaser of electricity changed that.

Once the state took over the purchasing of electricity on behalf of the utilities, purchase costs remained as high, just less visible. Rather than a transparent market—the PX—that was observable by the public, either directly through the web site or indirectly through newspaper reports, the purchases by the DWR were hidden from public view. However periodically, information would be issued about the purchase costs, often as press releases from the governor's office and later from the DWR.

Table 4.2 shows monthly data of DWR electricity purchases, including the price per MWh of electricity purchased under contracts,

TABLE 4.2
State Costs for Electricity Purchases

	Spot Cost ($/MWh)	Contract Cost ($/MWh)	Average Cost ($/MWh)	Fraction Spot	Fraction Contract	Total MWh (in thousands)	Total Cost ($ Millions)
Jan. 17–31	321	368	332	77%	23%	1,654	549
February	308	279	304	86%	14%	4,743	1,442
March	271	239	261	69%	31%	6,903	1,801
April	331	207	269	50%	50%	6,913	1,860
May	271	216	243	49%	51%	8,222	1,999
June	113	194	168	32%	68%	6,201	1,041
July	78	160	146	17%	83%	6,212	909
August	53	153	131	22%	78%	6,228	815
September	36	172	134	28%	72%	5,069	679
October	34	104	89	21%	79%	4,658	415
November	41	109	94	21%	79%	3,768	355
December	36	107	88	27%	73%	4,256	373
January	33	110	92	23%	77%	3,396	313
Total						68,223	12.5 Billion

THE FINANCIAL CRISIS OF THE UTILITIES: THE SAGA CONTINUES

In the months after the state had started purchasing electricity on be-half of the investor-owned utilities, the governor and the legislature began addressing the financial plight of the utilities. Initially, rather than accepting a rate increase to allow the utilities to work their way back to solvency, the governor started a process of negotiating with the utilities, offering to purchase the electricity transmission facili-ties, some generating facilities, and other assets. The colorful phrase characterizing the process was "I give you a dollar, you give me a hot dog."[24] The State Legislature and the governor took the view that for the utilities to get financial relief from the controls imposed by the state, they would be required to sell significant proportions of their physical assets to California.[25]

By late March and early April there had been little real progress in the negotiations. However, with much fanfare, Governor Davis announced he would deliver a live address to Californians on the electricity crisis. At that time the CPUC had proposed retail electric rate increases that could at least stabilize both the utility financial conditions and the State budget, but that would not repair either. It seemed an appropriate time for the governor to lend his support to that plan. In addition, many expected to hear positive progress on his negotiations with the utilities. However, he instead proposed an alternative and significantly lower set of rate increases. On his ne-gotiations with the utilities and on his rate increase he stated: "Unlike the PUC, my plan includes funds to restore the utilities to financial stability—if they agree to three main conditions: They must provide low-cost regulated power to the state for ten years, agree to sell us their transmission system, and dismiss their lawsuits seeking to double your electricity rates."

After PG&E executives listened to Gray Davis's live address, the next day, April 6, PG&E declared bankruptcy. Their filing for reorganization under Chapter 11 of the U.S. Bankruptcy Code cited "unreimbursed energy costs which are now increasing by more than $300 million per month, continuing CPUC decisions that economically disadvantage the company, and the now un-mistakable fact that negotiations with Governor Gray Davis and

---

[24]The characterization originated with Senate leader, John Burton.

[25]This requirement was part of the policy framework developed by the Governor in January. See section on state policy.

his representatives are going nowhere."[26] Gray Davis had finally pushed the largest utility over the brink.

Later that day Governor Davis met with John Bryson, CEO of Southern California Edison (SCE), announcing, "We are determined to work out the few remaining issues that we have between us. . . . But I am hopeful we will have a satisfactory result for the people of this state within the next few days, proving that negotiation, not bankruptcy, is the appropriate path." The SCE did not file for bankruptcy protection but continued the negotiations with the governor and the State Legislature.

The governor's "next few days" became the next six months. By September, the issues with the SCE had not been resolved, and Governor Davis called for a special session of the legislature to examine a possible bailout plan for the SCE. The financial crisis for the SCE was finally resolved on October 2, 2001, through negotiations between the SCE and the CPUC, before the special session was to begin.

In this settlement, the SCE agreed to release the PUC from all claims under its Filed Rate Doctrine lawsuit and agreed to withhold payment of dividends to its stockholders for at least three years. By the time of the agreement, wholesale electricity prices had declined to precrisis levels and the second round of retail rate increases had been implemented, so that retail prices were by then well above wholesale prices. Under the agreement, the CPUC agreed to keep SCE retail rates at the elevated levels for several years, providing the SCE with sufficient cash flow that it should be able to pay its debts. Thus, the agreement ensures that the people of Southern California will pay high electricity bills over the course of years. The CPUC expressed confidence that the agreement would restore the SCE to creditworthiness so it could, at some time, begin purchasing electricity for its customers. However, many creditors, including many electricity generators and traders, have not yet been paid, and the settlement terms are still purported to give the CPUC significant control over which wholesale electricity purchase bills will ever be paid. The settlement did not reach any resolution on the filed rate doctrine. The SCE withdrew the claim and the CPUC made no concessions about its own or State regulatory authority over the SCE. However, the SCE was able to keep all its physical assets, including its transmission and generation facilities.

---

[26]PG&E News Release, April 6, 2001.

Governor Davis rescinded his request for a special session of the legislature, officially signaling the end of SCE's crisis, stating, "Their settlement has protected the public interest and will allow the state's second-largest utility to return to financial health."

The terms of the settlement suggest that, had the CPUC been willing to raise rates in autumn of 2000 to the same extent they were raised in spring 2001, the entire financial crisis could have been avoided.

PG&E remains in bankruptcy court. On September 20, 2001, it filed a proposed reorganization plan, which promised to pay all creditors in full. The plan would separate PG&E into four separate companies, completing the vertical disintegration. One company would own and operate the retail electric distribution functions and operate as a regulated utility local distribution company,[27] selling most of its assets, including its electric generation and transmission assets, to the other three companies. These companies would operate as deregulated entities, each owned by its parent, PG&E Corporation. Proceeds from the sale of assets would allow PG&E to pay all creditors. Under this plan, the state would have very few options to control retail prices well below wholesale costs since the retail entity would own none of the generation and transmission assets. The plan would allow PG&E to escape much of the state's regulation of its activities and avoid legal restrictions imposed by the CPUC or the State Legislature. Governor Davis, the CPUC, and several consumer groups opposed this change, citing the possibility that retail price increases could occur under this plan.

On February 7, 2002, the federal bankruptcy judge (Judge Dennis Montali) refused to approve PG&E's reorganization plan and rejected PG&E's argument that U.S. bankruptcy law must supersede state law. The judge's ruling allowed PG&E to attempt to establish "with particularity" specific state laws and regulations that should be preempted by federal bankruptcy law. Nevertheless, he made it clear that PG&E must establish that the preemption is based on conflicts with particular provisions of federal bankruptcy law, not simply a general preemption.

On February 13, 2002, the CPUC submitted an alternate reorganization plan that would keep almost all PG&E activities under control of State regulators. The CPUC-proposed plan has many

---

[27]The natural gas components would be divided in a similar way, with natural gas transmission going to the unregulated entity and the retail natural gas functions staying with the regulated utility.

similarities to the one negotiated between the SCE and the CPUC. Similar to the SCE situation, retail electricity rates significantly exceed costs of acquiring electricity (for quantification, see Figure 4.12 in a subsequent section of this chapter), now that wholesale prices have dropped. Thus, PG&E is now accumulating revenues well in excess of its costs. The CPUC proposal would keep PG&E retail rates at the elevated levels for at least several years, providing PG&E with sufficient cash flow that it should be able to pay its debts over the next few years. The PG&E would not pay any dividends to its stockholders from 2001 through 2003. The PG&E proposal, if accepted, would assure that the people of Northern California, like those of Southern California, would pay high electricity bills over the course of years. The CPUC expressed confidence its proposal would restore PG&E to creditworthiness so it could begin purchasing electricity for its customers by January 2003.

The judge has not ruled on the CPUC proposal and PG&E has not yet filed a response to the judicial decision. However, it appears that the end of the PG&E crisis could be in sight, even though complete resolution may not come quickly. Nevertheless, until a full settlement is reached, PG&E is precluded from paying most of its debts, including the money it owes for purchasing wholesale electricity in the pre-January 2001 time. Thus, more than a year after PG&E purchased the electricity, many generators and electricity traders still have not been paid.

STATE AND FEDERAL POLICY RESPONSES

The time of crisis, even more than the challenge period, was a time for strong, wise political leadership. Faced with the reality of the crisis at its peak, the California governor and the legislature made energy one of the highest priorities for communication and for policy development. However, as in the challenge period, much of the policy action seemed primarily intent on casting blame outside of California, hiding the short-term problems and shifting the consequences to the future, even at the cost of greatly increasing the overall difficulties for California.

The policies favored by the California political leadership emphasized direct government intervention in the market place, reliance on retail and wholesale price controls, and strong regulatory intervention. The CPUC, now with different leadership than when AB 1890 had been passed, stopped trying to improve markets, strongly enforced retail price controls (which the state could control), and lobbied for wholesale price controls (which the state could not control). The California governor intensified his public relations campaign of blaming California's electricity problems on the federal government, federal regulators, electricity generators, and "deregulation," without mentioning his own policy inaction. He continued his lead role in militating for strong price control regimes at both the retail level and the wholesale level. The legislature failed to modify the most damaging problems of the system but did take leadership in encouraging energy conservation and energy efficiency measures. When the governor and legislature were forced to respond to the financial crisis, their response relied on direct governmental wholesale purchases of electricity and negotiations to acquire assets of the utilities, therefore moving the state toward public power and direct state participation in electricity markets.

At the same time, federal action through the FERC, though slow, sometimes misdirected, and inconsistent over time, seemed designed to address the underlying flaws in the market design and implementation, to avoid simple ineffective palliatives, and to strengthen the role of markets. Like the CPUC of the early through mid-1990s, the FERC operated as a regulatory agency trying to move away from direct control of market transactions and market pricing. The FERC policy actions, overall, had the hope of providing longer-term solutions to California's energy crisis by attempting to identify, analyze, and correct fundamental problems.

The ideological conflict was painful between state leadership, which continued to favor dominantly public sector roles, and the FERC, which continued to favor dominantly private sector roles. The state and the FERC each had jurisdiction over important parts of the restructured system, so neither could fully impose its views on the other, and each needed actions of the other to be fully effective. The fundamental ideological differences were never fully resolved and continue to this date.

ACTIONS BY THE STATE EXECUTIVE BRANCH
AND LEGISLATIVE BRANCH

Public Relations and Rhetoric

First, starting during the challenge period and extending through the crisis, Governor Davis waged a public relations campaign in which he sought to assign blame for California's electricity problems to many organizations outside of his own office. Perhaps his most frequent target was the electricity generators and marketers. In speech after speech and press release after press release, Governor Davis made it clear that he believed the generators were engaging in wrongful and possibly criminal activities. Words and phrases such as "profiteering," "plunder," "unconscionable," "price gouging," "exorbitant profits," "market marauders," "pirate generators," "privateers," "obscene profits," and "outrageous wholesale prices" peppered his formal statements.

Governor Davis often associated these words with phrases such as "out-of-state generators," which, like so much of his rhetoric, was a distortion of reality: electricity sales by in-state entities were at negotiated market prices, just as were spot market sales by out-of-state sellers (as would typically be the case in any markets). In fact, the two largest municipal utilities in California, the LADWP and the SMUD, were selling electricity at negotiated prices[28] just like every other seller. Yet it seemed politically expedient for the governor to shift all blame to entities outside California, completely distorting reality.[29]

---

[28]The DWR data for the first half of 2001, presented previously in Figure 4.5, show that the DWR paid California sellers, including California municipal utilities, higher prices than it paid the out-of-state suppliers Governor Davis had so often accused of price gouging. The DWR paid an average of $276/MWh to the LADWP, $268/MWh to the SMUD, and $305/MWh to the City of Burbank. It paid San Diego-based Sempra Energy an average price of $366/MWh. Among the ten largest out-of-state sellers to the DWR, only two (both Canadian entities) were able to negotiate prices higher than SMUD: private sector TransAlta ($298/MWh) and public sector Powerex Corporation ($425/MWh). The DWR paid an average of $236/MWh to the ten largest out-of-state suppliers, less than to any of the in-state sellers (with the exception of DWR purchases from itself).

[29]As of January 8, 2002, Governor Davis had shifted his rhetoric to focus attention on California municipal utilities. In his 2002 State of the State address he asserted: "Merchant generators, even some of our own municipal utilities—were gouging us unconscionably." Shortly thereafter, Governor Davis launched a daily series of political advertisements implying that Richard Riordan, former mayor of Los Angeles and a contender for the Republican gubernatorial nomination for California governor, was responsible for the LADWP charging prices "twice as high" as the prices charged by other sellers of electricity. The pure political motivation for Governor Davis's changing rhetoric and his distortion of reality had become painfully apparent.

The rhetoric included the governor's well-publicized announcements that the State of California was initiating a criminal investigation into the actions by the generators and marketers. However, to this date, the state has not announced that it has ever uncovered such illegal activities, suggesting that the criminal investigation never uncovered any illegal activities since, given the governor's pattern of public rhetoric, he would have broadly publicized any evidence of wrongdoing that the state found.

Federal organizations, particularly the FERC, were also subject to his biting attacks. A particularly vicious Gray Davis attack was prompted by the FERC's decisive steps to deny California's various attempts to extend state-managed price controls. In a communication for public consumption, he stated:

> *The Federal Energy Regulatory Commission has abdicated its responsibility to the people in the West. Their responsibility is to ensure just and reasonable rates. Instead, they have chosen to ensure unconscionable profits for the pirate generators and power brokers who are gouging California consumers and businesses. . . .*
>
> *This is an inexplicable decision by armchair Washington bureaucrats fixated on economic ideology that has no practical application to the dysfunctional energy market in California and the West. Instead of acting in the best interests of consumers and businesses, the FERC commissioners have acted as pawns of generators and power sellers whose only interest is to plunder our economy. . . .*
>
> *The public health and safety of California's citizens and the economy of the State cannot be subject to the blackmail of a few greedy privateers working in concert with a handful of Washington bureaucrats.*[30]

Governor Davis became fond of labeling electricity deregulation as the villain, rather than his own leadership, or lack of leadership, in managing the challenge and crisis. He referred to FERC actions as a "reckless deregulation experiment" that would make "guinea pigs of California consumers" and described California's problems as the "ravages of a dysfunctional marketplace." Governor Davis's language was colorful but did not serve the interests of the people

---

[30]Press release issued by Governor Davis on December 15, 2000.

of the State of California. The colorful language served only his personal political interests.

Regrettably, Governor Davis made threats that the assets of the generators would be subject to eminent domain procedures. Such threats, far from solving any of the real problems of the state, tend to chill the desire of other firms to invest in new generation in California and thus were counterproductive to electricity system solutions.

The low point of the rhetoric from the California Executive Branch came when California's chief law enforcement officer, Attorney General Bill Lockyer, managed to utter one of the most offensive statements imaginable from a person charged with the integrity of the criminal justice system in California. Lockyer stated in a *Wall Street Journal* interview (May 2001) that he hoped to imprison—and more than simply imprison—Kenneth Lay, the chairman of Houston-based Enron Corp, a person who was not charged with any crime in California, much less convicted: "I would love to personally escort (Enron Chairman Kenneth) Lay to an 8-by-10 cell that he could share with a tattooed dude who says, 'Hi, my name is Spike, honey.'"

The State Framework for Policy

In addition to the rhetoric that emanated from the Executive Branch of the California government, there did emerge an overall framework for policy making. Unlike Governor Davis's policy framework from the challenge period, this framework, developed in combination with the leaders of California's legislature, recognized both the electricity crisis and the financial crisis. In addition, unlike the governor's price control policy framework from the challenge period, it recognized the importance of electricity supply and demand to the electricity problems. Announced on January 26, 2001, as a "rough consensus reached with bipartisan leadership of California's Senate and Assembly," the policy framework was stated as:

1. Aggressively promote energy efficiency, conservation, and demand reduction among consumers, businesses and public entities.

2. Increase the supply of electrical generation in California through continuing efforts to streamline permitting and construction of new plants, while protecting the environment, and remove obstacles to the development of distributed generation.

3. Authorize the state to purchase the "net short" electricity needed to serve investor-owned utility customers. The "net short" is the power needed beyond that generated by the utilities themselves or available to them from "qualifying facilities" (QFs) and other long-term contracts. It is anticipated that most of this power will be purchased through long-term contracts with power suppliers.

4. Provide that the state will sell power directly to ratepayers with the investor-owned utilities collecting and remitting a dedicated portion of rate revenues to the state.

5. Reduce the price of power delivered by QFs to the utilities by changing the contracts between the utilities and QFs through action by the PUC and/or the legislature to a reduced rate agreed to by the QFs.

6. Provide ratepayers with an asset of value such as stock warrants as equity participation in the financial recovery of the utilities. This equity participation will be used either to help retire bonds or otherwise provide tangible benefits to consumers.

7. Continue negotiations with the investor-owned utilities and others on a plan to deal with the unrecovered costs that threaten the economic viability of the utilities while protecting the ratepayers.

8. Resolve outstanding regulatory and legal actions initiated by the utilities to recover all their undercollections.

9. A public authority that could ensure adequate power supply and adequate transmission capacity.[31]

This overall framework included five major points—numbers 3, 4, 6, 7, and 9—that, as implemented or negotiated by the state, would increase the public sector's direct participation in the energy markets as a buyer or seller of electricity. One major point—number 1—would involve increases in direct governmental regulation in energy markets. Point number 5 would require the state to use its regulatory or legislative power to alter the long-standing contracts QFs had with utilities. One point—number 8—would involve resolving the legal challenges brought by the utilities challenging the right of California to maintain retail price controls. Only point number 2 would involve increasing the ability of markets to work effectively.

---

[31]This can be accessed through http://www.governor.ca.gov/state/ govsite/gov_homepage.jsp. Once on the govenor's homepage, click on "Press Room," then on "Press Releases," and finally on "January 2001."

Elements missing from the framework were significant. There was no part of the framework designed to move the state away from the price controls imposed on investor-owned utilities, only a point to resolve the challenges to the price controls. There was no part of the framework proposing to allow the utilities to participate in a much broader range of contracts to buy electricity. Nothing in the framework addressed the dangers of energy emergencies, including blackouts. There were no points about working constructively with federal agencies to improve the operations of electricity markets.

Moreover, the subsequent policy actions taken or attempted by the state were roughly, although not completely, consistent with this policy framework. And similarly, the omissions in the policy framework remained omissions in state policy implementation. Some policies have already been discussed; some will be discussed in what follows.

Governor Davis called two concurrent extraordinary sessions of the legislature, the first on January 3, 2001, and the second on May 17 at the expiration of the first session. The work of these special sessions proceeded in parallel to the work during the (simultaneous) regular sessions but served to focus legislative policy attention on the electricity and financial crises.

Policies Impacting Energy Demand

The most beneficial of its policy actions in terms of loosening the supply/demand balance were designed to reduce electricity demand in both the short run and the long run. Although only the short-run programs would reduce the severity of the energy crisis, the long-run programs could help ensure there would not be a repeat of the crisis.

One of the most publicized was the "20/20 plan," which encouraged all residential and small commercial purchasers of electricity to reduce their use of electricity by 20 percent from the previous year. Those who did so would be rewarded not only with the reduction in the electricity bill based on less usage but also would enjoy a 20 percent reduction in their overall electricity bill. The 20/20 plan accomplished two objectives. It was effective in dramatizing a goal for reducing electricity consumption and making it clear that the goal was achievable. In addition, the plan had embedded in it a significant financial incentive that essentially increased the marginal price of electricity to consumers without increasing the average price.[32]

The state, with help from the Advertising Council, launched the "Flex Your Power" campaign featuring the image of a light switch and a finger turning off the switch, which further sensitized people to the public value of reducing electricity use.

The governor issued an Executive Order requiring retail business to reduce substantially "unnecessary outdoor lighting wattage" during nonbusiness hours.[33] Failure to do so would subject the commercial establishments to fines. Police were authorized to search out those companies using too much electricity and cite them. Whether this had any real effect or simply served to dramatize the goal of reducing electricity use was unclear.

The AB 1890 had included a component of the retail electricity price to pay for public benefit programs, including $228 million a year to pay for energy efficiency, conservation activities, and other demand-side management programs. However, the particular expenditures of these funds, earmarked for these specific purposes, needed state approval, which was forthcoming during the crisis. These funds paid for costs incurred by utilities in promoting energy efficiency improvements throughout California's economy. Perhaps the most successful was the subsidy offered for the sales of compact fluorescent lights at high-volume discount retail stores, such as Costco. The PG&E alone reported around 3.5 million sales of compact fluorescent lights under its 2001 incentive programs.[34] This initiative reduced electricity usage very quickly and can be expected to have a continuing impact on consumption.

---

[32]The incentive was a discontinuous one. There was a benefit for meeting or exceeding the goal, no benefit for almost meeting the goal, and no further benefit for exceeding the goal. Thus this plan increased the marginal cost only for reductions of 20 percent, not for increases.

[33]Executive Order D-19-01, February 1, 2001.

[34]A typical compact fluorescent light (CFL) uses about 20 watts to produce the same light as a 75-watt incandescent bulb. Thus, a CFL substituted for an incandescent light reduces electricity consumption by 55 watts during times either light would be on. If 50 percent of the PGE-subsidized CFLs were lighted at a given time, that would reduce electricity use by about 100 MW (0.5×3.5 million $\times$ 55 watts = 96 MW), roughly equivalent to the maximum output of two typically sized peaker generating plants.

In January 2001 the California Building Standards Commission adopted comprehensive emergency modifications to California's statewide building efficiency standards (effective in July 2001), giving California the toughest building efficiency standards for new construction in the nation. Among other features, the standards require more efficient air conditioning and heating ducts in new homes and impose standards on new windows designed to reduce solar radiative heat transfer. These modifications had no effect on the immediate crisis but can be expected to have a longer-term impact on electricity demand.

The legislature passed two major bills to reduce electricity use during the time of the crisis: SB 5X and AB 29X. The latter allocated $35 million to acquire and install real-time meters for industrial customers using more than 200 KW of power, many of which have been installed. However, to this date, the CPUC has yet to approve a tariff that would allow electricity to be sold at real-time prices, and thus this investment had no beneficial effect during the energy crisis.

The AB 29X also allocated $20 million to distribute compact fluorescent lights through the California Conservation Corps. SB 5X allocated about $430 million in general fund revenues to emergency energy efficiency incentives and $220 million in funds to reduce electricity prices for low-income households. The latter could be expected to increase slightly the usage of electricity while easing the financial impact of high electricity prices on low-income families.

Policies Impacting Electricity-Generation Capacity

In February 2001, Governor Davis signed six Executive Orders to expedite the review and permitting process of power-generating facilities in California. One order allowed small peaking plants to be quickly approved and constructed and was limited to those that could be completed before September 2001. The other orders envisioned a four-month and a six-month licensing process, where the time period was based on expectations of permitting time after all data to the California Energy Commission were deemed to be adequate, a process that itself could take months. The four-month licensing process was limited to simple cycle, thermal power plants, which had to be able to be on-line by December 31, 2002, and would be required to convert from a simple cycle mode to combined cycle mode or cogeneration within three years. The orders do have the longer-run potential of increasing the supply responsiveness by reducing the time for new plants to be approved and ultimately come on-line.

The governor negotiated with those companies that were in the process of constructing new generating plants in order to provide them with an incentive to come on-line earlier than they otherwise would have. The financial incentive offered for coming on-line early may have moved the on-line date for plants by a small amount but did not result in any plants coming on-line during the crisis. These incentives were politically valuable, however, since press releases from Governor Davis continued to suggest that his actions were responsible for construction of those plants, even though they had already been under construction when he took office.

Policies Impacting Risk to Electricity Suppliers

Throughout 2001, state actions continued to create financial risk for sellers of electricity and thereby reduced the supply of electricity from generating units within California. Those risks also discouraged those generating electricity outside California from selling into the California market. Such California electricity supply reductions could be expected to raise the wholesale price of California electricity. Financial risks stemmed from four classes of California actions (or inactions) continuing through much of 2001: change of the CAISO board composition, failure of the DWR to pay for spot electricity purchases through the CAISO, CPUC refusal to allow investor-owned utilities to pay challenge-period bills, and California's continued demands that the FERC order large refunds.

First, by the end of January 2001, Governor Davis had replaced the CAISO stakeholder board with a new five-person board, three of whom were closely associated with the Davis administration.[35] Control of the CAISO board had moved to the state. Once the PX stopped operating, the DWR was purchasing all its spot market electricity through the CAISO. Thus, the State of California had become the largest market participant and had gained control of the CAISO. The harsh rhetoric by Governor Davis castigating the

---

[35]Governor Davis appointed Maria Contreras-Sweet (California Secretary of Business, Transportation, and Housing), Tal Finney (Director of Policy, Governor's Office), Mike Florio (Attorney, The Utility Reform Network), Carl Guardino (President and CEO, Silicon Valley Manufacturing Group), Michael Kahn (Attorney; Chairman of Energy Oversight Board). Maria Contreras-Sweet left the board after the September 11 terrorist attack.

electricity generators and marketers was continuing. Thus, it was reasonable for all generators and marketers to believe that CAISO would not treat them fairly but rather would act to favor the State of California and electricity buyers whenever possible. This rational belief could be expected to increase significantly the perceived risks facing generators and marketers.

Second, from January through November 2001, the DWR purchased about $1 billion worth of spot market electricity through the CAISO. During this time, however, the DWR did not pay any of its obligations for purchasing electricity through the CAISO, and since the CAISO had no resources of its own to pay for purchases, as of November, the CAISO had not paid the generators. Nor could the generators be sure that either the DWR or CAISO would ever pay them.

It appeared that the CAISO had established policies that encouraged the DWR not to pay, or at least did not discourage its nonpayment. The CAISO had argued in a sequence of FERC filings that sellers were required to supply electricity for the CAISO's real-time markets whether they were paid or not. The DWR and CAISO argued to the FERC that the DWR might not be required to pay for all electricity it purchased on behalf of the investor-owned utilities. Until November, the CAISO and the DWR had not even reached a satisfactory agreement on how the CAISO would bill the DWR, and thus the CAISO never even billed the DWR for its electricity purchases until that month.

The FERC repeatedly ordered the CAISO to enforce its tariff provisions, requiring all buyers of electricity to be creditworthy. Finally, on November 7, 2001, the FERC found the CAISO in violation of its tariff and ordered that it pay all overdue amounts within three months:

> We have repeatedly directed the ISO to enforce its creditworthy standards under the Tariff. . . . Although DWR represents that it is the guarantor of transactions for the non-creditworthy UDCs [utility distribution companies] DWR has yet to pay for these net short positions. . . . Moreover, a creditworthy party pays its bills when they are due.[36]

---

[36]FERC, "Order Granting Motion Concerning Creditworthiness Requirement and Rejecting Amendment No. 40" (November 7, 2001). Available at http://www.ferc.gov/electric/bulkpower/er01-889-008-11-7-01.PDF.

Only after the FERC had issued the November 7 Order did the CAISO begin to bill the DWR for the power it had been purchasing since January. Until that time, the failure of the DWR to pay for its purchases created significant risk for the generators and traders that were selling to CAISO.

The FERC has quantified the risk to sellers resulting from DWR and the CAISO business practices. On June 19, 2001, the FERC issued an order outlining the methodology for calculating any noncompetitive overcharges in sales through the PX and CAISO. The FERC determined that a competitive price estimate could include a 10 percent "creditworthiness adder" for transactions after January 5, 2001, reflecting increased credit risks in California. As late as December 19, 2001, the FERC ruled that this 10 percent creditworthiness adder was still justified.

In the June 19 Order, the Commission instituted the 10 percent adder to recognize both the larger risk of nonpayment in California when compared with that in the larger West-Wide market, and the longer payment lag in the ISO spot markets when compared with that in the Western bilateral spot markets. The Commission also pointed out that questionable business practices have sent negative signals to future suppliers, credit rating agencies, and investors. . . . However, despite our repeated instructions to the ISO to ensure that there is a creditworthy party backing up each and every transaction, we have continued to receive complaints that suppliers are not being paid. Under these circumstances, we continue to believe that the circumstances that justified institution of a creditworthiness adder have not abated. Until the risk of nonpayment by purchasers in California has been relieved, the adder is still justified.[37]

Third, the state has taken actions to block the investor-owned utilities from paying their pre-January 2001 wholesale electricity acquisition bills. The PG&E's bankruptcy and the SCE's extended presettlement negotiations with CPUC have ensured that the two investor-owned utilities have not paid the generators and traders for their pre-January 2001 electricity purchases (see discussion in

---

[37]FERC, "Order on Clarification and Rehearing" (December 19, 2001). http://www.ferc.gov/electric/bulkpower/el00-95-001-12-19-01.PDF.

the section, "The Financial Crisis of the Utilities: The Saga Continues"). The CPUC proposal for the PG&E restructuring would significantly delay PG&E payments to the generators even after PG&E emerges from bankruptcy. Although the SCE now has large cash balances, the CPUC is still not approving complete payments of SCE debts for purchases from the generators. The total unpaid amount is greater than $10 billion. California seems to link blocking of payments to California's inflated $8.9 billion estimate of the refunds due from generators. This payment delay creates not only risks of nonpayment but also cash-flow problems for the relatively small electricity generators. Some implications of this refusal have already been discussed in the section entitled "Generators Off-Line."

Fourth, the state has continued to press the FERC for aggressively large refunds, asserting that the generators had overcharged California and continued to overcharge. The FERC initiated settlement hearings to reach an agreement on the appropriate amount of the refunds. However, attempts by FERC Chief Administrative Law Judge Curtis L. Wagner, Jr., to bring the parties to a settlement were blocked by California's unwillingness to budge in its refund demands. On July 12, 2001, Judge Wagner issued a report and recommendation in which he made it clear that California's claims were far too large:

> *That very large refunds are due is clear. . . . While the amount of such refunds is not $8.9 billion as claimed by the State of California, they do amount to hundreds of millions of dollars, probably more than a billion dollars in an aggregate sum.*
>
> *The State of California has publicly made it clear that the refund amount claimed by the State of California is $8.9 billion. It has not moved from that position and Governor Davis makes it publicly clear that it will not. . . . However, it is the opinion of the Chief Judge that the amount claimed by the State of California has not and cannot be substantiated.*[38]

Because California was never able to reach an agreement with any other parties, the actual amount of refunds will be settled by

---

[38]FERC, "Report and Recommendation of Chief Judge and Certification of Record" (July 12, 2001).

evidentiary hearing unless the parties are able to come to agreement beforehand. The schedule contemplates a sequence of hearings scheduled for March through July 2002. Absent settlement, the refund amounts will not be determined until after all hearings have been completed. The uncertainty about the outcomes of these hearings further increases the risk for market participants.

Policies Related to Energy Emergency Responses

The state took no leadership in mitigating energy emergencies until after the last of the blackouts had occurred, when the rules for managing blackouts were modified to reduce costs if blackouts were to continue. For example, large industrial users were allowed to enter contractual relationships in which they agreed, when requested during energy emergencies, to reduce their use of electricity by 20 percent from then current levels. In exchange, they were assured that they would be spared from rolling blackouts. However, as more and more electricity users became exempt from blackouts, the more those blackouts would be concentrated on the remaining users. By late spring 2001, an estimated 50 percent of electricity use had been exempted from blackouts, and therefore the remaining nonexempt users faced a doubled risk of being blacked out themselves. This plan had another drawback. For many companies, the easiest way of ensuring they could reduce demand by 20 percent on short notice was to keep demand at least 20 percent above their minimum needs for electricity. Thus, there was an incentive for companies to avoid reducing demand by as much as they might otherwise in order to assure their ability to cut back from then current levels when needed.[39] Although this system did enhance the demand reductions during emergencies, it probably increased the use of electricity in nonemergency times and thereby increased the probability of energy emergencies.

In addition, in a change from the practice during the early blackouts, when the area being blacked out was given only a very short warning, a plan was developed to provide more advance warnings about forthcoming blackouts. This change was intended to allow emergency personnel to be positioned more effectively

---

[39]This incentive comes about because the cutback was to be measured from consumption levels in the few weeks before the companies were called on to cut back. If the cutback was measured from consumption levels at some base time, say at the time the rule was passed, then there would not have been this perverse incentive.

during rolling blackouts and to allow companies to make some plans to cope with anticipated blackouts. However, no blackouts occurred after the decision was made to provide the warnings and thus it is unclear how well the system would have worked.

These actions were potentially useful for the most part but, other than the energy conservation and efficiency programs, did nothing fundamental to help solve the energy crisis.

Retail Electricity Pricing

Most needed to address the energy crisis (and the financial crisis) was for retail electricity prices to adjust to the changing wholesale prices. Increases in retail prices would have more sharply reduced electricity demand and therefore would have reduced wholesale prices. Nevertheless, that was the action most strongly opposed by the governor. Instead, even during the crisis period, the pervasive message from the governor and the other state institutions was their demands for expanding wholesale electricity price controls as a companion to continued retail price controls.

However, after many months of refusing to approve retail electricity price increases, the CPUC accepted the idea that it could keep the retail base prices of electricity and could add "surcharges" on to the retail rates to start bringing retail rates up toward the wholesale prices. On January 4, 2000, the CPUC took the first small step, approving a 1-cent/KWh, ninety-day surcharge on customer bills (equivalent to $10/MWh), an amount far smaller than desirable for encouraging the needed electricity demand reductions, but a step. This surcharge would increase residential rates about 9 percent, small business customers 7 percent, medium commercial customers 12 percent, and large commercial and industrial customers 15 percent.

Using conventional estimates of the elasticity of demand[40] for electricity, the average retail price increase of 10 percent could be expected to motivate a roughly 1–2 percent reduction in demand over a short run, starting almost immediately. Although this demand reduction was smaller than desirable

---

[40]The elasticity of demand is defined as the percentage reduction in demand motivated by a 1 percent increase in price. Here, and for other numerical examples, a short-run elasticity of demand for electricity will be approximated as 0.1–0.2. Long-run elasticities have typically been estimated to be as large as 1.0 and possibly larger.

with the very tight market, even the 1–2 percent reduction in demand could have some impacts on the wholesale price. Using the previous assumption that a 1 percent change in supply or demand leads to a 10 percent change in wholesale price, such demand reduction could motivate a 10–20 percent reduction in wholesale price. On the other hand, if a 1 percent change in supply or demand leads to a 2 percent change in wholesale price, such demand reduction could motivate only a 2–4 percent reduction in wholesale price. Thus, although this surcharge was far too small to solve the financial crisis facing the utilities, it contributed somewhat to the demand reductions that were observed during that time.

Perhaps more importantly, the principle had been established that retail price increases could be a viable response to the energy crisis.

Governor Davis seemed well aware that allowing retail prices to increase sufficiently would have been fundamental to addressing the energy problems. However, he still refused to allow that step. In one well-publicized February press conference, he stated: "Believe me, if I wanted to raise rates I could have solved this problem in 20 minutes. But I am not going to ask the ratepayers to accept a disproportionate burden."[41] And he did not raise the rates. At least not until the state was threatened with budgetary chaos.

By early March, with the California DWR purchasing the electricity, the economic realities of the high wholesale price and low retail price were now falling most sharply on the state, not on the utilities. The State budget had been decimated. Political leaders began seeing the wisdom of increasing retail electricity prices to compensate the State Treasury for the costs of its wholesale electricity purchases. Even Governor Davis grudgingly accepted retail price increases. On March 27, 2001, the CPUC voted to increase retail electricity rates by 3 cents/KWh for SCE and PG&E customers and to make permanent the 1 cent/KWh temporary surcharge. It was estimated at the time of its passage that this increase would be sufficient to allow revenues collected from the

---

[41]Transcript of press conference, Governor Gray Davis, February 16, 2001. By the time he had made this statement, Governor Davis had already developed the plan for selling state revenue bonds to pay for state purchases of electricity and for requiring ratepayers to pay all of the interest and principal of these bonds. Under this plan, the ratepayers would be forced to accept the entire burden, completely contrary to the public statement he was making.

sale of electricity to cover the cost of DWR purchases of wholesale electricity but would do little or nothing to bring the utilities
back to financial health.

Even then, Governor Davis worked to reduce the rate increase.
During a live address to the people of California on April 5, Gray
Davis proposed an alternative to the CPUC increase: an average
increase of 2.4 cents/KWh for PG&E residential customers, 2.2 cents/
KWh for SCE residential customers, and between 2.6 and 3.0
cents/KWh for commercial/industrial customers.

Although the CPUC announced that the increase would be effective immediately, the promised tiered-rate proposal had yet to
be designed. It was widely reported in the media that, although
the actual charges might not appear on consumer bills right away,
the customer billings would be implemented retroactively to the
end of March. Thus, even before the price increase was implemented, the belief by individuals and companies that there would
be a hefty price increase probably motivated a significant reduction in electricity consumption.

On May 15, the CPUC adopted the specific rate structure,
which would appear on June bills. The two retail rates together
increased retail rates by roughly 30–35 percent. Using the same
estimates of elasticity of demand, these price increases could be
expected to motivate short-run demand reductions of 3–7 percent, reductions large enough to affect significantly the tight
electricity markets.

As implemented, the rates adopted by the CPUC are highly
tiered, with households that use low amounts of energy paying
prices slightly lower than the cost of delivery services plus acquisition cost of electricity and those using larger amounts paying almost twice the cost of that electricity for additional units
purchased. Figure 4.12 illustrates the rate structure for PG&E in
December 2001.[42] The red line shows the marginal price of electricity at various levels of monthly electricity consumption, ranging from zero electricity use through 2,000 KWh per month. For
reference, the average use of electricity per residential customer in
California (548 KWh) is noted.

For those who use less than 130 percent of the "baseline" quantities per month (the winter baseline for the San Francisco Bay Area

---

[42]These particular data are for a home in the San Francisco Bay Area not
using electricity as its primary source of space heating and are included in bills
PG&E sends to its residential customers.

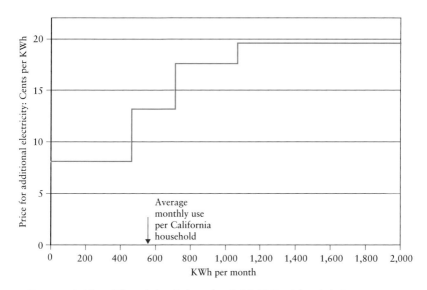

FIGURE 4.12:   Electricity Prices for PG&E Residential Customers
(San Francisco Bay Area), December 2001

is 356.5 KWh), the customer pays 8.0 cents/KWh; for those that
use more than 300 percent of the baseline, the marginal price rises
to 19.5 cents/KWh.

These figures can be compared with the pre-restructuring
price of about 9 cents/KWh, the current spot cost of wholesale
electricity plus service fees (transmission, distribution, and
public purpose programs), totaling about 6 cents/KWh, or the
cost of the DWR electricity purchases plus service fees, totaling
about 13 cents/KWh. By any of these measures of cost, this rate
structure greatly overcharges those residential customers who
use a large amount of electricity relative to the baseline. The retail price for the greatest users of electricity (more than 300
percent of the baseline) is over twice as high as the 9 cents/KWh
average price of retail electricity prior to restructuring. Thus,
even though the electricity crisis is over, those customers who
use over 300 percent of the baseline quantities of electricity pay
twice the rate they faced before the crisis.

FERC RULE MAKING

Early in the challenge period, the FERC started to carefully examine problems of wholesale electricity markets throughout the
United States. On July 26, 2000, the FERC ordered its staff "to
conduct an investigation of electric bulk power markets so that it

can determine whether markets are working efficiently and, if not, the causes of the problems." The commission asked its staff to "investigate the markets, including volatile price fluctuations, and report their findings by November 1, 2000." After San Diego Gas and Electric filed a complaint with the FERC in August 2000, the commission directed staff to accelerate its analysis in California and the western region of the United States.

Federal policy implemented through the FERC was necessarily more limited than state policy could be, since the FERC did not have jurisdiction over any retail market operations, electricity consumers, plant siting, or utility electricity purchases. It did have primary authority over wholesale markets, although it had allowed California institutions to take the lead in designing the wholesale markets within the state. Those wholesale markets commanded most of the FERC attention.

In November 2000, the FERC released the staff report and simultaneously issued a Market Order proposing remedies for California wholesale electric markets. Through that November Order proposing remedies and the subsequent December Order directing those remedies to be implemented, the FERC had started the process of taking control of market design from California institutions and providing that leadership itself. Governor Davis and other California political leaders strongly resisted that shift in control. The painful process of wresting control over wholesale markets from California officials while California leaders fought to retain control continued throughout the entire crisis.

For the most part, the FERC was pursuing a market approach, attempting to repair defects in the California wholesale markets rather than controlling prices. However, as an organization that operated for the most part as a judicial body, with operational procedures comparable to those in litigations, FERC decision making, with one exception, was typically slow and laborious. Moreover, FERC decision making depended not only on judicial rules but also on the beliefs of FERC commissioners. The change in the composition and leadership of the FERC during the process itself implied that FERC decisions were not necessarily consistent over time. Ultimately, the FERC implemented temporary wholesale price controls, primarily in the form of bid caps, initially throughout California and then throughout the western region, as the crisis was nearing its end.

November 1 and December 15, 2000, Orders

On November 1, 2000, the FERC issued a Market Order that proposed a set of remedies for California's wholesale electricity markets. The remedies were, for the most part, to take effect at the end of 2000. The Order provided a three-week period during which anyone could comment on the various proposals. The FERC followed, on December 15, with an Order directing the remedies. Except for the more extensive discussion, the December 15 Order was very consistent with the November 1 Order.

In these orders, the FERC reiterated its earlier conclusion that the wholesale prices were not "just and reasonable" and stated the two issues fundamental to the problem:

> *The existing market structure and market rules, in conjunction with an imbalance of supply and demand in California, have caused and, until remedied, will continue to have the potential to cause, unjust and unreasonable rates for short-term energy during certain time periods.*[43]

The FERC went on to propose measures designed to repair the defects in the wholesale markets and, while the defects were being repaired, to keep prices lower than they would otherwise be. The FERC had started the process of removing from California formal leadership in wholesale electricity market design. A first goal was to reduce the overreliance in California on the spot markets for wholesale electricity.

The FERC eliminated the requirement that the investor-owned utilities buy and sell all power on the PX or CAISO. This change, in principle, permitted utilities to participate in bilateral markets and forward markets, not simply in spot markets. It allowed them to use the electricity they had generated without selling the electricity and buying it back. This was an important long-term change, but given the precarious financial situation of the utilities by that time, its short-term impact was probably limited to allowing the utilities direct use of the electricity they generated.

However, for this Order to have any significance, it was necessary for the CPUC to eliminate the requirements it had set on the utilities. The FERC noted that without CPUC cooperation, this portion of the Order would be ineffectual:

---

[43]Language from the November 1 Order.

We cannot emphasize enough that the California Commission must act decisively and immediately to eliminate the requirement for the IOUs to buy the balance of their load from the PX. This is the most serious flaw in the market design created by AB1890 and the California Commission's implementing Orders. . . . In addition it is crucial that the California Commission move quickly to provide the IOUs with approval of their forward purchases. The specter of after-the-fact disallowance for transactions other than PX purchases has certainly chilled the decision making process and continues to subject California's ratepayers to the volatility of spot prices.[44]

In addition, the FERC imposed strong incentives on utilities and generators to complete almost all scheduling of load and generation with the CAISO ahead of time, rather than in real-time transactions. These incentives were designed to move electricity transactions away from the real-time market. The FERC required all California market participants to preschedule all resources and loads with the CAISO and imposed a large penalty on all real-time energy transactions greater than 5 percent of the prescheduled amount.

The CAISO's Replacement Reserve capacity market rules were modified so that a supplier bidding into this market would receive only the energy payment if it were called on to deliver energy, not the capacity payment in addition. These modifications could be expected to make market scheduling more rational, the acquisition process more deliberate, energy emergencies less frequent, and ancillary market manipulation more difficult.

In addition to reducing the reliance on spot markets, these Orders rejected a central component of the governor's policy framework from the challenge period. The FERC Orders decisively rejected the proposal that the PX be given authority to implement wholesale price caps and denied the request that the CAISO continue its authority to manage price caps. However, in order to keep continuity, the FERC ordered that the CAISO implement a $250 price cap on its purchases, without modifying the $100 price cap it had imposed for replacement reserves, until the end of December. Thus, the CAISO was precluded from further

---

[44]FERC, "Order Directing Remedies for California Wholesale Electric Markets" (December 15, 2000).

changing these price caps during that period without the express permission of the FERC; after the end of December, the state would no longer have the authority to manage or modify any wholesale price controls.

The FERC substituted its own price mitigation measures to begin at the end of December, ordering that all single-price auctions run by the CAISO or the PX be temporarily modified to a hybrid system, often described as a "soft price cap." Under this system, a single market-clearing price would be used if it were no greater than $150/MWh. However, if the market did not clear at $150/MWh or below, any accepted bid above $150/MWh would be paid the bid price, which would not be used to set the market-clearing price. Typically, suppliers bidding less than $150/MWh would be paid an amount at or near $150/MWh, and those bidding above would be paid their actual bid.

This rule changed optimal bidding strategies for those times participants expected that the market would not clear at a price at or below $150/MWh. Under these changed rules, it was no longer optimal for independent firms to bid at their marginal cost but rather to guess the cut-off price and to bid a little below that price, as in any as-bid auction system. Thus such a soft price cap system leads to a lower total cost of purchases for a fixed set of bids but motivates firms to increase their bid prices. Thus, it is dubious whether the partial move to an as-bid system would in fact have led to expenditure reductions. It could have increased total costs.

In addition, the PX and CAISO were required to report confidentially to the FERC all bids in excess of $150, and each seller was required to file bid price, electricity quantity, and marginal generation cost of each such transaction. The expressed intent was for the FERC to monitor the market and to observe attempts to exercise market power. Those bidding above $150/MWh would be asked to justify their bids, and lack of justification could result in the supplier being forced to refund the higher price.

Such a requirement for bid justification could provide strong motivation for limiting bids if generators believed that price bids above costs would be detected and that the refunds would include a penalty in addition to the difference between price and marginal cost. However, if generators believed that bids well above costs were unlikely to be detected and that, if detected, the only penalty would be a requirement to refund the difference, then this requirement would prove ineffective.

In addition to changes in the market rules, the FERC required changes in the governance of the PX and CAISO, rejecting stakeholder boards and requiring that the boards of the PX and CAISO be replaced with independent nonstakeholder boards. The FERC promised to give further guidance on the selection of these boards.

The state seemed to agree with the last of the requirements, subsequently passing its own legislation that would eliminate the stakeholder boards. However, in another test of state versus federal authority, the governor pointed out to the FERC that he had the power to make appointments within the State of California. The California legislation made it explicit that the governor would appoint the CAISO Board of Governors,[45] which he subsequently did, apparently without consulting the FERC about its composition.

The Board of Governors consisted of Maria Contreras-Sweet (California Secretary of Business, Transportation, and Housing), Tal Finney (Director of Policy, Governor's Office), Mike Florio (Attorney, The Utility Reform Network), Carl Guardino (President and CEO, Silicon Valley Manufacturing Group), and Michael Kahn (Attorney; Chairman of Energy Oversight Board). Although unquestionably each board member was highly talented, the board composition led immediately to the appearance, if not the reality, that the CAISO—the California *Independent* System Operator—would no longer be independent.

The FERC had ordered that CAISO be governed by an "independent non-stakeholder board." A California state agency was the largest buyer of electricity in the state and thus the state was clearly a market stakeholder. Two members of the new CAISO Board of Governors were members of the Davis Administration. One was chair of Governor Davis's Energy Oversight Board. Thus a voting majority of the board was clearly associated with the State government, in particular, with the Davis administration. It would be difficult to characterize this as an "independent non-stakeholder board."

---

[45]This legislation is AB 5X by Assembly member Fred Keeley (D-Boulder Creek). It replaces the existing governing board of the Independent System Operator (ISO), composed of twenty-six so-called "stakeholders," with a governing board composed of five members appointed by the governor. Board members were required to be independent of any ISO market participant but could be members of the State Admininstration.

However, other than the last issue of who had the authority to appoint the members to the PX and the CAISO boards, these Orders very clearly wrested control from the state and moved it to the federal level. However, with members of the PX and CAISO boards appointed by the governor, and with board members having authority to implement the FERC rules, this structure promised to prolong the jurisdictional conflict.

CAISO Tariff Amendment No. 33

Shortly before CAISO's authority to maintain price caps had expired, it requested that the FERC allow a change of its purchase rules (Tariff Amendment No. 33, issued December 8, 2000). In what may have been its only very fast response on an important policy issue, FERC agreed immediately. The CAISO replaced the cap on imbalance energy bids with a soft price cap system, with the interim break point set at $250/MWh (rather than the $150 in the November 1 Order). Under this interim procedure, the CAISO stopped rejecting bids priced above the then current $250/MWh price cap and began evaluating those bids in merit order, from low price to high price. Bids in excess of the $250 break point would not set the market-clearing price for imbalance energy, but rather would be paid as bid.

The CAISO's reason for this change underscored the difficulties of the price cap system under which California had been operating.[46] The CAISO noted that it had been forced to declare Stage 2 emergencies for the previous four days, and saw no immediate relief. The change was designed to allow the CAISO to compete for more needed electricity. Terry Winter, chief executive officer of the CAISO, explained, "I couldn't keep the system working if we didn't get relief."[47] It is very likely that the new plan did make more electricity available and reduced the severity of energy emergencies. It is also likely that the plan allowed wholesale prices to increase in California by essentially eliminating the price cap in the real-time market several weeks before FERC's order would have done so.

These were intended as interim plans, to remain in effect while the FERC led the process of developing more comprehensive price mitigation plans and systematically improving market operations.

---

[46]FERC Docket No. ER01-607-000, "Order Accepting Tariff Amendment on an Emergency Basis" (December 8, 2000).

[47]Nancy Vogel, *Los Angeles Times*, Nov. 7, 2000.

However, the FERC Orders did not stop the drumbeat of demands from the governor and the CPUC that more rigid price controls be imposed on the wholesale markets. The pressure operated through press releases and press conferences, communication by members of the California delegation in the U.S. Congress, and direct appeal to other decision makers in Washington. Finally, on April 26, the FERC did issue an Order that accepted wholesale price controls, or in FERC vocabulary, "price mitigation."

April 26, 2001, FERC Price Mitigation Order

This Order established a prospective "mitigation and monitoring" plan for the California wholesale electric markets, scheduled to become effective May 29, 2001. The plan included several central elements that the FERC described as intended to strike a balance between market-determined prices and controlled prices.[48]

The plan included provisions designed to control the number of generating plants that would be off-line at any time (see Figure 4.6), since by then the problem of plants off-line was well recognized. It required that all planned outages by units with Participating Generator Agreements[49] (PGAs) with the CAISO be coordinated with and approved by the CAISO, presumably making it easier to ensure that any outages of generating units were for legitimate reasons, not simply to increase market prices. Perhaps more importantly, it would allow the CAISO to develop a central body of information that would give early warning of tight markets.

The price mitigation plan moved a step back from the hybrid auctions of the November 1 and December 15 Orders and toward restoring single-price auctions. Rather than keeping the soft cap, which was set at a fixed, somewhat arbitrary level, all price caps would be removed. Replacing the soft caps would be "bid caps," limitations on the prices that given generation units could bid. Each generation unit would be required to bid a price no higher than an

---

[48]See www.rtowest.org/Doc/FERCOrder_April262001_EL00-95-012_CalISOMktMitigation.PDF.

[49]A Participating Generator Agreement is a legal agreement between a generator and the CAISO that establishes "the terms and conditions on which the ISO and the Participating Generator will discharge their respective duties and responsibilities under the ISO Tariff." The agreement allows the Participating Generator to schedule energy and submit bids to the CAISO through a Scheduling Coordinator.

administratively determined estimate of the marginal cost of operating that plant. The estimated marginal cost would be based on the unit's heat rate and emissions rate, the price of natural gas and emissions credits, and a $2/MWh fee for operation and maintenance costs. These bids, limited by bid caps, would be processed in a single-price auction to give the market-clearing price, a price each generator would receive if its bid were below that level.

There was an opportunity for an exception to the bid caps. If a firm could establish that its cost was in fact above the calculated bid cap, that firm could submit a higher bid; however, that bid would not be used to determine the market-clearing prices. In addition, these firms would be required to justify their costs or pay refunds. Similarly, resources located outside California could bid, but their bids would not be used in setting the market-clearing price during mitigated periods.

The bid caps would not always be imposed. Rather they would be imposed whenever any energy emergency had been declared. No caps would be imposed in the absence of an energy emergency, following the theory that competitive forces would be sufficient in those times.

However, this structure left open the possibility that the bid caps would limit prices during an emergency at levels lower than the market-clearing prices in nonemergency situations. Whether this would occur, however, depended on whether the competitive forces would be sufficient during nonemergency times.

In addition to the bid cap requirement was a rule designed to stop generators from exercising market power by simply not bidding at all, rather than just bidding a high price. The plan imposed a "must offer" requirement, stating that all sellers with PGAs offer all their available power to the ISO in real time if it is available and not already scheduled to run, which would apply to all sellers with PGAs, as well as nonpublic utility generators located in California that use any CAISO facilities. The requirement would not be imposed on hydroelectric plants.

The Order prohibited other bidding practices if they were seen as potentially allowing anticompetitive market manipulation, such as bids that vary with the output of a unit in a manner not related to the known cost characteristics of the unit, thus excluding the types of bids—described in a previous chapter—in which the last MW of electricity is bid at a very high price relative to most of the electricity from the same unit. Similarly, a single unit in a portfolio could not be bid at a very high level compared to the remainder of the portfolio unless there was a clear performance or input cost basis. Bids that appear to change only as electricity demand goes up, independent of the operations of the generating unit, would be outlawed.

Finally, the Order made it clear that demand response should be part of the market response. Load-serving entities were required to establish demand response mechanisms in which they identified the price at which load should be curtailed.

This mitigation plan was conditioned on the CAISO and the three investor-owned utilities filing a proposal for a Regional Transmission Organization (RTO) by June 1, 2001. This requirement was meant to develop regional responses to regional problems; however, the plan was California-specific in all other respects.

FERC June 19 Order Broadening the Scope of Price Mitigation

Ultimately, after comments were received, a more comprehensive plan was adopted on June 19, extending the price control regime to all of the western states and to all times, including times when there was no energy emergency. The Order primarily extended the scope of the April 6 Order. It was scheduled to remain in effect until September 30, 2002.

As opposed to the April 6 Order, the June 19 Order set rules to be implemented in a common manner[50] across all of the markets in the western region. As in the April 6 Order, whenever there is an energy emergency, it forces the generators to offer bids at some estimated marginal cost.[51] In addition, however, in nonemergency times the mitigation order sets price controls based on the market-clearing price in the last Stage 1 emergency. Moreover, it further attempts to eliminate California's reliance on spot markets.

In addition to the bid cap system of the April 6 Order, the June 19 Order imposes price caps on bilateral sales. These bilateral trans-

---

[50]A 10 percent price premium was allowed for sales to California to compensate for California-specific risk. Whether this premium is larger than needed to compensate for risk or is too small has been debated intensively. See an earlier section of this chapter on the "creditworthiness adder."

[51]FERC, "Order on Rehearing of Monitoring and Mitigation Plan for the California Wholesale Electric Markets, Establishing West-Wide Mitigation, and Establishing Settlement Conference" (June 19, 2001).

actions would be based on whatever prices are negotiated between the buyer and the seller, but the market-clearing price in the single-price auction would set an upper limit on the allowable prices for these transactions.

Different bid caps were applied to generators and marketers. During energy emergencies, the bid by a generator could be no higher than an administratively derived estimate of marginal cost of electricity from that generator. The estimate would be equal to the marginal cost of the gas used (with that gas purchased at that moment on a spot market for gas) plus variable operations and maintenance costs.

The costs of emissions credits or other emissions costs and start-up fuel costs would not be included in setting the market-clearing price. Rather these costs would be directly billed to the CAISO. Such a system would no longer ensure that the lowest-cost units would have their bids accepted. In particular, emissions and start-up costs would not count in determining which plants would be dispatched. Unfortunately, this would create a bias toward selecting the plants with weaker environmental performance if their costs otherwise were low.

In addition, generators would be given an opportunity to justify costs higher than the administratively determined bid caps, but these higher costs would not be used in setting the market-clearing price.

Marketers, as opposed to generators, would not be allowed to bid higher than the market-clearing price. That is, they would act as price takers.

Simple price caps would be imposed for spot market sales in times other than energy emergencies. The price for spot market sales could be no greater than 85 percent of the highest CAISO hourly market-clearing price established while the last Stage 1 emergency (not Stage 2 or 3) was in effect. When the next Stage 1 emergency is declared, the new price cap, which could be higher or lower than the one that had been set before, would be set for the subsequent time.

This FERC Order currently sets all price mitigation rules throughout the western region. As such, it sharply changes the California system from one that used blunt price caps in California markets, which were viewed in isolation from the rest of the interconnected region, to one that uses caps on bids tailored to generation costs and that fully reflects the interconnected nature of the western region. Moreover, its lifetime is limited to one additional year.

Some Impacts of the Current FERC Price Mitigation Rules

It is difficult to access definitively the impacts of the FERC April 26 and June 19 Orders. Just before they came into effect, wholesale prices fell to below the maximum prices allowed under these mitigation rules and soon fell to well below the maximum prices. Although it is conceivable that FERC price control rules caused a sharp decline in prices, price controls typically do not cause prices to fall well below the controlled levels. Therefore, it is unlikely that either the bid caps or the nonemergency price caps can account for the observed reduction in prices.

However, it is possible that the rule prohibiting anticompetitive bidding practices changed the pricing dynamics in the market, though the impact of this rule could not be assessed without careful evaluation of the confidential CAISO data on the nature of bids before and after this change. These confidential data, if ever made available to researchers, might provide some information about the significance of that rule.

The price mitigation rules do have one troubling feature. The non–energy emergency price caps for the entire West are fundamentally controlled by a California organization, the CAISO. This price cap is set equal to 85 percent of the highest CAISO hourly market-clearing price established when the last Stage 1 emergency was in effect, but only if that emergency was in effect for a full hour. However, the CAISO itself declares energy emergencies and in some circumstances can control whether or not the Stage 1 emergency lasts for more than one full hour, and thus can decide whether or not to reset the price cap. Though there has been no evidence that this power has been misused, the potential is troubling.

CALIFORNIA POLICY DURING THE CRISIS: A CRITIQUE

The sad history of a challenge that grew into a full-blown crisis need not have occurred. At every step of the way, there were alternatives that the state could have taken to address the financial crisis, the electricity crisis, or both. However, the steps would have taken leadership at the gubernatorial level.

The first alternative that could have been taken, but was not, would have been to allow the utilities in spring 2000 to start purchasing electricity on medium- or long-term contracts. This action could have been taken by the CPUC, since by that time, the purpose being served by the restrictions was no longer valid. Presumably, the governor, having appointed the president of the CPUC, could have worked with her to accomplish that action if he had chosen. Alternatively, if the CPUC had been unwilling to cooperate with the governor (an unlikely possibility), he could have taken action by exercising his broad emergency powers. Neither the governor nor the CPUC ever took this first crucial step.

This single step would have had a large direct impact on avoiding both the financial crisis and the electricity crisis, since the financial crisis was exacerbating the electricity crisis. If the utilities had entered into long-term contracts for a large share of their electricity supplies, they could have remained financially viable throughout the time, and if they had remained financially viable, the generators of electricity could have remained confident of being paid for electricity sold. Without uncertainty about whether they would be paid, their bid prices would have been lower and suppliers would not have been forced to shut down plants because they could not pay for generating electricity. Although wholesale prices would have risen, it is very doubtful that they would have risen to such high levels had there not been the financial crisis.

With the failure to authorize long- or medium-term contracts, the governor and the CPUC kept the investor-owned utilities facing a high risk. Ironically, this solution, initially denied to the utilities, was an action taken by the state at the height of the crisis. Thus rather than the utilities entering into long-term contracts at relatively low prices, the state entered into long-term contracts later, at much higher prices.

Second, the political leadership failed to allow the retail price to move with the wholesale price. This failure was fundamental to the financial crisis and, as discussed above, was a fundamental reason the energy crisis remained as severe as it did.

Although the leadership failure must rest squarely with the governor, the overall failure was fundamentally bipartisan. Neither the Republicans nor the Democrats in the California Legislature were as a whole demanding increases in the retail prices. Some isolated exceptions were pointing out the importance of retail price increases.[52] Nevertheless, legislators of both parties, fearing adverse voter reaction to any dramatic increases in retail prices, acquiesced

---

[52]For example, early in the crisis, Representative Joseph Simitian, a Democrat, was calling for retail rate increases, at least in the marginal prices of electricity.

to the governor's position, seen by Democratic legislative leaders as the "bookends" of Governor Davis's policies. At least a high cost to the state was less visible to voters than would be the high cost of increased utility bills if retail prices had been allowed to increase. In addition, if the state were able to issue bonds to cover the cumulative state shortfalls, the high cost would be seen by ratepayers over the long, distant future and would not be as obvious during the next election. The political calculus seemed very strong and neither party took leadership by fighting to bring about retail price increases until the State budget had been decimated.

Given that the actions actually undertaken by the governor were primarily politically expedient actions and those that he avoided were more difficult, politically riskier actions, the question arises whether the governor understood the seriousness of the problem that California was facing. If there was any doubt that Governor Davis was aware the state faced a serious challenge, the report[53] he received on August 2, 2000, from two of his key energy appointees— Michael Kahn, Chairman of the EOB, and Loretta Lynch, President of the CPUC—confirms that he had been fully informed early in the challenge period and that he had been advised by people whom he trusted that strong actions were needed. With this advice, he soon afterwards developed a policy framework relying exclusively on price controls. He sent letters to the CPUC, the PX, the CAISO, and the EOB strongly urging them to take actions following the strategy he had developed.[54] In addition, Governor Davis did his part to communicate his perspectives on the energy situation externally, as was discussed in a previous section. Thus, it is clear that Governor Davis was very personally involved from the early days of the challenge period, that he felt comfortable exerting his power as governor to direct these California agencies, and that it was he determining the central policy choices taken by the California government.

Throughout the entire emergence, growth, peaking, and remission of the California electricity crisis there was a frequent stream of advice to the state from the FERC in the form of responses to California requests, orders initiated by FERC in response to complaints filed by participants in the California markets, FERC stud-

---

[53]Report discussed more fully in previous section "State Policy Responses during the Challenge Period."

[54]More complete discussion appears in previous section "State Policy Responses during the Challenge Period."

ies and other reports, and direct communication by FERC members and staff with Governor Davis and other California state or private agencies. This advice made it clear that the FERC was willing to work in a cooperative manner with the State of California, but that California had much to do in order to correct its internal policies. Although much of this advice may not have been welcome by Governor Davis, the information was brought forcefully to his attention.

In addition, advice to Governor Davis was not limited to advice from Washington but was forcefully communicated both personally and publicly. One of the more public communications was issued in late January 2001 by an ad-hoc group of energy and public policy experts[55] convened through University of California, Berkeley. This group, including university faculty, former public officials, and energy consultants, issued a call to action entitled "Manifesto on the California Electricity Crisis," outlining a set of

---

[55]Signed by: Sanford Berg (Director, Public Utility Research Center, University of Florida); Tom Campbell (Professor, Stanford Law School); John Chandley (Principal, Law & Economics Consulting Group); Carl Danner (Former Chief of Staff to the President of the CPUC); Harold Demsetz (Professor Emeritus, Economics, UCLA); Roger Farmer (Professor, Economics, UCLA); Lee Friedman (Professor of Public Policy, U.C. Berkeley); Richard Gilbert (Professor, Economics, U.C. Berkeley); William Hogan (Professor, John F. Kennedy School of Government, Harvard University); Paul Joskow (Professor, Economics and Management, Director, MIT Center for Energy and Environmental Policy Research); Paul Kleindorfer (Professor of Operations & Information Management, Professor of Public Policy & Management, The Wharton School, University of Pennsylvania); Amartya Lahiri (Assistant Professor, Economics, UCLA); Robert Lawrence (Professor, John F. Kennedy School of Government, Harvard University); Tracy Lewis (Professor, Economics, University of Florida); Chris Marnay (Staff Scientist, Lawrence Berkeley Nat'l Laboratory); Daniel McFadden (Nobel Laureate, Professor of Economics, U.C. Berkeley); Phil McLeod (Principal, Law & Economics Consulting Group); Robert Michaels (Professor of Economics, California State University, Fullerton); Lee Ohanian (Associate Professor of Economics, UCLA); Shmuel Oren (Professor of Industrial Engineering and Operations Research, U.C. Berkeley); Joseph Ostroy (Professor of Economics, UCLA); Larry Ruff (Consultant); Richard Rumelt (Professor of Business and Society, UCLA); Pablo Spiller (Professor of Business, U.C. Berkeley); Robert Solow (Nobel Laureate, Professor of Economics, MIT); James Sweeney (Professor of Management Science and Engineering, Stanford University); David Teece (Professor, Director, Institute of Management, Innovation & Organization, Haas School of Business, U.C. Berkeley); Phillip Verleger (PK Verleger LLC); Mitch Wilk (Former President and Commissioner CPUC); Oliver Williamson (Professor, Haas School of Business, U.C. Berkeley); Janet Yellen (Professor, Haas School of Business, U.C. Berkeley).

public policy solutions designed to help California solve the energy crisis.[56]

The Manifesto made it clear that the financial crisis:

must be dealt with immediately before it gets further out of hand. If the creditworthiness of the investor-owned utilities can be restored, California can both solve the immediate supply shortage problems resulting from credit risks and then look to proper long-term solutions to its electricity problems.

The Manifesto urged four key elements to these long-term solutions:

freedom to engage in long-term contracts, retail price flexibility, competition at both the wholesale and retail levels, and more effective cooperation between federal and state regulators to fix a variety of market imperfections and resulting market performance problems.

The Manifesto stressed the importance of avoiding actions that would make matters worse:

In particular, a State takeover of the business would make matters worse, as would turning the State into a permanent electricity purchasing authority. It would also be unfortunate if the State were itself to commit to long-term contracts for a large portion of California's electricity needs. The State's credentials as an astute player in the electricity market aren't impressive, and there is no reason to expect major improvement in the future. Accordingly, emergency state contracts should be avoided if at all possible. Nor would the State buying up existing generation assets add to supply. In the end, new power plants are needed, and the State should focus on creating a supportive environment for necessary new private investment. State ownership is not a solution at all—merely a guarantee that the taxpayers will be saddled with additional obligations for decades to come.

---

[56]The complete document is available at http://www.haas.berkeley.edu/news/california_electricity_crisis.html.

The advice from within California was clear, forceful, and well publicized. It could not have been missed. Unfortunately, Governor Davis chose to reject this advice, as he continued to reject the advice of federal authorities, doing almost exactly the opposite on every count. California continues to suffer the consequences of his decision making.

5

FROM CRISIS TO BLIGHT

Although the electricity crisis itself was a short-term event, the policy actions—or inactions—during the challenge period and the crisis have left a continuing harmful legacy that threatens to remain for years or even decades to come. This legacy continues in terms of the fundamental financial problems with which investor-owned utilities are struggling, in terms of deep financial obligations incurred by the state in purchasing electricity, obligations the state intends to transfer to purchasers of electricity within the service areas of the two investor-owned utilities, and in terms of financial obligations ratepayers will be forced to meet if they wish to remain in California.

Pacific Gas and Electric (PG&E) remains in bankruptcy court. Its most recently proposed restructuring plan has been opposed by the State of California but is under consideration by the court and as such provides the possibility that PG&E will ultimately return to financial health. The second-largest utility, Southern California Edison (SCE), has agreed with the CPUC on a retail price structure that promises but does not guarantee that SCE will return to financial health, although not quickly. Although the peak of the crisis has passed for these two firms, they face a continued high risk.

The state has been purchasing electricity on behalf of the investor-owned utilities since January and has accumulated a short-term net financial shortfall exceeding $6 billion as a result.

In addition, the state has signed long-term contracts to purchase electricity, with contractual commitments to pay prices around twice as high as the expected future market prices. These contracts together represent long-term financial obligations to pay more than $40 billion to purchase electricity that is likely to be worth around $20 billion. The difference between the contractual price and the value of the electricity represents an expected future net loss of roughly $20 billion. Thus, because of its actions, the State of California has accumulated a combination of short- and long-term financial losses exceeding $25 billion. These near- and long-term financial losses are the basis of the blight the state now faces.

However, who will pay these financial losses is still an issue. If these losses are added to the future retail prices of electricity in the service areas of the investor-owned utilities, retail electricity prices in those areas will be elevated for many years above prices in surrounding states or prices in parts of California served by the municipal utilities (Los Angeles and Sacramento are the two major locations). If these losses are paid by California taxpayers, taxes must be increased in California or state-supported public services must be diminished. Either allocation of the financial obligations would be damaging to the people of California.

The legislature and the governor have made their intentions clear that these financial losses must be paid, not broadly by the California taxpayers, but by the families and companies that will remain as or will become customers of the investor-owned utilities. These financial obligations were incurred by the state "on behalf of" those families and companies that were customers of the investor-owned utilities during the crisis. A large majority of these families and companies can be expected to remain as customers of the investor-owned utilities during the next decade or so. Thus, imposing the financial obligations on the future customers of the investor-owned utilities would result in a rough correspondence between those who would be forced to pay the costs and those on whose behalf the state incurred the obligations.

However, this allocation of the costs will not lead to anywhere near a perfect correspondence between those who would be forced to pay the costs and those on whose behalf the state incurred the obligations. Families and businesses moving into the service areas of PG&E and SCE would be required to pay costs of these past mistakes. Those moving out of the service areas, either to other parts of California or away from California, will avoid paying the costs.[1] This allocation of costs thus creates incentives for families and businesses to move out of areas served by the investor-owned utilities to other states or to areas served by the municipal utilities. In addition, it penalizes families moving into the service areas of investor-owned utilities.

Another perspective, one not adopted by the governor or the legislature, is that the financial obligations resulted not from the mistakes of the electricity ratepayers—either those purchasing electricity from the investor-owned utilities during the crisis or those that may be located in the service areas of the investor-owned utilities in the future—but rather from the decisions made by the governor, the CPUC, and the legislature prior to and during the crisis. The governor and legislators were elected by the voters; the CPUC members were appointed by governors. It was the entire electorate, or at least the majority voters of the electorate, who had empowered the governor and the legislature. Thus, the alternative perspective is that these costs should be distributed broadly among the California voters, and that these financial losses should be paid over a period of years through the State Treasury. To date, however, the governor and the legislature have definitely not adopted this perspective. Moreover, it is unlikely that the voters who purchase electricity from the municipal utilities would welcome a solution involving their paying for electricity they did not use. But this solution would not create the same incentives for families and businesses to move out of the service areas of the investor-owned utilities.

Which groups should or will ultimately pay the costs of these state obligations is a long-term issue that need not be fully resolved during the next year. Currently, the state has incurred the obligations and is taking steps to delay payment in the short term and ensure that the financial obligations are ultimately paid by future customers of the investor-owned utilities.

In the short run, perhaps California has no choice but to defer the payments. Because of the economic slowdown, California is

---

[1]To some extent this will be mitigated. The future obligation may reduce the value of real estate in the service areas of the investor-owned utilities, decreasing the price of real estate and imposing costs on those leaving the area. But one cannot expect this capitalization process to be perfect.

now facing a State budgetary deficit exceeding $10 billion, not counting any financial shortfalls from electricity purchases. Unless the state can find a way to recover the electricity-related shortfalls from the retail electricity consumers or can find a way to defer payment for years, the State budgetary deficit will increase sharply, perhaps to untenable levels. Thus, the state has little choice but to ensure that the financial shortfalls from electricity purchases will not become short-term obligations for the State Treasury.

The California Legislature has authorized the state to defer payments of the shortfall and to shift obligations to ratepayers in the service areas of the investor-owned utilities. First, the state has authorized the issuance of $12.5 billion of revenue bonds, which would be financial obligations not of the state, but of retail electricity purchasers within the PG&E, SDG&E, and SCE service areas.[2] The retail electricity purchasers in California would be obligated to pay back the principal and interest on those bonds through increased retail prices of electricity. In addition, the state requested that the CPUC provide long-term guarantees that the retail electricity price will be kept high enough to ensure that ratepayers will pay the entire cost of the long-term electricity contracts plus the costs of repaying any revenue bonds the state is able to market. Until recently, the CPUC was unwilling to make such a commitment, citing very legitimate concerns that the various obligations made by the state "on behalf of" electricity purchasers could result in unreasonably high retail prices over many years.

Absent the guarantee, the state plan to sell revenue bonds was in limbo. The long-term electricity purchase contracts include clauses that obligate the state to pay for that electricity ahead of all bonds, notes, or other indebtedness. Therefore, if the state were to issue revenue bonds, the payment of their interest and principal would be subordinated to payments for the long-term contracts. This subordination would not create particular risks if the CPUC guaranteed that the retail electricity prices would always be kept high enough to adequately cover both obligations. However, until the CPUC agreed to the guarantee, it was highly unlikely that the bonds could have been issued as investment-grade instruments.

---

[2]Under current plans these bonds would not be obligations of anyone purchasing electricity within the service areas of the municipal utilities because electricity was not purchased on behalf of these consumers.

The state had financed its electricity purchases using a short-term bridge loan, anticipating that it would be able to market long-term bonds. Because the bonds have not yet been sold, however, the bridge loan rolled over to become a medium-term loan at a higher interest rate. It remains an obligation of the State of California. Now that the CPUC has agreed to keep retail rates high enough to ensure payment of the long-term contractual commitments and assure the bond repayments, the state should be able to market the bonds as investment-grade instruments and repay the medium-term loan.

These continuing financial ramifications of the dual crisis are major components of the blight that threatens California, but they do not encompass all long-term adverse consequences of the state's policy choices.

One of the important provisions of AB 1890 was direct access for electricity consumers to wholesalers, generators of electricity, or other electricity aggregators so consumers would have the ability to bypass utilities. Although the option of going directly to generators was unlikely to be taken, at least at first, by residential consumers, the option could be important for commercial or industrial users. The option promised to create legitimate retail competition that, over the course of years, could be expected to reduce retail markups and increase the range of electricity supply services available to all consumers.

But the California Legislature has voted to repeal provisions allowing direct access: companies and individuals are precluded under State regulation from entering into contracts to purchase electricity except from their local utilities, which are obligated to pass revenues on to the state to cover the state's financial obligations. The legislation repeals direct access during the time that the state continues to purchase electricity on behalf of utilities. The purchase contracts extend for the next twenty years and the legislative intent seems to be that direct access would be abolished during that entire time. Thus, unless the current legislation is changed, meaningful retail competition will not be a reality in California for a very long time.

Although elimination of retail competition is a restrictive step backward, the state's financial obligations provide a strong motivation for such a step, since the governor and legislature have decided that the financial obligations of purchasing electricity through increases in the retail electricity prices are to be paid by future customers of the investor-owned utilities. That allocation of costs provides strong incentives for customers, particularly large customers, to stop purchasing electricity from these utilities. The easiest alternative for most would be to bypass the utilities, thereby avoiding payment of some portion of the state-incurred financial obligations.[3]

Since the total amount of the obligations is fixed, the more customers are able to avoid paying a share of these obligations, the greater will be the remaining share to be paid by the rest of the customers. Such a restriction therefore helps to ensure that the state's financial obligations for electricity purchases will be borne broadly within the service areas of the investor-owned utilities.

In addition, California has created a State Power Authority that would develop and operate new electric-generating plants, selling state-generated electricity in competition with private sector generators. This agency has the potential for moving California even further down the path to becoming a public power state and pressuring consumers to purchase the state-generated electricity in preference to possibly lower-cost electricity generated by private sector firms.

Collectively, these long-term consequences of State actions threaten to leave California with more severe versions of the problems that motivated restructuring in the first place—high retail prices, no consumer choice, and pervasive government control in electricity supply. This, then, is the blight toward which California is being led.

LONG-TERM ELECTRICITY PURCHASE CONTRACTS

At the height of the electricity crisis, Governor Davis announced that the state would not limit its wholesale electricity purchases to the quantities needed during the crisis period but rather would enter long-term contracts to buy electricity over the next two decades. The state subsequently requested bids to sell large quantities of electricity to California through long-term contracts. This was the first of several policy actions under which the state would start becoming a long-term direct participant in

---

[3]For most large firms the other two alternatives—move to areas of California that will not face these high prices or move out of California—are more difficult and may not be economically viable.

the electricity markets, substituting direct state control for private sector control. Ironically, entering long-term contracts was one of the actions proposed by the utilities but precluded under State regulations.

As had been pointed out in the "Manifesto on the California Electricity Crisis," the height of the crisis was not the time to lock the state into long-term contracts. Long-term contracts, negotiated by even the utilities, could have been expected to result in many years of high electricity prices. Yet the governor chose a time shortly after the peak wholesale prices to start negotiating the long-term contracts. Rather than the state entering long-term contracts at that time, several alternatives were available.

First, the state could have waited until the crisis had subsided and negotiated long-term contracts only after spot prices had fallen significantly, which would have left the state vulnerable to even higher wholesale prices during the crisis and to even larger budgetary deficits. In hindsight it would have avoided many years of elevated wholesale prices, although at the time the state entered the contracts it could not have known with certainty whether spot prices would increase or decrease.

Alternatively, the state could have encouraged the investor-owned utilities to negotiate medium- or long-term contracts appropriate for their needs, which would have left the long-term control of these purchases with the private sector, not with the State. However, once the utilities were not creditworthy, sellers would have been unwilling to enter such contracts or, at best, would have required very large risk premiums. To counter that problem, the state could have provided guarantees to the sellers for those obligations. In that way, the state could have reduced the risk without taking on the purchase obligation itself.

The state could have waited until the crisis had subsided and allowed the utilities, once they were again creditworthy, to themselves negotiate medium- and long-term contracts. This solution, however, depended on the state allowing increased retail electricity rates so that the utilities could have become creditworthy within a reasonable time. However, during early 2001, the governor was still opposing any retail price increases beyond the $10/MWh temporary surcharge. Thus, given the governor's opposition to retail price increases, this option was not realistic, although the state could have still guaranteed payment of the financial obligations under the contracts and thus could have facilitated private sector contracting.

In short, at the peak of the crisis there were no good alternatives for California to ensure lower wholesale prices. The time for the state to sign long-term contracts or to let the utilities sign those contracts was gone by the end of the year 2000.

However, Governor Davis continued on the path of establishing the state as the direct buyer of electricity, rather than following the other alternatives. He chose to do so at the peak of the electricity crisis, authorizing a team to negotiate long-term contracts for the state to buy electricity, and the team did so.

During the negotiations, both the generators and the state were well aware that there were many generating units under construction. Therefore, the governor could rationally expect that the negotiated long-term contractual prices would be well below the then current spot prices. This expectation made it possible for Governor Davis to assure the voters that, although the contract negotiations and terms would be confidential, the contracts would specify electricity prices well below the spot prices they were hearing about daily. In fact, the negotiated prices are lower than the then current spot prices but much higher than the wholesale prices that could reasonably be expected during the life of these contracts.

Figure 5.1 shows the total MW under these contracts for each month up to the year 2011. One contract continues beyond this

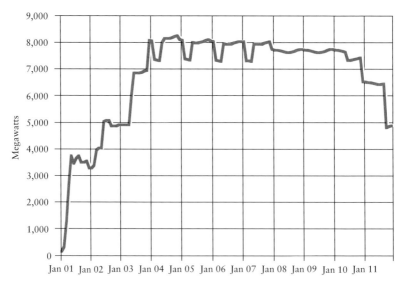

FIGURE 5.1:   Total MW under Long-Term State Contracts

point to the year 2021, providing 1,000 MW of electricity. These long-term contracts obligate the state to purchase roughly 8,000 MW over the peak usage times each month (typically sixteen hours per day, six days per week) for each year between 2004 and 2010, about 20 percent of the total generating capacity in California.

Some of the contracts specify the source of the electricity. In each such case, the source is electricity from California plants that already had been under construction before the challenge period or crisis had developed.

The total contract quantity does not reach its peak until January 2004. Fully half of the contracts do not promise to deliver electricity until after January 2002, more than seven months after the end of the crisis, and some do not begin delivering electricity until January 2004. Thus, the governor's justification for the contracts—that they were used to solve the crisis—seems inconsistent with the timing of several contracts. Since observers at that time generally believed that the biggest difficulty would be during summer 2001 and that California would be past the crisis by fall 2002, long-term contracts that do not begin until January 2004 are not consistent with the goals announced by the governor.

These contracts are consistent with California moving along the path to becoming a public power state, with fundamental control of electricity supply resting with the state government, rather than with the private sector. Thus, the timing of these contracts suggests that part of their purpose may have been to help transform California into a public power state.

It would be easier to justify the contracts if the contractual prices were low, but they are not. Figure 5.2 graphs the contractual prices under these contracts to the year 2011 if there are no natural gas price adjustments. For 2001 and 2002, the price varies on a month-to-month basis but averages over $90/MWh.[4] During 2003, the prices decline from an initial $90/MWh to $75/MWh. The price from the year 2004 through the end of the contracts averages slightly above $70/MWh.

These prices are significantly higher than the expected market-clearing prices for electricity once the new generating plants come on-line. Figure 5.2 illustrates an estimated range of average electricity prices that could be expected to characterize the market

---

[4]These prices include not only the price stated in the contract but also the capacity payments obligated under these contracts.

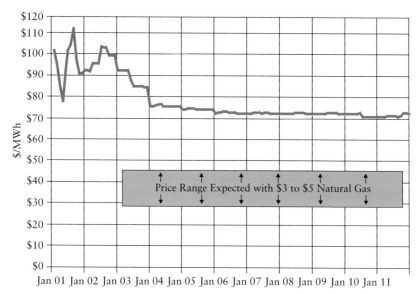

FIGURE 5.2:   Prices in State-Negotiated Long-Term Contracts versus
Expected Future Wholesale Prices

once new electric-generating capacity comes on-line, under the assumption that delivered natural gas prices range between $3/mcf and $5/mcf.[5] These natural gas prices would result in wholesale electricity prices ranging between about $30/MWh and $45/MWh. Though these are simply predictions about an expected range, they would have been very reasonable projections at the time the long-term contracts were being negotiated. Such predictions suggest that the contracts negotiated by the state will require California to pay between $25/MWh and $40/MWh higher than the market prices that could have been projected at the time the contracts were negotiated. This additional cost applies to roughly 20 percent of California's electricity supply during the next ten years and 10 percent over the subsequent ten years.

In addition to the high contractual prices are more subtle problems of delivery location and risk-bearing provisions of the contracts. Each contract includes a firm guarantee that the state will purchase the contractual quantities. For the most part, they are take-or-pay contracts in which the state guarantees to pay for the

---

[5]This calculation assumes new generating plants have a heat rate of 8.6 MMBtu/MWh plus a fixed cost of $3/MWh.

contractual quantities whether or not it actually takes the quantities. The risk-bearing issues were examined by California State Auditor Elaine Howle, who, on December 20, 2001, reported that the contracts did not include adequate protection from price spikes and outages. Most of the contracts provide little or no penalties to suppliers if they fail to deliver the contractual quantities.

Some defenders of the contracts have argued that the prices in the long-term contracts should not be criticized without taking into account the short-term contracts that were tied to the long-term contracts. The assertion is that the state agreed on prices higher than fair-market prices for the long-term contracts in exchange for receiving electricity during spring and summer 2001 at a price lower than the market price.

Sempra Energy Resources is one of the sellers cited as agreeing to contracts that would exchange future costs in place of costs during 2001. In a November 5 article in *Utility Spotlight*, Sempra Energy Resources CEO Stephen Baum was quoted as saying: "To complete the long-term deal and to help stabilize prices during the state's energy crisis, (we) sold this summer's power to California at a discount-to-market basis, creating a loss in the second and third quarters. . . ." Sempra in fact did contract to sell California 250 MW of power for peak periods in the four months from June 2001 through September 2001 at $80/MWh. This sale occurred at a time when futures prices for electricity during summer 2001 were around $400/MWh. Thus, for Sempra, it may be true that the state agreed on prices higher than fair-market prices for the long-term contracts in exchange for receiving electricity during spring and summer 2001 at a price lower than the market price. However, in the same contract, Sempra agreed to sell California electricity for the six-month interval, April 2002 through September 2002, at high prices. The contract committed California to buy 300 MW of power during peak periods in those six months at a price of $160/MWh and 150 MW during all hours (peak as well as off-peak) for those six months at a price of $100/MWh, which helped to compensate Sempra for sales at below market levels, leaving very little justification for substantial increases in the long-term contractual prices. The long-term contractual quantities vary from 1200 MW to 1900 MW from June 2003 through September 2011, at prices averaging $67/MWh.[6]

---

[6]All the Sempra prices, including the year 2001 prices, are included in Figure 5.2.

On the other hand, some firms, such as Calpine, did not have any short-term contracts with the State of California and thus could not have reduced the short-term prices in exchange for above-market long-term prices.

Thus, it is possible that some energy generators did link the prices for short-term sales to the terms for long-term sales. To the extent that did happen, the long-term contracts should be evaluated in the context of linked short-term sales. However, the state was ordered by the court to release the terms of the long-term contracts, which it did. If low prices in linked short-term contracts were part of the considerations the state received for signing the long-term contracts, the state was obligated to release information about those linkages. Since the state did not release such information, it is reasonable to conclude that there were no linkages other than those embedded in the contracts released by the state and whose prices are summarized in Figure 5.2.

Figure 5.3 estimates the financial obligations to be paid by the State of California for these long-term contracts. For the years between 2004 and 2010, California will be obligated to pay somewhat more than $4 billion per year.

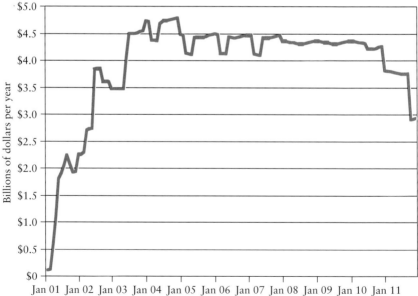

FIGURE 5.3:   State Financial Obligations for Long-Term Contracts

Currently, the State of California does not sell retail electricity directly to customers but only through the utilities on whose behalf the state purchases the electricity. In doing so, it could choose either of two very different options about the pricing of this electricity.

First, it could charge the utilities a price for this electricity consistent with the market price, under a belief that the market price will be much less than the contractual price the state has negotiated; it would lose money on each such transaction. The difference would come directly from the State budget, which would then be burdened by about $2 billion per year for the next ten years. Under such a pricing policy, the costs of contractual mistakes would be distributed broadly among the California voters, as suggested in the introduction to this chapter. Retail electricity prices would not be elevated and these contracts would not lead to incentives for families and businesses to move away from service areas of the investor-owned utilities.

This has not been the announced intention of the state. Rather, it has announced that the utilities would be required to purchase the electricity from the state at a price equal to the contractual prices that it negotiated. This would imply that for the next ten years the utilities would face an annual $4 billion financial obligation based upon decisions made by the state "on their behalf." This financial obligation would provide electricity worth about $2 billion annually. If the investor-owned utilities were to pass that cost on to their customers, the financial loss would increase their retail prices of electricity by about 10 percent for the next ten years and perhaps 5 percent for the subsequent ten years.[7]

The CPUC initially voted against guaranteeing that the DWR would be allowed to cover all of these costs from future retail electricity rates. However, the CPUC has now agreed that all state-negotiated contractual costs will be charged to consumers through electricity rates.

There is now a broad recognition in California that entering into these contracts was a mistake, or at least that the terms negotiated by the state were so unfavorable that it was a great mistake to agree to them. This recognition has led to efforts by the state to "renegotiate" the contracts. The state has been in or has scheduled

---

[7]These calculations assume that the revenues these utilities receive during the next ten years will be about $15 billion per year.

contract revision discussions with at least five holders of major contracts (Calpine Corp., Coral Power, Dynegy, PacifiCorp, Sempra
Energy, and Williams) and has brought legal actions as well,
requesting the FERC to invalidate the contracts or to reduce the
prices in them.

The position taken by the electricity generators is well summarized
in a statement by Williams Co.'s spokeswoman Paula Hall-Collins:
"Our position has been clear from the very beginning. We do have a
contract and we feel it was fairly negotiated. But as with any of our
long-term deals, we're interested in developing a relationship."[8]

The state's position is summarized by two statements, one by
Loretta Lynch, President of the CPUC—"We can do it easy or we
can do it hard, but it will be done"[9]—and one by state senator
Richard Alarcon (D-San Fernando)—"Everything short of extor-
tion that we can do . . . we should."[10] The state seems to be pursuing a wide variety of approaches to the renegotiation that go
beyond attempting to find mutually advantageous contractual
changes. The attorney general has continued the investigation to
find improper actions in the wholesale electricity markets and
appears to be trying to make that investigation a component of
the renegotiation talks. The CPUC has challenged several of the
contracts in complaints to the FERC and has recently filed a comprehensive complaint to that body.

ELECTRICITY REVENUE BONDS

As discussed in the previous chapter, central to the governor's
plan to buy wholesale electricity on behalf of the investor-owned
utilities' customers was the plan to issue bonds, also on behalf of
those customers, to finance the purchase of that electricity. The
bonds, currently proposed to total $12.5 billion, would be sold as
DWR revenue bonds, not as State general obligation bonds.[11] The
$12.5 billion would cover, after discounts and other costs of mar-
keting the bonds, about $6 billion borrowed from the California

---

[8]Quoted from article by Carrie Peyton, *The Sacramento Bee*, Jan. 10, 2002.
[9]Ibid.
[10]Statement from hearing by the Joint Legislative Audit Committee.
[11]Under the California Constitution the State cannot issue bonds backed by
the full faith and credit of the State of California unless the voters of
California vote to do so. However, neither the ratepayers nor the California
voters need to vote on these revenue bonds.

general fund and the $4.3 billion bridge loan the state negotiated during the electricity crisis. If the sale were successful, it would be the largest government bond sale in U.S. history.

Under the current plan, the revenue bonds, when (and if) sold, would represent an obligation to the future buyers of electricity in California, in particular the customers of the investor-owned utilities. This obligation would be in addition to the obligation stemming from the state's long-term electricity purchase contracts.[12]

If they were sold as fifteen-year bonds with an interest rate between 4 percent and 5 percent, they would require an annual payment of roughly $1.2 billion per year over the next fifteen years, which would correspondingly increase the average price of electricity sold by the investor-owned utilities. Annual payment on the bonds would increase the price of electricity to these consumers by about 6 percent,[13] in addition to the price increase associated with the long-term contracts signed by the state.

However, whether these bonds would be marketable as investment-grade instruments was, for a long time, questionable. As revenue bonds, the guarantee of repayment would be based only on revenues from future sales of electricity. The state's long-term contracts to purchase electricity obligate it to pay for the electricity it purchases using monies collected in the DWR's Electric Power Fund (the Fund) established in the California State Treasury. These contracts have clauses that state: "payments under this agreement shall constitute an operating expense of the Fund payable prior to all bonds, notes or other indebtedness." Therefore, if bonds were issued as obligations of the Electric Power Fund, payment of the interest and principal of these bonds would be subordinated to payments for the long-term contracts.

---

[12]This obligation is particularly ironic in light of the governor's statement on February 16: "Believe me, if I wanted to raise rates I could have solved this problem in 20 minutes. But I am not going to ask the ratepayers to accept a disproportionate burden." This obligation seems to have been part of the governor's intention from January 19 when he first authorized the DWR to start buying electricity. He apparently planned even then to require ratepayers to accept the entire burden, since he never formally proposed any alternative means of paying the interest and principal on the revenue bonds other than asking the ratepayers to pay the entire amount.

[13]In 1999, investor-owned utilities sold 153 million MWh of electricity (see Table 2.1). If that electricity were to sell at a bundled average price of $130/MWh (including distribution services), total revenues of the investor-owned utilities would be $20 billion per year. Six percent of $20 billion is $1.2 billion.

Thus, the principal and interest might not be paid unless retail prices for electricity sold by the investor-owned utilities will be high enough to pay costs of the state-issued long-term electricity purchase contracts and the continued electricity purchases, in addition to the debt service on the bonds.

As discussed in the chapter introduction, subordination would not create risks if the CPUC guaranteed that the retail electricity prices would always be kept high enough to cover both obligations adequately. Initially, however, the CPUC explicitly rejected such a guarantee. Therefore, absent changes in the CPUC decision, it seemed likely that the bonds could not be issued as investment-grade instruments.

If the bonds were not issued, the state could continue with its current $4.3 billion loan, which it would be obligated to pay back over several years, unless it is refinanced. The State budget would remain in deficit from its past electricity purchases, but ratepayers would not necessarily face the additional 6 percent increase in the retail electricity price over the next fifteen years. In any event, the State of California currently has incurred a debt that it will be obligated to pay. Either it will cause a long-term drain on the electricity ratepayers or it will cause a shorter-term drain on the State Treasury. Either adds to the blight.

On January 31, 2002, the CPUC announced that it had reached a tentative agreement with the DWR and was negotiating with the offices of the governor and the treasurer about the amounts and provisions of a bond issue. The agreement would make it possible for the state to sell the revenue bonds as investment-grade instruments. The bond proceeds, after marketing costs, would repay the $4.3 billion short-term loan, and the remainder would replenish the state's general fund. Under the agreement, the DWR would put in best-faith efforts to renegotiate the long-term contracts and would allow the CPUC to take legal actions to try to overthrow the contracts.

INCLUSION OF THE UTILITIES' PAST CRISIS COSTS IN FUTURE ELECTRICITY RATES

Retail electricity prices can be expected to remain elevated above wholesale electricity costs for a third reason. The utilities incurred massive losses during the challenge and crisis periods, and there remains a legal argument that they be allowed to recover some significant share of those losses. The CPUC has made such an agreement that would allow SCE to earn back in the future some portion of losses incurred during the challenge and crisis periods. As part of the agreement, SCE agreed to drop its "filed rate doctrine" lawsuit. The PG&E is still proposing that it be allowed to recover some share of the losses. Whether such an option will be allowed for PG&E is not clear, but the decision is likely to be part of the final plan to allow PG&E to emerge from Chapter 11 bankruptcy proceedings.

The SCE agreement with the CPUC would allow it to recover much of its losses over the next several years. In particular, the agreement would allow SCE to keep charging its customers the current level of retail electricity prices even though the wholesale price has decreased to pre-challenge period levels. The current price includes an average increase in retail electricity rates of $40/MWh. This is an average increase of 33 percent above the historical average retail prices charged by SCE. Thus, if wholesale prices of electricity remain at their current levels, then, because of the need to recover the past losses, the retail price of electricity purchased from SCE will be 33 percent higher over the next several years than it otherwise would be.

Whether the 6 percent increase in electricity prices associated with the electricity bonds plus the 10 percent increase associated with the state long-term contracts would be added to the 33 percent increase associated with SCE recovering its past losses is not clear. What is clear, however, is that customers of SCE will be paying a significant increase in electricity prices over and above the wholesale cost of electricity and over and above the price of electricity in other states.

PAYING SUNK COSTS THROUGH FUTURE ELECTRICITY PRICES

There is little doubt that—absent very large refunds from the electricity generators and complete renegotiation of the long-term contracts—the state faces many billions of dollars of electricity purchase costs beyond the future wholesale costs. These are sunk costs that have already been incurred (although they may not have to be paid until some future time) and whose magnitudes will not depend on whether Californians buy much or little electricity in the future.

There is no easy way to pay these large sunk costs; however, some ways of paying them are likely to be more damaging than others. The current state plan—increasing retail electricity prices for many years in the future—is likely to be one of the more damaging options. The damage will come about because the elevated prices of electricity will motivate consumers to take actions that would not be economically justifiable given the future wholesale electricity costs and the costs of distributing electricity. Those actions can increase the blight facing California.

The introduction to the chapter has discussed how elevated prices may distort locational decisions of businesses and families both within California (from the service areas of investor-owned utilities and to the service areas of municipal utilities) and between California and other states. For businesses, the locational distortions may be more subtle than decisions to move away from areas with high electricity prices. Rather, firms may simply shift some fraction of their electricity-intensive activities away from California or away from service areas of the investor-owned utilities. They may compensate by moving back the same fraction of their non–electricity intensive activities or they may choose not to compensate at all.

Businesses will face incentives to self-generate electricity since self-generation will allow them to avoid paying some share of the sunk costs. This incentive to self-generate will remain even if self-generation costs exceed costs of electricity delivered by investor-owned utilities. This will occur if the inclusion of sunk costs makes the price of electricity delivered by investor-owned utilities higher than the per-unit cost of self-generation. Businesses will look for ways of substituting other energy, such as natural gas or petroleum, in place of electricity.

In addition, there may be incentives for municipalities, such as San Francisco, to municipalize their utilities if the sunk-cost allocation rules are written so that the newly created municipal utility can avoid paying its share of sunk costs. This possibility seemed to be part of the debate in 2001, when San Francisco residents were voting whether to create a municipal utility and take over PG&E distribution assets.[14]

---

[14]This proposal was defeated by a very narrow margin. During the debate, S. David Freeman, head of the California State Power Authority, speaking to a rally of those supporting municipalization, promised that the State Power Authority would sell the new municipal utility electricity at a low cost. Perhaps he meant that the electricity would be sold at a low cost but that San Francisco would still pay the same share of the sunk costs, but newspaper reports of his speech never suggested that caveat.

The inclusion of sunk costs in future electricity prices can also distort capital investment decisions by businesses and families. Electric vehicles currently represent only a very tiny fraction of the personal passenger vehicles on the road today. With the advance of hybrid electrics and technologies needed for dedicated electric vehicles, it is likely that more dedicated electric vehicles will be introduced into California markets. However, elevated electricity prices would create incentives against purchase of these vehicles. At a less esoteric level, elevated electricity prices would provide incentives for families to buy clothes dryers and water heaters fueled by natural gas rather than those powered by electricity. Although these individual distortions are each unlikely to be important to the California economy, their cumulative impacts can add to the blight.

ELIMINATION OF DIRECT ACCESS

One of the important and very positive elements of the restructuring under AB 1890 was a provision for direct access by users of electricity to electricity generators. Electricity users and generators were allowed to negotiate bilateral contracts directly for the purchase and sale of electricity. Although it is not reasonable to expect that small users would negotiate such contracts, the ability for large users to do so is a step toward creating retail competition.

In addition, direct access created the possibility for retail aggregators to compete with one another and with the utilities. A retail aggregator could enter agreements with many users of electricity to supply their electric needs and possibly additional energy needs, contracting with generators to supply electricity that it would in turn provide to its customers. The opportunity for such aggregators to enter the market potentially provides an element of retail competition, although it is most likely that such aggregators would initially participate only in niche markets. Direct access is a potentially useful step toward retail market competition, although, in itself, it is far from sufficient to create that competition.

However, direct access would conflict with the intention of the state to pay for the sunk costs through increased future electricity prices. The price elevation is creating an incentive for large users to enter bilateral contracts directly with generators to provide the electricity, rather than purchasing electricity through investor-owned utilities. Whenever a large electricity user bypasses utilities, or otherwise avoids purchasing electricity from the utility, more of the sunk costs fall on the remaining customers, further increasing the retail price of electricity.

Members of the California Legislature understand this phenomenon and have voted, as part of Assembly Bill 1X (AB 1X) to eliminate direct access. It adds Section 80110 to the Water Code:

> *After the passage or such period of time after the effective date of this section as shall be determined by the [Public Utilities] commission, the right of retail end use customers . . . to acquire service from other providers shall be suspended until the department [the Department of Water Resources] no longer supplies power hereunder.*

The CPUC most recently ruled that the suspension shall begin as of September 20, 2001, but kept open the possibility of setting that date retroactively to July 1, 2001. The DWR has entered contracts to purchase power extending until the year 2021. Thus, under AB 1X, direct access would be suspended for the next twenty years, absent legislative or contractual changes.

STATE POWER AUTHORITY (CALIFORNIA CONSUMER POWER AND CONSERVATION FINANCING AUTHORITY)

The most recent and explicit step toward turning California into a public power state was the creation of the new State Power Authority, established by Senate Bill 6X (SB 6X). This authority, headed by S. David Freeman, has broad power to construct new electric-generating facilities and to acquire existing facilities by use of eminent domain procedures.

Governor Davis first proposed creating a state power authority during his January 8, 2001, State of the State speech, when he proposed ". . . either a joint power authority among the State and our thirty municipal utilities to develop the additional power we need, or a California public power authority that can buy and build new power plants." Passed in May 2001, SB 6X created the State Power Authority, more formally known as the California Consumer Power and Conservation Financing Authority.

The State Power Authority has broad powers to construct, own, and operate electric generation and power facilities and finance energy conservation programs. It "will be able to finance natural gas transportation or storage projects; issue up to $5 billion in bonds; have the power of eminent domain; and make loans and grants."[15] The State Power Authority "will be authorized to build, own and operate new power plants on behalf of consumers."[16] Although the State Power Authority currently has a $5 billion limitation on its bond-issuing authorization, the authorization may increase once the initial $5 billion has been spent.

The Authority initially signed[17] forty-eight letters of intent with nineteen separate bidders, allowing it to begin negotiations to have 2,271 MW of renewable energy constructed. As of October 4, 2001, it had signed thirty-one letters of intent from sixteen separate bidders for 3,214 MW of natural gas–fired peaker units to be on-line for next summer.

Had the State Power Authority continued on this path, it would have spent large amounts of State money without achieving any long-term increase in California generation capacity. To the extent the State Power Authority were to build new generating units, these units could be expected to substitute explicitly for generation, transmission, and contractual activities by private corporations.

The expected displacement of private investment is most obvious for gas-fired peaker units that would be owned by the Authority. Peaker units can be constructed rapidly by private sector firms; however, corporations will do so only if such construction is profitable. The State Power Authority has indicated that it will sell electricity from its peakers at "cost"; thus, no profit margin would be included in the wholesale prices of electricity generated by these units. Private sector owners of peaker units would expect some profit margin. Thus, if the State Power Authority generates electricity as efficiently as private sector firms, the Authority would be willing to sell electricity for a lower price than private sector firms. This would not reduce the equilibrium price of electricity (that would be set by overall supply/demand balance), but it would ensure that the State Power Authority operates its peaker plants for a greater fraction of the time than private sector firms. For every MWh of electricity the State Power Authority generates, some private sector firms will generate one MWh less. With less opportunity to sell power, private sector firms will invest in fewer peaker units. In general, then, it can be expected that the investments by

---

[15]Press release issued by Governor Davis, 05/16/2001.
[16]Ibid.
[17]See: www.capowerauthority.ca.gov/projectlist/main.asp.

the State Power Authority would displace private sector investment on a one-for-one basis.

In addition, California Power Authority projects would be
exempt from franchise fees and property taxes, even though they
would impose as much cost on cities and counties as would equivalent private sector projects. This subsidy to California Power
Authority projects implies that even if the State Power Authority
generates electricity less efficiently than would private sector
firms, the Authority could still sell electricity for a lower price
than private sector firms, with cities and counties bearing financial losses. Thus there would be less pressure for the California
Power Authority to manage its projects efficiently, even though its
projects would displace more efficient private sector generators.

Now that it is becoming clear that California is likely to have
sufficient capacity before next summer, the California Power
Authority has been backing away from its intention to build new
gas-fired peaking plants, issuing a draft request for bids for
microturbine, solar photovoltaic, and fuel-cell projects. Its current investment plan emphasizes renewable forms of energy, such
as wind, biomass, and solar. Currently, there is very little private
sector investment in these emerging technologies, and thus there
is little private sector investment to be replaced. As such, the current investment plan of the California Power Authority can be
expected to increase the number of plants in California that use
renewable energy to generate electricity.

Thus, the creation of the State Power Authority and its initial
activities were moving California down the road toward public
power generation. However, that path seems to have changed
somewhat with the emphasis on harnessing renewable energy for
public power generation. Whether the Authority will revert to its
initial direction of investment or remain on its current path is not
obvious at this juncture, but will be very dependent on the policy
options encouraged by the next California governor and legislature.

6

POLICY OPTIONS

What Next?

Now that the crisis has passed, blight is threatened, and public attention has subsided, California and all the western states still face important policy issues relating to both the electricity system and the financial implications of the two crises. Some of the decisions may be driven at the federal level through the FERC. Others involve state regulatory or other policy decisions. However, most involve opportunities—or requirements—for cooperation at the state, regional, and federal levels. In the remainder of this chapter, these policy issues are discussed in terms of a series of prescriptive recommendations.

IMPROVE REGIONAL INTEGRATION

Integrated physically through an extensive grid of electricity-transmission capacity, the electricity systems of the eleven western states are highly dependent on one another. The electricity crisis made it clear that long-run supply and demand trends and short-run variations in those trends in any part of the region can have important ramifications throughout the entire region. Regulatory policies in one state can influence electricity markets throughout the region. Information about new capacity development in one state can influence decisions about whether new capacity development will be profitable in other states. Yet the regulatory policies, information flows, and market management rules of the eleven western states have not been well integrated. Thus, there are opportunities for mutual gain among the states through actions that increase regional integration of decision making and information flows.

PUBLICLY AVAILABLE SUPPLY/DEMAND INFORMATION

Many decisions made by either public sector or private sector entities depend largely on good information about regional electricity supply, demand, and prices, in addition to state-specific information. For example, decisions to invest in generation capacity made by either public sector or private sector entities depend on beliefs about future supply and demand balances and/or future wholesale electricity prices. If potential investors—in either the public sector or private sector—believe there will be surplus generating capacity for many years, they tend to avoid making new capacity investments, recognizing that it is unlikely that they will recover the costs of the investment, much less earn a profit. If they believe there will be shortages over the relevant future, potential investors are likely to choose to invest in new capacity. Thus, good information about historical and current conditions and reasonable projections of future conditions throughout the region can help to avoid boom and bust cycles in the electricity markets. Monitoring to detect exercise of market power can be more effective if based on information from throughout the interconnected region rather than information from simply one state. Evaluation of the relative impacts of energy conservation programs, retail price changes, and reductions in economic activity would be improved by high-quality state-specific and regional data, and such evaluations would be helpful in improving policy interventions in response to possible future electricity challenges or crises.

The nature and extent of publicly available electricity information vary radically among the various states. California, the largest state, provides a rich array of information through the CAISO and the California Energy Commission; much of these data is readily available on the Internet. The California Energy Commission periodically publishes projections of electricity supply and demand. The Northwest Regional Planning Council develops periodic estimates of electricity demand and supply for the northwestern states. However, some of the states provide relatively little information through readily available sources.

The Energy Information Administration, an agency of the U.S. Department of Energy, regularly publishes state-by-state electricity data on a comparable basis. However, these data are too limited to guide private sector and public sector decision making. The Western Governors' Association and the FERC have both published studies that examine the entire region, as have several researchers.[1] Yet these sources do not provide sufficient information for continued decision making.

Cooperative efforts among the states to coordinate either information development or information communication could provide mutual gains. Whether such cooperative efforts would best be organized through direct cooperation among state agencies, the Western Governors' Association, a regional transmission organization, the Western Systems Coordinating Council (WSCC), research institutes, or some federal agency is not clear. What does seem clear, however, is that better publicly available region-wide data could improve private sector and public sector decision making and provide the general public better opportunities to evaluate the policy decisions being made and communicated by public officials.

REGIONAL TRANSMISSION ORGANIZATION

In December 1999, the FERC issued Order 2000, calling for the formation of regional transmission organizations (RTOs) spanning large geographic regions and responsible for providing reliable, nondiscriminatory, and efficient transmission service for regional competitive wholesale electricity markets. In Order 2000, the FERC expressed its belief that the creation of such RTOs could reduce any remaining transmission-related impediments to competitive wholesale electric markets—in particular, any remaining engineering and economic inefficiencies in the operation and expansion of transmission grids and any opportunities for transmission owners to discriminate to favor their own (or affiliated companies') wholesale market purchases and sales.

In April 2001, the FERC accepted the proposal for the creation of RTO West, an RTO that would control all transmission within the eight western states (Washington, Oregon, Idaho, Montana, Nevada, Arizona, Utah, and parts of California not controlled by the CAISO). The FERC noted, "RTO West can serve as an anchor for the ultimate

---

[1]For example, Jolanka V. Fisher and Timothy P. Duane have published such a study.

formation of a West-wide RTO."[2] The new RTO West will serve as the independent system operator for its entire area and "will operate more than 90 percent of the high voltage transmission facilities from the U.S.-Canadian border to southern Nevada."[3]

An important issue for California is whether to combine the functions of the CAISO and RTO West into one RTO that could more efficiently control transmission services over almost all, if not all, of the interconnected western region of the United States. Such an integration could remove any problems of transmission coordination between California and the rest of the West. However, in principle, any remaining problems could be eliminated without creating a single organization but rather through sufficient coordination between the two existing organizations. In practice, however, as long as operational rules of the two entities remain different from one another, such coordination is likely to be imperfect. If California wholesale electricity purchases and sales return primarily to spot market transactions while bilateral contracts continue to characterize most of the transactions in the other areas, the structural differences in wholesale electricity markets may make integration of the two entities more difficult. In addition, the integration would take the power to appoint the members of the governing board out of the hands of the California governor and may therefore reduce the degree of political control over the transmission system.

Whether the CAISO should remain as its own RTO and simply cooperate with RTO West or the two entities should become one is not clear. However, the California governor and legislature need to address this issue in the near future.

IMPROVE CALIFORNIA ELECTRICITY MARKETS

REDESIGN WHOLESALE MARKETS FOR ELECTRICITY

In examining causes of the energy crisis in California, this book has focused most attention on issues of regional energy supply and demand, California price regulation of the retail and wholesale markets, risk management, and long-term problems stemming from decisions made by California's political leaders. Issues of California

---

[2]FERC press release April 25, 2001, re Docket Nos. RT01-35-000 and RT01-15-000.
[3]Ibid.

market design have been important but not central to understanding the fundamental causes of the crisis. No matter how perfectly the wholesale market had been designed in California, the fatal flaws in the regulation of the investor-owned utilities coupled with the perfect storm leading to supply/demand imbalances would have created a challenge, and the failure of the political leaders to address the problem meaningfully would have led to the crisis.

However, the wholesale markets in California remain severely flawed. They are unnecessarily complex and uncoordinated. Although the degree to which market power has been exercised, generating capacity has been strategically withheld, or market rules have been manipulated for financial gain, may not be fully resolved, it is clear that the currently flawed markets continue to create risks that costs will be increased and prices will be elevated above the appropriate levels. There is a great need to modify these markets to reduce the chance that another garden-variety storm will produce perfect-storm symptoms.

Restructuring Principles

Many authors have addressed means of restructuring the market. A clear and cogent statement of some of the principles is incorporated in Hogan's statement to Congress, from which the following passage is taken:

> *The experience is now sufficient for FERC to go beyond its previous deferential approach to markets created by stakeholders without regard to a set of detailed standard design principles. The good experience is concentrated in New York and in PJM, which serves the Mid-Atlantic region. These two markets now function under independent system operators (ISO) who employ a standardized spot market design for system coordination. . . . The common elements of this standard design include a bid-based, security-constrained, economic dispatch with locational prices, bilateral schedules, financial transmission rights, license-plate access charges and a broad scope for market-driven investment. Efficient pricing consistent with the ISO coordination functions then permits maximum commercial freedom without undermining reliability. The market monitoring and market power mitigation rules follow from the design. . . .*

These principles would include:

1. *The ISO must operate, and provide open access to, short-run markets to maintain short-run reliability and to provide a foundation for a workable market.*

2. *An ISO should be allowed to operate integrated short-run forward markets for energy and transmission.*

3. *An ISO should use locational marginal pricing to price and settle all purchases and sales of energy in its forward and real-time markets and to define comparable congestion (transmission usage) charges for bilateral transactions between locations.*

4. *An ISO should offer tradable point-to-point financial transmission rights that allow market participants to hedge the locational differences in energy prices.*

5. *An ISO should simultaneously optimize its ancillary service markets and energy markets.*

6. *The ISO should collaborate in rapidly expanding the capability to include demand side response for energy and ancillary services.*[4]

The CAISO's Wholesale Market Redesign Efforts

The CAISO has recently taken policy leadership by developing proposals for fundamental improvements in the wholesale market design through its "Market Design 2002" project. A team within the CAISO has been assigned the responsibility of developing a program of market changes that would address the most fundamental of the wholesale market problems. On January 8, 2002, the CAISO issued a preliminary draft of its proposed market changes.[5] Although the draft is still explicitly a "work in progress," it proposes substantial changes to repair some of the most troublesome aspects of the current wholesale markets in California and represents an excellent step

---

[4]"Statement of Professor William W. Hogan before the Subcommittee on Energy Policy, Natural Resources and Regulatory Affairs, United States House of Representatives" (August 2, 2001).

[5]California Independent System Operator, "Market Design 2002 Project: Preliminary Draft Comprehensive Design Proposal" (January 8, 2002). http://www.caiso.com/docs/09003a6080/13/58/09003a6080135879.PDF.

toward adopting restructuring principles consistent with those outlined above.

Central elements proposed by the CAISO include the following:[6]

- *Available Capacity (ACAP) Obligation on Load-Serving Entities*

- *Day-Ahead Congestion Management*

- *Firm Transmission Rights (FTRs)*

- *Forward Spot Energy Market*

- *Residual Day-Ahead Unit Commitment*

- *Real-Time Economic Dispatch Using Full Network Model*

- *Real-Time Bid Mitigation for Local Reliability Needs*

- *Damage Control Price Cap on CAISO Markets*

Most of these proposed elements represent much-needed and
appropriate reforms to the well-identified market flaws. Under
the *day-ahead congestion management* proposal, the CAISO
would start using a "fully accurate model of the CAISO grid for
the purpose of adjusting generation and load schedules to mitigate transmission overloads and ensure local reliability, instead of
today's simplified three-zone model." This change will allow the
CAISO to move toward nodal pricing and control, which recognize that economic conditions at various nodes of the grid may
vary significantly from one another even within a given geographic zone.

Firm transmission rights are financial instruments that would
allow market participants the right to ensure their electricity
would be transmitted at a particular time between particular generator locations and load locations. These would allow participants to hedge risks of possible high congestion charges.

The proposal for a *forward spot energy market* would replace
the now-defunct PX with an organized short-term futures market
for electricity. However, rather than a market run totally separate
from the CAISO, the new forward spot energy market could and
should be integrated into the CAISO operations (although the

---

[6]Each of the following elements is a direct quote from "Market Design
2002 Project: Preliminary Draft Comprehensive Design Proposal." Quotations
in the paragraphs that follow are from this document as well.

CAISO believes the market could be operated by another entity). As the CAISO team has recognized, under the proposed congestion management changes, there will be spot market transactions among electricity market participants; creation of a formal forward spot market would improve the efficiency of these trades.

The proposal for *residual day-ahead unit commitment* would allow the CAISO to assess whether the day-ahead schedules include enough resources to meet the next day's demands. If needed, the CAISO could make commitments to pay electricity-generating resources that have long start-up times for both the times they are generating and the costs they incur for start-up and for remaining in operation even when the electricity may not be needed.

Under the proposal for *real-time economic dispatch using full network model*, "every 10 minutes during each operating hour the CAISO would run a 'security-constrained economic dispatch' program to determine which resources to dispatch at what operating levels to meet real-time needs." Such an approach would allow the CAISO to use cost-minimizing, modern optimization models, taking into account the relevant constraints facing the system ("transmission constraints, local reliability needs, and generator operating constraints, as well as system imbalance energy needs"). This proposal would be consistent with the move toward nodal real-time pricing in the wholesale market. In addition, it would eliminate the requirement for scheduling coordinators to submit balanced loads. The overall optimization program would perform the balancing function and thus individually balanced loads would not be important.

Finally, the proposal for *real-time bid mitigation for local-reliability needs* would allow the CAISO to mitigate locational market power that could be exercised by generators that are the only units operating at a constrained location on the grid.

Although the detailed implementations of these plans undoubtedly have not yet been completed and, once completed, will be subject to much debate, these proposed changes together represent a very strong and useful movement toward improving the design of California wholesale markets.

Two of the proposals, however, may not be appropriate in their current form, or at least require significantly more design. The proposal for an *available capacity (ACAP) obligation on load-serving entities* would place on the utilities (and other load-serving entities) the responsibility "to procure adequate capacity to meet their expected peak monthly loads plus reserve requirements," which would move the California wholesale markets sharply away from spot markets and is likely to lead utilities to enter into a mix of long-, medium-, and short-term contracts to purchase electricity. This allocation of responsibility would be a very positive step, as would the shift away from spot markets. However, it is not yet clear whether the CAISO-proposed mechanisms for accomplishing this end would be workable. Under this proposal, each load-serving entity would be required to have contractually available electricity generation capacity equal to "a fixed margin above the next month's forecast peak load (for example, in the area of $(1.15)\times$ forecast monthly peak load)," which could be met "by a combination of own generation, firm energy contracts, . . . capacity contracts, and physical demand management."

Before the beginning of each month, each load-serving entity would be required to demonstrate to the CAISO that it has procured adequate capacity for the following month. Those entities that had shortfalls would be assessed a substantial penalty.

Whether such a plan will improve the market operations is unclear. It would increase the demand for electricity contractual commitments and, at least in the short run, would increase the wholesale price of electricity. The CAISO would be required to evaluate the demand forecasts of each utility and substitute its own forecasts for the utility forecasts if they differ from one another. The proposed incentive structure is likely to lead to more unused generating capacity in times of short supply than would be desirable. The plan might encourage somewhat more capacity development than would otherwise be the case and might reduce the degree of price volatility. In short, though this plan has many desirable characteristics, more design and analysis is still required.

Finally, the proposal for a *damage control price cap on CAISO markets* has been designed to "limit the adverse cost impacts of an unusually severe price spike." However, this proposal cannot be evaluated until the level of that price cap, the conditions under which it is applied, and the structure of prices under the cap are specified. Whether price caps, bid caps, or no controls at all are more appropriate to deal with severe price spikes has not been settled.

The CAISO has clearly communicated its intention to use the preliminary draft as a starting point in the redesign process, not as the ending point. As such, the CAISO is now taking a very appropriate and much-needed leadership position in working to improve the California wholesale electricity markets.

ENSURE COMPETITION IN WHOLESALE MARKETS

The California experience suggests that particular attention must be paid to ensuring that there is true competition and only a minimum chance for the exercise of market power. Because there are so many constraints on the electricity system—based on the nonstorable nature of electricity, the locational structure of electricity generation and use, and limitations associated with transmission capacity—enforcement of antitrust laws and other procompetitive laws is important. However, in doing so, the empirical rules that have been developed for other industries may be difficult to apply directly.[7]

Public visibility of actions taken by the various participants in the system—generators, local distribution companies, traders, and governmental agencies—is also crucial for appropriate policy making and enforcement of market rules. Thus, reliable, publicly available data would allow analysts and members of the public to see more clearly the actual workings of the system. Appropriate data include both the regional supply and demand data described above plus more detailed data (possibly made available only after several months) about actions by individual market participants.

Finally, given the possibility of complex bidding structures, it is important that the system be designed to reduce the possibility that firms with relatively small market share can exercise market power. Some of the market redesign issues discussed above can be important for this goal.

PROMOTE RETAIL COMPETITION BY RESTORING DIRECT ACCESS

As discussed above, retail competition for serving small residential customers may be problematic. However, retail competition for serving large industrial loads is feasible and would have several important benefits. If industrial customers can negotiate contracts with electricity generators, absent requirement for CPUC intervention, those contracts can provide appropriate risk-sharing mechanisms

---

[7]For example, given the almost vertical demand functions and the supply functions (when capacity is low), empirical rules based on conventional measures of market concentration are likely to understate the opportunities for exercise of market power.

that are mutually beneficial to the generator and the user of the electricity. For example, such contracts could implement a real-time pricing system, with real-time prices varying along with some objective measure of spot wholesale prices. The real-time pricing system could be implemented as a two-part system, so that marginal prices can vary along with wholesale prices while the average payment for the electricity varies only by a much smaller amount.

Direct access could allow those companies that need a much higher degree of supply reliability and are willing to pay for it to be able to acquire such reliable electricity supplies. Direct access could also promote the development and installation of micro turbines or fuel cells that are located very close to the point of electricity use.[8]

Finally, direct access for large industrial customers could be the starting point where we begin to experiment with the possibility of more complete retail competition.

As discussed above, however, current law precludes direct access for all customers. The California Legislature recognizes that direct access would conflict with the intention of the State to pay for the sunk costs it has incurred through increased future electricity prices.

There are viable alternatives for recovering the sunk costs that do not require elimination of direct access. For example, the State could impose a tax on electricity sales, either for sales in service areas of the investor-owned utilities or throughout the state. Alternatively, the CPUC could adopt an exit charge, under which any industrial customer choosing to bypass utilities would be obligated to pay into a fund designed to cover the State's sunk costs.

An even better alternative would be to recognize the nature of the problem—the State of California agreed to a large number of unwise financial obligations, which were the responsibility of the governor and the legislature as representatives of the California citizens. The State could keep these mistakes as financial obligations through the State Treasury. The State of California would still pay the financial burden of the errors made by the governor and the legislature, but the payment, over many years, would remain strictly a financial

---

[8]It is possible, however, that the *lack* of direct access could encourage distributed generation located on the facilities of the customer wishing to purchase electricity, if that customer were precluded from the opportunity of directly negotiating an appropriate contract for electricity generated off of its premises.

problem rather than the cause of restrictions on the freedom of California's economy to operate effectively.

Thus, it is both desirable and possible to restore direct access at least for large electricity customers. The failure to do so is a step backwards, toward direct governmental controls rather than market operations.

IMPROVE PRICING IN RETAIL MARKETS

Markets for electricity, like markets for other commodities, can allow people the freedom to choose the goods and services they wish to consume while at the same time ensuring that the quantities they purchase are economically efficient. Markets can encourage consumers to buy goods and services whenever those products are more valuable to the consumer than their cost and can discourage purchases whenever the value to the consumer is less than the cost. However, markets can function in such an efficient and free manner only if prices correspond to costs, in particular to marginal costs.

One of the fundamental problems during the challenge period and the electricity crisis was that retail electricity prices were not allowed to follow marginal costs even approximately. Retail prices were artificially constrained to well below marginal costs of electricity production and distribution during the entire challenge and crisis periods. When retail prices are kept well below cost, consumers are not naturally encouraged by market forces to reduce their use of electricity. The resultant overuse of electricity provides motivations for governmental organizations to impose restrictions on personal freedom to choose how much electricity to use. Now retail prices charged by the investor-owned utilities remain well above marginal costs and promise to remain at elevated levels for decades to come. When retail prices are kept well above cost, consumers find ways of using less electricity than would be optimal from their own perspectives and incur excessively large costs for reducing their use of that electricity. Thus, both underpricing of electricity during the challenge period and crisis and overpricing of retail electricity afterwards cause economic inefficiencies.

The functioning of retail electricity markets could be significantly improved if retail prices were allowed to track costs of providing that electricity to customers. Tracking of costs could be improved in two dimensions. First, during times of particularly high wholesale prices, average retail prices should be elevated to correspond to the high average wholesale prices and during times of low wholesale prices, average retail prices should decline: the retail price level should on average correspond to costs. Second, during the course of the day, as wholesale prices fluctuate between high levels during peak times and low levels at off-peak times, retail prices should follow this daily variation in wholesale costs.

The problems of failing to allow the retail prices to increase during times of exceptionally high wholesale prices have been extensively discussed in previous chapters of this book. The discussion need not be repeated here. However, the problem of failing to allow retail price variations during the course of the day to correspond to cost variations has not been adequately discussed and will be the subject of what follows.

Allow Real-Time Retail Pricing

Wholesale electricity prices vary sharply over the course of a day, week, or month, with high prices during times of high demand and low prices during times of low demand. Figure 6.1 illustrates this price variation using data on wholesale prices and transactions volume on the California PX during July 1999, a normal period. The volume, shown by red lines, has a scale from 0 to 40,000 MW. Wholesale price, shown by blue lines, has a scale from $0 to $160/MWh.

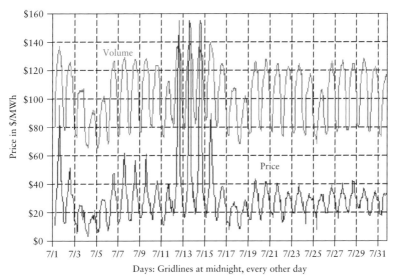

FIGURE 6.1:   PX Price and Volume during the Course
of a Month: July 1999

SOURCE: California Energy Commission

Figure 6.1 shows that during the course of the month, wholesale price varied from a low of $2/MWh to a high of $155/MWh, roughly an eighty-fold variation. During the days with least variation, the high price was roughly twice the lowest price and during days of medium price variation, the high price could be six times as high as the lowest price.

Figure 6.1 also shows that prices were high during periods of high volume, when demand reductions would be appropriate, and prices were low during periods of low volume, when there is no particular need for demand reductions. If consumers could be motivated to shift the timing of their electricity use away from the peak times toward off-peak times, wholesale price increases during peak periods could be substantially alleviated, inducing only small increases in the off-peak prices.

Even in the face of these large normal variations in wholesale prices, and thus in costs of acquiring electricity, regulated retail prices for all but the largest customers remained constant. For example, for PG&E, the retail price of electricity during this time was $125/MWh, including $60/MWh for delivery services and $65/MWh for electricity. Thus, for most times during that interval the retail price of electricity itself exceeded the marginal cost of electricity, but for some times the price was much lower than marginal cost.

Efficiency in the use of electricity could be significantly improved if customers faced retail prices that varied on a real-time basis, corresponding to marginal cost variations. Such a time-varying system is generally referred to as "real-time pricing." In principle, real-time pricing would promote economic efficiency since it could be designed to ensure that retail prices closely tracked marginal costs of electricity on an hour-by-hour basis or more frequently.

In practice, however, installing meters, designing and operating the communications systems, and managing the billing system would be costly, even though the meters are currently being installed for the largest customers. For the largest customers and those most able to change their electricity purchases in response to time-varying prices, the costs of metering will be smaller than the economic gains from real-time pricing and, on net, real-time pricing would lead to net economic benefits. For the smallest customers and those least able to adjust electricity purchases in response to changing prices, the costs of metering would exceed the economic gains from real-time pricing, which, on net, would not be attractive. Thus, although real-time pricing is an attractive option for many electricity users, it is not economically attractive for all.

Real-time pricing is likely to grow as a contractual structure for the larger users if retail competition, particularly direct access, is restored. Under such a competitive system, electricity users who would, on net, benefit from real-time pricing would be free to choose such a pricing arrangement, and those who would not benefit would be free to keep prices that remain constant within a given day. In addition, for those under CPUC tariffs, real-time pricing should be made broadly available.

Under a pure system of real-time pricing, the price of all electricity purchased by large customers would vary on an hourly basis with the wholesale market price. Such a system is referred to as a "one-part real-time pricing" system. The difficulty of a one-part real-time pricing system is that the total expenditure for electricity by large electricity users could vary radically from week to week or month to month. If an electricity user wishes to avoid large fluctuations in electricity purchase costs, one-part real-time pricing may be unattractive.

An alternative, especially for large industrial customers, is a "two-part real-time pricing system," under which a contractually determined base-load quantity of electricity purchased by the large user is made available at some more stable price. For increases or decreases in the quantity of electricity used around that level, the price for incremental increases or decreases in use of electricity would be set equal to the real-time price. Under such a two-part system, the large customer bears less risk of price variations but still faces incentives to reduce demand during high-price times, since the marginal retail price of electricity would move with the wholesale price. Two-part real-time pricing would allow a balance between the stability of average expenditures and the variability of marginal prices responding to changing conditions.

The disadvantage of a two-part real-time pricing system, however, is that if the base-load quantity is set at a price lower than expected for the future, each user will fight to have a large base-load quantity. The allocation of the baseline in that case becomes a difficult political process.

Even this problem can be solved if the price of the base load is set equal to or slightly above the expected price of the electricity in the future. In that case, the customer can freely choose the base-load quantity for the future and sign a binding contract to that effect.[9] However, the problem cannot readily be solved if the base load is made available at a subsidized price, as was the case during the electricity crisis. Thus, although real-time pricing would have been useful during the challenge period and the crisis, those times would have been the most difficult to introduce such a system. Thus, it perhaps should not have been a surprise that, although the California Legislature voted for $35 million to install real-time meters, a real-time pricing system has not yet been approved and implemented within the state.

IMPROVE RISK MANAGEMENT

Risk management for the electricity system involves identification and appropriate reduction of both the physical and the financial risks and involves improving the response of the system to adverse events. Physical risks are discussed first. A subsequent section addresses financial risk protection.

REDUCE INFRASTRUCTURE-RELATED RISKS

Improve Fuel Supply Infrastructure

In California, the infrastructure to transport natural gas both into the state and within the state has been a bottleneck causing natural gas prices to soar; this infrastructure should be expanded. With these pipelines at or near capacity, whenever there is a significant increase in the use of natural gas to run generating plants, we can expect sharp increases in natural gas price, with a consequent increase in wholesale costs of electricity.

High prices for infrastructure services provide market signals that greater amounts of that infrastructure would be economically efficient and profitable for investors. The price for natural gas transportation services within California can be measured by the difference between the delivered natural gas price and the price at the California border, a difference that rose to $50/mcf. Although this price persisted for only a short time, transportation services prices exceeding $5/mcf persisted for months, which strongly suggested the need for additional pipeline capacity.

---

[9]Pricing of mobile telephone service is organized that way. The buyer decides how may "free" minutes to have available each month and pays a fixed cost for the fixed availability of these free minutes. Additional minutes, purchased as spot transactions, are at a much higher rate.

Now that the crisis is over and the very inefficient gas-fired generating plants are not being used, natural gas pipeline capacity currently appears sufficient. However, the new gas-fired electricity-generating plants soon coming on-line will again increase the use of natural gas and will thus require an increase in natural gas pipeline capacity. In order to minimize the risk of similar natural gas price spikes, California's natural gas pipeline system needs expansion. The California Public Utilities Commission needs to support, and even encourage, future proposals for pipeline expansion.

Improve Transmission Infrastructure

The infrastructure for electricity transmission is currently too limited at a few important bottlenecks on the grid. Significant increases in the electricity price in Northern California, relative to the Southern California price, were associated with the inability to move adequate quantities of electricity from Southern California to Northern California when needed, along Path 15. An expansion of the transmission capacity between Northern and Southern California would be a significant infrastructure improvement, but a very costly investment.

In October 2001, Secretary of Energy Spencer Abraham announced that a power transmission line would be built to relieve congestion along Path 15. Estimated to cost about $300 million, the line will be built by a consortium of private companies and public agencies.

In addition, the crisis made it painfully clear that the western United States is electrically virtually isolated from the rest of the country. The West had very high spot wholesale electricity prices, whereas prices to the east of the Rockies remained much lower. The construction of new tie lines connecting the western part of the United States with the rest of the nation would allow a sharing in either direction as needed and would reduce the likelihood of regional electricity shortages. On the other hand, transmission facilities are expensive. Costs of such investments would likely dwarf the $300 million expected for the Path 15 upgrades. In addition, investment in new gas-fired electricity generators is relatively cheap. Whether investment in such new transmission capacity would be economical, relative to the alternative of new generation capacity, remains to be seen, but an assessment of that option is needed.

Make Energy Infrastructure More Secure from Terrorism
The infrastructure serving California's electricity system, including natural gas pipelines and electricity transmission systems, is vulnerable to terrorist attacks. Successful attacks have the potential of creating another electricity crisis, although probably of shorter duration than the 2000–2001 events.

The natural gas pipelines that serve California cover long distances, in many places above ground. The above-ground sections could be vulnerable to terrorist attack, although the below-ground sections are likely to be difficult to attack. Successful attacks could reduce California's ability to generate electricity using natural gas, the energy source for 50 percent of California's electricity generation. Pipelines coming into California each have the capacity to supply on average less than 10 percent of California's electricity generation. Unless the system is near full capacity, only successful attacks on multiple pipelines can create such a crisis. Moreover, a decrease in natural gas availability would cause the least efficient gas-fired generating units to be taken off-line, not the most efficient. Thus, although California is vulnerable through the natural gas pipeline system, the potential for damage is smaller than that for the electricity transmission system.

Electricity transmission lines remain very vulnerable to terrorist attacks, although successful attacks on most lines themselves could be repaired relatively quickly. In addition, local transmission grids are designed to operate effectively if one transmission line is out of operation. However, there are several transmission lines essential to system operation. Given the large fraction of electricity moved along Path 15, between Northern and Southern California, and the large fraction moved on the two interties from the Pacific Northwest, successful terrorist attacks at these parts of the grid could precipitate a short-term physical shortage of electricity.

Even more damaging than attacks on transmission lines would be attacks on substations, which cannot be repaired quickly because the large transformers and the switching equipment typically cannot be made available quickly.

How one can best protect this vulnerable infrastructure is not clear; however, the solution should involve some combination of protection, redundancy of infrastructure, and equipment stockpiles allowing rapid facility repair. Each of these strategies adds costs to the electricity system.

IMPROVE SYSTEM RESPONSE TO ADVERSE EVENTS

One approach to improving risk management involves reducing the likelihood that adverse events, such as supply shortages, will occur. That approach, discussed in the previous section, may lead to a focus on reducing the infrastructure-related risks. There is another, complementary approach: reducing the harm that results from adverse events, should they occur.

Typically, harm can be reduced by making the system more flexible and more responsive to changing economic conditions. The responsiveness then allows, even encourages, individual consumers and producers to adjust in ways that reduce the harm they face and, in so doing, reduce the harm to the entire system. Generically, such approaches involve increasing the electricity demand responsiveness and electricity supply responsiveness to changing conditions.

Increase Electricity Demand Responsiveness

As has been discussed in previous chapters, one of the fundamental causes of price volatility in the wholesale electricity markets was the lack of responsiveness of electricity demand to wholesale prices. Figures 3.14 and 3.15 illustrated that if the demand for electricity were more responsive to wholesale price changes, the wholesale price changes caused by variability in supply and demand would be greatly reduced. Thus, price-spike-related economic damages would be reduced if electricity demand were more responsive to wholesale price increases.

A significant factor ending the electricity crisis has been the reduction in use of electricity. Some of the underlying demand reductions are transient and some are permanent. The permanent reductions in demand, although beneficial, will not provide the "shock absorbers" needed to increase the demand responsiveness of the system. Market participants and governmental agencies will take into account these permanent demand reductions as they evaluate or forecast future electricity demand. Such expectations of future electricity demand strongly influence new generation capacity.[10] Therefore, permanent

---

[10]The influence may be direct in that firms estimate the future generating capacity needed to satisfy future demand. Or it may be indirect in that firms evaluate the supply/demand balance and assess the likely future market prices of electricity. Through either route, expectations of future demand influence capacity investment decisions.

demand reductions will ultimately lead to equivalent reductions in electricity-generation capacity, just compensating for the demand reductions. Therefore, once all adjustments are completed, permanent reductions in electricity demand will not enhance the ability of the state to respond to future price volatility.[11]

Policies that lead to greater demand reductions that occur quickly in response to wholesale price increases could significantly reduce future wholesale price spikes. Implementing such policies in California would be good, although implementing them throughout the West would be much better.

One strategy would be to make retail prices quantitatively more responsive and more quickly responsive to wholesale prices, counting on consumers to reduce electricity purchases in their own interest when retail electricity prices increase. This strategy could involve many different approaches.

At the most basic level, this strategy would require electricity regulators to abolish fixed-price retail price controls. California's dogged maintenance of retail price controls in the face of sky-rocketing wholesale prices was the single most harmful California policy failure. If Governor Davis and/or the CPUC had allowed retail rates to increase appropriately during the challenge period, demand would have dropped enough to allow California to avoid the crisis.[12]

Even without such retail price controls, most utilities, municipal or investor owned, charge retail rates to approximate the cost of delivery services plus the average cost of acquiring electricity. Moreover, most utilities acquire the vast majority of their electricity

---

[11]One should remember that California has a long tradition of successful policies designed to reduce electricity demand. In 1999, California per capita residential electricity use was 37 percent below the national average. This history of relatively low electricity intensity did not save California from the crisis.

[12]One might reasonably conclude that, after observing the great harm caused by California's maintenance of retail price controls into the crisis, no state would ever make such a fundamental mistake in the future. But price controls have been a resort of political leaders in the United States before and they are likely to be again. And Governor Davis seemed to understand fully the great damages his policy was causing. Moreover, because the economic factors underlying California's restructuring are common across many electricity systems, the reasons underlying California's initial imposition of price controls may be relevant elsewhere. However, even if retail price controls are imposed during times of relatively stable wholesale prices, California's plight should make it clear that such controls must be eliminated during times of sharply rising wholesale prices.

through long-term fixed-price contracts or their own generation (incurring costs not closely related to the wholesale price). Thus, the average acquisition cost of electricity increases by far less than does the spot wholesale price.[13] Therefore, under average cost pricing, retail prices increase by only a small fraction of the increase in spot wholesale prices. The magnitude of the resultant retail price increase is much smaller than the magnitude of the spot wholesale price increase.

In addition, regulated retail electricity prices generally respond only slowly to wholesale price increases. Typically, regulators calculate average cost in a backward-looking manner, based on many months of historical experience. Regulator agencies seldom, if ever, calculate the average of current acquisition costs. Therefore, calculated average costs respond only slowly to changes in spot wholesale prices. As a result, the retail price increase is often delayed for many months, and the speed of its increase is much slower than that of the spot wholesale price increase.

Regulatory agencies could take steps to make the speed and magnitude of retail price increases correspond more closely to the speed and magnitude of changes in the spot wholesale market by quickly adding surcharges onto the standard retail rates in times of rapid wholesale price increases. These surcharges can be larger than the increase in average acquisition cost and yet may be smaller than the increase in the spot wholesale price. Such surcharges would increase the net revenues of the utility during wholesale price spikes. Regulators could require the utility to accumulate these excess revenues in a special account that could be drawn on during times of sharp reductions in spot wholesale prices.[14] In this way, state agencies could still regulate utilities so that prices *averaged over time* corresponded to average costs while varying retail prices by more than the variation in average acquisition cost.

In addition, retail pricing could include two-part tariffs, either with or without real-time pricing, allowing the marginal retail

---

[13]As an example, if a utility acquires 90 percent of its electricity on long-term fixed-price contracts and 10 percent on the spot market, then a $100/MWh increase in the spot wholesale price would lead to a $10/MWh increase in the average wholesale price.

[14]This statement assumes that regulators allow retail prices to fall by more than the decrease in average acquisition cost during times of sharp drops in spot wholesale prices.

prices—that is, the prices for increases or decreases in the quantity of electricity purchased—to increase or decrease by as much as wholesale spot prices while keeping the average retail price equal to average acquisition costs. Such a system—if one could transcend the problem of customers fighting to increase their low-priced base quantity—would enhance the efficiency of retail markets and greatly increase the responsiveness of demand to wholesale market conditions.

A further step would be for utilities to institute real-time pricing broadly, as discussed in a previous section. Real-time pricing, with variations in marginal prices corresponding to wholesale price variations, would give the fastest, most complete incentives for demand to respond to wholesale price movements.

The farther utilities move along this sequence, the more responsive retail demand will be to wholesale prices. The more responsive retail demand is to wholesale prices, the less volatile the wholesale price will be. However, the farther utilities move along this sequence, the more volatile the retail prices will be and the greater the political impetus to reestablish retail price controls will be.

Retail price variations are not the only means of increasing energy demand responsiveness. Utilities could introduce a system of demand-side bidding, in which large users of electricity could agree to reduce their use of electricity while being compensated financially for those reductions. Utilities could establish a formal auction to allow such demand-side bidding to proceed efficiently, which the CAISO's "Market Design 2002" project envisions.

In addition, utilities could increase the currently existing programs of direct control by the utilities of some loads—for example, air-conditioning loads. Many uses could be set under computer control and utilities could exercise that control in times of tight electricity markets. The equipment for that communication and control is available now. The utility and the customer would enter a contractual relationship that allows the utility to cycle the appliances, or to reduce the use of those appliances during hours of the day in which prices of electricity are particularly high. The utilities would need to negotiate ahead of time the contractual agreements to allow such widespread load-shedding in times of need. Under such a system, the customer would not pay large increases in electricity price but would still be motivated to reduce demand when needed.

Increase Supply Responsiveness

The most fundamental long-term solutions to the California electricity crisis were initiated four years ago with the boom in construction of new electricity-generating facilities. Including the plants that were completed this summer, 11,000 MW of new generating capacity is under construction. Of this total, about 6,000 MW can be expected to come on-line within the next year or is already generating electricity. Another 11,000 MW of new generating capacity is under review by the California Energy Commission.

A fundamental requirement for avoiding perfect-storm problems is adequate electricity-generating capacity. However, "adequate" must be defined in a regional context, not simply a California-specific context, since the regional markets are so tightly interconnected. Thus, there need to be incentives for new generation capacity throughout the region, including in California, where the issue is how not to discourage development of generation capacity. In the other states, the issue is how to encourage the appropriate amount of new construction.

Since the restructuring legislation of 1996, which included a significant deregulation of electricity generation, there has been a boom in construction of new generating plants in California. Nevertheless, it is important not to get in the way of this process. Threats to take over these plants by eminent domain or a return to the old regulated system, as well as a long-term system of wholesale electricity price control, could each dampen enthusiasm for new construction. These threats create large uncertainties for those considering investing in new electricity-generating facilities. Similarly, actions by the State Power Authority to use State funds to compete with private sector investment would be contrary to the goal of allowing the private sector to develop new generation capacity. State-created investment uncertainty is neither in the long-run interests of the citizens of California nor in the interests of investors in the electricity system.

Given the long lead-time from decisions to invest in new generating units until the time the new generation is on-line, increasing supply responsiveness must account for the responsiveness of investment decisions to forecasts of future market needs. However, future supply and demand conditions in electricity markets are not perfectly predictable. Hydroelectric generating capacity is very dependent on the amount of rainfall. Increased costs of natural gas can make some generating facilities uneconomical and thereby reduce supply. Construction of new generating facilities can be delayed for a host of different reasons. Prediction of the growth in electricity demand is at best an imperfect art. Air-conditioning loads are very dependent on weather, so consumption of electricity can vary greatly on a daily basis. And for states like California, which count on other states to supply a significant amount of electricity demand, supply and demand conditions in those other states may also be unpredictable. For that reason, improvements in the quality of prospective market information, including the breadth and quality of current and historical regional electricity market data, could be important contributors to the goal of increasing electricity supply responsiveness.

In addition, financial incentives could encourage utilities or generators to ensure that there will be reserve capacity in the system, which would increase the short-run supply responsiveness and thus help reduce the damages associated with adverse supply and demand conditions. One approach would be the creation of capacity markets. However, capacity markets are very difficult to develop and manage and thus may not be a viable means of increasing capacity to increase the short-run supply responsiveness. Another approach might be the implementation of something like the "available capacity obligation on load-serving entities" currently being proposed by the CAISO.

DISTRIBUTE FINANCIAL RISKS APPROPRIATELY

California's electricity crisis made it clear that the financial risks associated with rapid increases of wholesale prices were felt very unevenly by the various utilities in the West. Those that had secured all or almost all of their electricity needs through long-term fixed-price contracts faced little or no financial risk. On the other hand, those, such as California's investor-owned utilities, that were required to purchase more than one half of their electricity on the volatile spot markets faced tremendous financial risks. In addition, those utilities that could respond by increasing retail electricity prices were able to avoid risks by passing them on to their customers, whereas those utilities whose retail rates remained fixed bore all risks of wholesale price increases themselves.

Each utility and its customers will typically wish to reduce the risk of price spikes associated with short supplies of electricity. One method of any single utility reducing its risk and those of its customers would be to enter long-term contracts to purchase electricity at fixed prices. If a utility covered all of its electricity needs this way, variations in spot wholesale prices would have no necessary financial consequences. If the utility's retail rates were based on its average acquisition price of electricity, then its customers would also not be subject to financial consequences of wholesale price increases. In this way, the utility and its customers could avoid all risk of wholesale price variations.

However, long-term fixed-price contracts may reduce the risk facing the utility holding the contracts while increasing the risk to utilities (and their customers) buying electricity at spot market prices. In some sense, long-term contracts do not reduce the overall market risk but simply transfer that risk to other market participants. This occurs because utilities typically sell electricity to their customers at prices based on the average acquisition price of that electricity. If, when wholesale prices increase, the average acquisition price does not change, utilities typically keep retail electricity prices constant. Constant retail prices imply that the electricity users have no incentives to reduce their demands as wholesale prices increase. Therefore, long-term contracts tend to substantially reduce the electricity demand responsiveness and imply that larger wholesale price increases are needed to balance supply and demand after a given reduction in electricity supply or increase in demand.

The role of contracts in distributing the financial risk, rather than reducing the overall risk, can be illustrated by a group of five identical utilities each purchasing 10,000 MW of electricity. Under one assumption, none use any long-term contracts, compared to another assumption that each covers 80 percent of its initial purchases using long-term contracts. Assume that in either case, some event reduces the electricity supply by 5,000 MW. Then, each firm, being identical to every other firm, would ultimately reduce its consumption by 1,000 MW.

Assume now that every $2/MWh rise in the retail price of electricity reduced the demand for electricity for a given firm by 100 MW. Therefore, the retail price of electricity would need to increase by $20/MWh in order to motivate the 1,000 MW demand reductions for each firm. This required retail price increase would be $20/MWh, no matter whether no utilities or all utilities used long-term contracts.

If no firms had any long-term contracts and all priced retail electricity at the average wholesale cost, then in response to the 5,000 MW reduction of supply, the wholesale price would increase by \$20/MWh, which would apply to all 9,000 MW that each utility was still purchasing. Thus the cost increase for the 9,000 MW ultimately purchased would be \$180,000 per hour of purchases (9,000 MW × \$20/MWh).

If each firm had long-term contracts covering 80 percent of its initial electricity needs and all priced retail electricity at the average wholesale cost, then in response to the 5,000 MW reduction of supply, the wholesale price would now increase by \$180/MWh, not \$20/MWh. The \$180/MWh increase in price would apply to the 1,000 MW the utility would continue to purchase on the spot market; there would be no price increase for the other 8,000 MW under long-term contract. A \$180/MWh increase in price applied to one-ninth of the purchases would increase the average wholesale price and the average retail price by \$20/MWh. Thus the cost increase for the 1,000 MW ultimately purchased on the spot market would be \$180,000 per hour of purchases (1,000 MW × \$180/MWh), identical to the increase that would occur if no firms had long-term contracts. A similar equality would hold for increases in electricity supply leading to reductions in wholesale electricity price.

Thus, although each individual utility could use long-term contracts to protect itself from the risks of wholesale price increases stemming from supply reductions, it could do so only if the other utilities continued to purchase on the spot markets. If all utilities tried to protect themselves using long-term contracts, none ultimately would be any more protected than when all electricity was being purchased on the spot markets. Long-term contracts simply protect those utilities that have entered long-term purchase contracts and transfer the risks to the other utilities.

Equal distribution of the financial risk among utilities, therefore, requires that each utility be given an equal opportunity to protect itself with long-term contracts.[15] If most utilities are so

---

[15]A numerical example illustrates different firms having different contractual protection. Assume three utilities had long-term contracts for 80 percent of initial electricity needs and two had no contracts. In response to the 5,000 MW reduction of supply, wholesale price would increase by \$42.86/MWh. The \$42.86/MWh price increase would apply to 1,000 MW of 9,000 MW for utilities with contracts, increase average price by \$4.76/MWh, and reduce demand by 238 MW for each of these three utilities, for a total reduction of 714 MW. The \$42.86/MWh increase in price applied to all purchases of the other two utilities would increase average price by \$42.86/MWh and reduce demand by 2,143 MW for customers of these two utilities, for a total reduction of 4,286 MW.

protected but some are required to purchase the majority of their electricity on spot markets, those purchasing on spot markets will bear a disproportionate share of the risk. A similar phenomenon would occur if utilities were not allowed to increase retail prices when wholesale prices increased, as was the case in California.

To keep the example simple, assume that public utility commissions, to protect consumers, allowed only 10 percent of the wholesale price increase to be passed on to retail customers and that utilities purchased all electricity on the spot market, as in the first case. Then, in response to the 5,000 MW supply reduction, wholesale prices would increase by $200/MWh, not $20/MWh. Since 10 percent of this $200/MWh increase in wholesale price would be passed through to consumers, consumers would face an increase in retail price of $20/MWh, just enough to motivate the requisite demand reduction. Consumers, although protected by the Public Utility Commission, would face exactly as much of a price increase as they would with no such protection. However, now the utility would lose $180/MWh for each of the 9,000 MWh it purchased, for total losses of $1,620,000 per hour of purchases.[16]

The examples illustrate the fundamental point. Every restriction that keeps wholesale price increases from translating to retail prices will result in greater increases in the wholesale prices, since each such restriction reduces the electricity demand responsiveness. If some utilities are allowed to enter long-term contracts while others are denied that opportunity, the latter group will face increased financial risk just compensating for the reduced financial risk of the former group. If wholesale price increases are only partially passed through to retail price increases, wholesale prices will go up even more to motivate the requisite demand responses, therefore harming the utilities without in fact protecting the customers.

This fundamental nature of the markets implies that if some utilities throughout the region are allowed, even encouraged, to cover most of their electricity acquisitions through long-term fixed-price contracts, then all utilities must be allowed to do so. If wholesale prices increase, these utilities must be allowed to increase the retail prices correspondingly. Any restrictions on the

---

[16]If consumers were ultimately required to pay some share of these losses through long-term bonds, the efforts to protect consumers would make them strictly worse off, since they would save no money during the crisis but would be burdened by high prices afterward, as in the California case.

ability of a utility to enter long-term contracts or to pass wholesale cost increases to retail prices will lead to an uneven distribution of risk among those utilities.

However, the simple examples do not give the complete story, since utilities differ in the financial agreements they have with their customers. Therefore, a wide array of contractual structures should be open to the participants in the system, so they can each choose appropriate contracts depending on their particular circumstances. Electric utilities that have fixed obligations to serve customers are likely to want electricity supply contracts whose time horizon is consistent with the long-time scale of the obligation to serve. Risk-sharing arrangements between the utilities and their large customers or between generators and large customers should be allowed or encouraged. Risk-sharing arrangements may include obligations to provide a fixed amount of electricity at a predetermined price with additional quantities of electricity or reductions in the use of electricity priced in real time. With such contracts in place, the utilities could make long-term contracts to acquire the electricity in sufficient quantities to cover such retail contracts and could thus be free to set up risk-sharing arrangements that are consistent with the preferences of their customers.

MANAGE CALIFORNIA'S FINANCIAL OBLIGATIONS

California has acquired massive financial obligations primarily because of the State's mismanagement of the electricity crisis. The total dollar value of these obligations is still not clear. The FERC has yet to rule on the size of the refunds to which California will be entitled from generators that charged more for electricity than allowable under FERC price mitigation rules. Moreover, the size of the bond offerings and their terms are still outstanding issues. Whatever the ultimate magnitude of the obligations, the State still needs to resolve two issues: how it should treat financial obligations to electricity generators under the long-term contracts and in what ways it should pay for these obligations. These will be the final two issues of this chapter.

LONG-TERM ELECTRICITY CONTRACTS

Now that it has become widely apparent that the State's long-term electricity purchase contracts are at prices well above the current and expected future electricity prices, there is a strong pressure among governmental officials to "renegotiate" the contracts. There seems to be a broad recognition in the State Administration and Legislature that these contracts are not now and never were in California's interest. Yet how the State should proceed is not obvious, since many options involve a trade-off between the credibility of the State as a contractual partner and the depth of the electricity blight.

Renegotiation of many contracts can be valuable for both contractual parties when economic conditions change; however, legitimate renegotiation implies the identification of contractual changes that are preferable for both parties. It typically does not imply changes that are preferable from one party's perspective and disadvantageous from the perspective of the other party. Nor does it mean unilateral reneging on commitments. Yet these distinctions are not apparent from California's policy pronouncements, where renegotiation seems to have lost the concept of mutual gain or mutual agreement.

Attempts by California to achieve unilateral gains can have long-term adverse consequences for California. The continuing ability of the State of California to negotiate contracts on reasonable terms with a wide variety of contractual partners depends largely on its *not* developing a pattern of attempting to avoid its contractual obligations. Thus, California must recognize that even though the long-term contracts are very costly to the State, unilateral attempts to avoid this obligation would be harmful to California's credibility. Thus, it is important that any renegotiations of the contracts be truly bilateral agreements, rather than unilateral attempts by the State to force the generators to provide it with lower prices.

Similarly, the State should not try to overthrow the terms of the contracts by legislation. In particular, one legislative proposal, no longer active, would give repayment of state electricity bonds, if issued, higher priority for payment than the electricity contracts, conflicting directly with terms included in the long-term electricity price contracts negotiated by the State of California. Passage of this bill would be just such a unilateral change in the essential contract terms. Not only would such a change reduce California's credibility as a contractual partner, but it is also likely to be subject to years of litigation. Given the litigation threats, such a legislative solution would not accomplish its end of ensuring that the bonds would be marketable as investment-grade instruments.

PAYING FOR LONG-TERM FINANCIAL OBLIGATIONS

Currently, Governor Davis has made it clear that he intends the elevated costs of long-term electricity purchase contracts and debt service costs of the long-term bonds (once issued) will be obligations of future retail purchasers of electricity in California. These obligations would keep electricity prices elevated for decades above the marginal costs of electricity acquisition. Such long-term electricity price elevations will lead to long-term distortions within electricity markets unless this method of payment is changed. Two possible changes would reduce the distortions.

The first alternative would be for Californians to pay for these contractual obligations in their role as taxpayers rather than as electricity purchasers, which would not reduce the direct costs to California for these contracts but would reduce the long-term electricity market distortions and thus the depth of the blight. Such a change would allow the State to return direct access as an option for large electricity users.

Fairness issues associated with such a plan can be seen through several different perspectives. The obligations were incurred for purchases of electricity on behalf of the customers of the large investor-owned utilities. From one perspective, it thus seems unfair that all taxpayers should pay the costs. However, the California governor and members of the legislature made the fundamental mistakes. These were officials elected by all of California. Thus, from a second perspective it seems unfair that only a portion of the taxpayers should incur the costs of their mistakes. In addition, the mistakes were made in the years 2000 and 2001. Thus from another perspective, it seems unfair that new firms or consumers entering California after the crisis should be responsible for the mistakes made before they moved to California. In addition, some people and firms will move to or from service areas of the investor-owned utilities. One perspective suggests that it would be unfair for these to avoid the costs or pay the costs of the past decisions, simply because they chose to or are required to relocate within California. It is highly likely and extremely unfortunate that such fairness debates will be central to any policy debates about whether to convert the contractual obligations from an electricity ratepayer obligation to a taxpayer obligation.

Alternatively, a nonbypassable fixed charge, sufficient to pay for the financial obligations of the long-term contracts plus the debt service on the bonds, could be assessed to electricity users. Utility customers who continue to purchase their electricity from investor-owned utilities would simply pay the elevated price. However, those who no longer chose to purchase their electricity from the investor-owned utility would be required to pay an exit fee calculated to cover their share of the financial obligations. Firms and consumers who were not customers of the investor-owned utilities in 2001 would be entitled to a price reduction, the opposite of the exit fee.

In principle, this approach would allow the State to allocate the financial obligations of the long-term contracts and the long-term bonds to those customers who purchased from the investor-owned utilities in the year 2001. In practice, however, such a plan would not be simple. It could create a set of incentives for firms and customers to take actions to avoid the fee; for example, by reducing their scale of operations within the service area of an investor-owned utility but not actually leaving. Hence, though in principle such an approach would be viable, in practice the difficulties may be too great.

Between the two options, considering the difficulties of implementation and the remaining distortions, conversion of the obligations from ratepayer obligations to taxpayer obligations is likely to be the better course of action. However, it is likely that the fairness concerns will dominate the debate and the current California governor and legislature will take no action. If that is the result, California's electricity system could remain in blight for decades to come.

7

SOME REFLECTIONS

The story of the California electricity and financial crisis is far from finished. At the time of this writing, Pacific Gas & Electric is still struggling to develop a plan to emerge from bankruptcy that is acceptable to both the judge and its creditors. Southern California Edison is regaining financial health but still faces obstacles. Various state agencies are attempting to renegotiate the long-term contracts and/or to challenge the contracts in court or through the FERC. The CPUC and the DWR are discussing options for issuing long-term revenue bonds. Wholesale price mitigation measures established by the FERC are scheduled to expire in September. Litigations spawned by the crisis are working their way through the courts. The fall of Enron has brought into question the viability of some electricity contracts. In addition, Enron's fall has led commentators to blame that corporation for its roles in electricity market restructuring and the crisis. The FERC recently initiated a fact-finding investigation into whether Enron or any entity manipulated electricity or natural gas prices (or "otherwise exercised undue influence over wholesale prices") during the crisis. The CAISO is developing proposals for correcting flaws in California electricity markets. The FERC continues to promote and support regional transmission organizations. Other regions, including the Northeast, are successfully operating restructured electricity systems. Texas is moving forward with its deregulation. The House Energy and

Commerce subcommittee is working on legislation to promote deregulation. Researchers are striving for deeper understanding of western electricity markets, further sorting out the underpinning of the crisis and working to design better electricity market structures.

Even though the story is far from final, it may be valuable at this point to reflect on lessons that emerge from the sad history, even though any lessons will be, by necessity, somewhat subjective.

Unfortunately, one message repeatedly communicated is that the California experience proves that electricity deregulation has been a failure in California, and by extension, is likely to be a failure elsewhere. For example, Governor Davis stated, "But we must face reality: California's deregulation scheme is a colossal and dangerous failure. It has not lowered consumer prices; it has not increased supply. In fact, it has resulted in skyrocketing prices, price-gouging and an unreliable supply of electricity. In short, an energy nightmare."[1] Governor Davis has even used the California experience in Mexico to condemn any move toward privatization of the Mexican electricity system. Governor Davis during early December 2001, speaking in Mexico, urged Mexican authorities to keep complete governmental ownership and control of the electricity system: "Don't hand over your electricity infrastructure to private interests, unless you have 15 percent more energy than you need. In private meetings, [Mexican] President [Vicente] Fox and I agreed on this."[2]

Yet a fair assessment of the California experience cannot reach such an anti–private sector conclusion, nor can it lead to a negative conclusion about the viability of electricity system deregulation.

First, as has been well documented by researchers such as William Hogan[3] and by Robert Crow,[4] electricity system restructuring, including deregulation, has been very successful in other nations and in other regions of the United States. Successful deregulation has been proven possible, even though California's particular system is flawed and has been managed terribly.

---

[1]January 8, 2001, State of the State Address.

[2]Quote from UPI wire: http://www.upi.com/view.cfm?StoryID=14122001-070000-9884r. Story by Ian Campbell, UPI Economics Correspondent.

[3]For example, William W. Hogan, "Electricity Market Restructuring: Reforms of Reforms" (Harvard University: May 25, 2001).

[4]Robert Thomas Crow, "Not Invented Here: What California Can Learn from Elsewhere about Restructuring Electricity Supply" (Stanford Institute for Economic Policy Research Working Paper, December 2001). Available at http://siepr.stanford.edu/papers/pdf/01-10.html.

In California, deregulation has set the stage for widespread wholesale market competition and adequate electricity-generation capacity. California's restructuring has resulted in a dramatic increase in the number of new electricity-generating plants proposed, approved, and under construction. Deregulation is having the desired impacts on wholesale electricity supply.

The contention still seems to be that deregulation caused the electricity crisis. However, a fair examination of the western electricity crisis shows this contention to be invalid. The crisis stemmed primarily from two factors. For over a decade, population growth and economic growth in the western states steadily increased electricity consumption, but very little new electricity-generating capacity was added. As a result, by the year 2000, western electricity markets had become very tight even under normal conditions. But 2000 and early 2001 were not characterized by normal conditions. Exceptionally low rainfall in the Pacific Northwest and Northern California led to sharp temporary reductions in hydroelectric generation that triggered the electricity crisis. California deregulation played only a minor role, if any at all, in creating the crisis.

The financial crisis, on the other hand, was the direct result of California regulatory actions. It was not the result of *deregulation,* but rather of overly stringent *regulation.* Even though all municipal utilities and investor-owned utilities throughout the entire West faced the electricity crisis, investor-owned utilities located in California were the only ones that experienced the financial crisis.

Two regulatory rules forced California investor-owned utilities into a financial crisis. First, these utilities had been precluded from using long-term electricity purchase contracts to protect themselves financially from wholesale market price spikes. This lack of protection was in stark contrast to practices of other utilities: investor-owned utilities in the other western states and municipal utilities throughout the West, including California. The regulatory-imposed absence of financial protection set the stage for the financial crisis.

Second, once electricity prices on wholesale spot markets skyrocketed, the California governor and the CPUC refused to allow the retail price increases needed to keep the investor-owned utilities financially viable. The legislature even reestablished retail price control for San Diego Gas and Electric. The regulations forced the investor-owned utilities to purchase electricity at very high wholesale prices and to sell the same electricity at retail prices controlled to be far below purchase costs. These utilities were required to sell as much electricity as their customers wanted to buy, even though utilities were losing money on all their sales. The CPUC never allowed any increases in retail electricity prices until after the largest two utilities had been drained of all financial assets and of all borrowing capacity and were on the verge of bankruptcy. Only then did the Commission approve any retail price increases. However, the initial increase was far too small to balance sales price and purchase costs. Thus retail price regulation, not deregulation, was fundamental to creating the financial crisis for the utilities.

Once these utilities had become so credit unworthy that generators and marketers were no longer willing to or required to sell them electricity, the State stepped in to buy electricity on their behalf. The State itself began buying electricity at high wholesale spot prices and selling it at the low regulated retail prices. Buying high and selling low was just as costly to the State as it was to the investor-owned utilities. During the winter and spring of 2001, this program completely drained the State Treasury of its projected $8 billion surplus. This ill-conceived scheme was not the result of deregulation, but was the deliberate choice of the State of California. In short, the financial crisis was *not* the product of deregulation, but rather was the product of overly aggressive and inappropriate regulation.

The California experience should make it clear, once again, that actions that economically isolate the supply side of markets from the demand side create major problems. In California, retail price control was the primary regulatory mechanism that isolated the demand side from the supply side of the electricity markets. Such price controls typically reduce system responsiveness and eliminate incentives for consumers to adjust to changing economic conditions. The lesson had been brought home forcefully to the United States during earlier energy crises, including 1973–74 and 1980–81 when gasoline price controls and governmentally imposed oil allocation controls led to hours-long gasoline lines. Yet California political leaders, ignoring lessons of the past, maintained rigid retail electricity price controls until the bitter end.

Maintenance of retail price controls thus discouraged energy demand reductions—energy conservation—by consumers. However,

energy conservation was California's best hope for forcing wholesale prices to decrease. Thus, California's decision to keep retail
prices at artificially low levels allowed wholesale prices to remain
at painfully high levels. Consumers did save money in the short
run through lower rates, but will pay all of the high wholesale
costs through long-term increases in the retail rates. Therefore,
public officials, by isolating consumers from wholesale market
conditions, have brought long-term harm to California consumers of electricity as well as to California taxpayers.

The California experience also brought into sharp focus the
importance of managing the risks associated with implementation
of any policies, especially those that radically change the system.
California electricity restructuring was just such a policy. It radically changed regulation, altering an electricity system that itself
has never been free of economic risk. The history of the electricity
system should have made it clear that one cannot confidently predict changes that significantly influence generation costs. Cost of
fuels change, as has occurred for natural gas, oil, and coal. Public
acceptability of generating technologies can vary over time.
Hydroelectric generation depends entirely on rainfall, the amount
of which can vary sharply from year to year. Prediction of electricity demand growth is at best an imperfect art, and understanding
circumstances in which market power might be exercised—in fact,
even determining whether market power is being exercised—is
fraught with error. Risks exist and they must be managed.

Given the significant economic risks, the regulatory system
should distribute those risks appropriately. However, the restructuring left investor-owned utilities bearing a disproportionate share
of the risk. Subsequent regulatory implementation made matters
worse. Thus, with reductions in available hydropower, the financial
consequences of soaring wholesale spot market prices were borne
disproportionately by the California investor-owned utilities.

It is impossible to expect that policy choices will eliminate system-
wide risks. Risks will always remain. Nevertheless, one can expect
that good policy choices and regulatory implementation will fairly
distribute those risks and that the regulatory system will not disproportionately concentrate risks on a limited number of companies,
particularly if those companies are incapable of bearing the entire
risk. Unfortunately, that was not the case in California.

The California experience highlights something that is well
known to everyone who has managed, participated in, or observed

large-scale changes in complicated organizations or economic structures. Any major restructuring of such important systems will continue to require modifications well after the initial changes have been implemented. System operation requires monitoring and may require wise and strong leadership to identify and implement changes that are needed after unintended adverse consequences of the system change become apparent.

California's electricity system includes both complicated organizations and complex economic structures. The restructuring was fundamental and sweeping. No one was able to predict with complete certainty how all the changes would work. Thus, it was important that the State carefully monitored important features of the system operation.

No one should have been surprised to find important unintended adverse consequences of the electricity system restructuring. No one should have been surprised to find system flaws that required changes. And no one should have been surprised to hear that the Chief Executive of the State needed to provide the leadership to assure that the appropriate changes were implemented.

In California, the governor is the Chief Executive Officer of the State and thus had the leadership responsibility to assure that flaws in the changed electricity regulation system were identified and corrected early enough to avoid a crisis. At least, the governor could have corrected flaws enough to avoid the most damaging consequences of the crisis. The California experience shows the real lasting harm that can befall when the governor fails to take the appropriate role.

The California experience also highlights the dangers of failing to differentiate between short-run issues and long-run issues. California, like all of the western states, faced a short-term electricity crisis. Although during the crisis it was impossible to predict its exact duration, available information about new generation capacity under construction made it clear that the supply shortage, at the root of the crisis, would be of relatively short duration. During the crisis, it was also possible to foresee that any problems of market rules would become far less important once the anticipated new generating capacity was on-line. Thus, the short-term nature of the electricity crisis was predictable even during the crisis.

It was also predictable that the financial crisis, if allowed to proceed, could have long-term ramifications and that long-term contracts for electricity purchases at prices far exceeding the expected electricity prices would have long-term adverse financial ramifications. Thus, there were foreseeable long-term problems.

It is commonplace to note the need for careful differentiation between short-term problems and long-term problems. Careful differentiation between short term and long term helps ensure that new long-term problems are not created as "solutions" to short-term problems. Unfortunately, the California State Government did not seem to so differentiate. Thus, the State negotiated long-term contracts ostensibly aimed at the short-term crisis; these contracts quickly became long-term problems. The failure to implement rational short-term solutions, such as temporary retail price increases, implied that the State missed those solutions that could act quickly over a short time period, allowing the short-term challenge to become a crisis and leading directly to the long-term financial problems. Although reasonable people can disagree about the appropriate policy measures, appropriate matching of the time scale of the solutions to the time scale of the problems would have been far superior to those actions taken in California.

As a final reflection, it is important to recognize that California has had severe economic and policy problems in the past and will have problems in the future. But California has a robust economy, boasts a diverse and vibrant population, provides technological leadership for the world, and remains a wellspring of new ideas. California will survive the problems, both the short- and long-term problems, associated with the electricity and financial crises. And in decades to come, perhaps the lessons learned from this crisis will help California to avoid similar mismanagement.

Index